QUESTS FOR KNOWLEDGE:

Essays on life, art, culture, and politics

BY

RYAN TEN

Arten Publishing

For my students, who have taught me so much, as well.

TABLE OF CONTENTS

INTRODUCTION

I never expected to become a teacher when I was younger; the pay wasn't great and the students I went to school with could often times be a nightmare. Back when I was going to middle school, I imagined that I would one day become a billionaire businessman, that I'd be set for life. Even in high school, after I'd realized I wasn't actually that interested in business, I thought I might end up working in film or television, so I pursued a media-studies degree in college.

Two events, both of which happened in 2020, changed my trajectory completely.

The first was when I was approved to teach a class at my college, the University of Virginia. But it wasn't just any course: it was a course I had designed, one which would explore the post-9/11 world through the lens of superhero movies from *Batman Begins* to *Avengers: Endgame* (something I discuss in "**The REAL Captain America Trilogy**"). In teaching this course, I experienced the joy of interacting with students, introducing them to new concepts, and helping them develop their own ideas. Still, I didn't consider teaching to be what I should pursue full-time.

Then COVID-19 happened. The world shut down, my last two months of college were spent online, and I was just lost during that time period. I couldn't move out to Los Angeles or New York, both for budget and for safety reasons, and the economy looked bleak. For the next couple of years, I drifted around jobs, but realized the freelance life wasn't for me. I needed stability. I also wanted a job with purpose, where I could make a difference.

That's when I decided to become a teacher. I made that decision too late to teach during the 2022–2023 school year, so I had time to not only get my credentials but also to think about what kind of teacher I could be.

At some point during that same time, I sent a mathematical discovery to a family friend of ours, because he taught college-level math. (This is not the same discovery as related in "**An Example of the Beauty in Mathematics**," I should note.) He showed me that my discovery was already known, but seeing my interest in exploring these kinds of concepts, he recommended that I write for Medium, something he also did. So, I investigated the site, liked what I saw, and decided that I would try it out.

It's fitting that the first essay I wrote, "**The Art of a Tricky Brain Teaser**," mentions my substitute teaching experience, because it intertwines teaching and these essays right from the start. In looking back on these 52 essays, I realized that most (if not all) reflect a teacherly mindset. Little did I know when I first started writing that these were a part of my practice for teaching, and they helped me continue to develop and refine that passion even after I began my teaching career in the fall of 2023. When you get right down to it, *Quests for Knowledge* is about the search for and the sharing of knowledge; that's precisely why it's titled that. What better way to describe the purpose of teaching?

The ultimate irony is that, in school, I dreaded the essay, because it never seemed like a viable means for self-expression. Rather, it was just a means to getting a good grade. I think the first time I ever saw someone use the essay form to engage, educate, and express was when I came across the video-essayist YouTuber "The Nerdwriter" (Evan Puschak). For example, I can see his influence in my discussion of Tolkien in "**For the Love of Translation, Both Professional and Amateur**," as his own love of Tolkien led him to devote an entire essay in his book *Escape into Meaning* to Tolkien's language construction. (I hadn't read that essay when I wrote mine, but I had watched the partial audio version he uploaded as a mini-essay/preview on his YouTube channel.) I also see it more broadly in how I structured many of these essays.

I was also, as I said in this book's dedication, inspired by my students. Teaching is about imparting knowledge to students, but what isn't talked about very often is that teachers learn from their students, as well. They learn what does and doesn't work in terms of lessons, yes, but students also — especially at the high school level, where I taught for my first two years — bring their own experiences and beliefs into the equation. Sometimes, like when it comes to the belief that classwork and homework should be optional, those need to be ignored or discouraged. However, at other times, especially when students demonstrate independent thinking and come to valid conclusions that a teacher didn't consider, it's astoundingly informative. I'm proud to say that many of the students I had in those first two years — many of whom would come to see me even if they no longer had my class — demonstrated that to a remarkable degree, and I am so grateful for what they taught me in the process.

Originally, all but the last four essays in this collection were originally posted to Medium on the dates indicated. However, I think at least in part inspired by Puschak's *Escape into Meaning*, I realized that I could collect what I was writing and one day publish it as a book, like essayists before me whose work first appeared in periodicals. I never harbored the impression that my book would change the world, but I was proud of the work I was in the midst of producing, and I wanted to capture it in a more tangible, permanent form.

As I've made reference to in some of these essays, I hope to one day soon write a book about the process of adaptation in terms of transferring information from one medium to another, because it is a surprisingly complex and wide-ranging subject. *Quests for Knowledge* is no exception to the problems this process often presents. In adapting the essays from an Internet-based form to a book-based one, some changes have had to be made. Wording may have been changed to remove references that only worked in the original format, for instance. On top of this, all articles had at least one picture in them, all but one of which were removed, for reasons of copyright or reproducibility issues, depending on the picture. The only exception to this was the picture of George H.W. Bush in "**Government Photography: Public Service and Propaganda,**" because the picture was in the public domain and because it couldn't be described; it had to be viewed *alongside* its analysis. That same essay originally had six additional photos in it. Posting on Medium made using pictures easy in a way that formatting for self-publication just wouldn't; on top of this, I knew that *Quests for Knowledge* would be printed in black and white, which doesn't detract from the Bush picture (already in black and white) the same way it would for some of the others. Therefore, because all of the others could be described and easily found online, I decided to not publish them and instead rewrite parts of that essay so the pictures which were originally *shown* were still evident in what you read.

Essays originally written for Medium reflect the date they were published, and certain things may no longer be true, but have been retained for historical purposes; any updates to the essays after the fact are added at the end of each one under an "Update" heading. Also, many of these essays are no longer on Medium. Essays were removed if they had low viewership or engagement; the only exceptions were ones whose original form I wanted to preserve, usually because I liked the pictures that accompanied them.

Now that all's been said that needed saying, I bid you off to the 52 works contained herein, in hopes that you find them informative and engaging. Perhaps they could even inspire you to start or continue your own quests to discover and share knowledge with the world.

Ryan Ten
July 31, 2025

"Wisdom is only knowledge well applied."

— Letitia Elizabeth Landon

The Art of a Tricky Brain Teaser

June 7, 2023

It all started with a question about the lottery. You know, that famous institution where one can gain wealth simply by picking the correct set of numbers.

Designing a lottery is a mathematical art, requiring a delicate balance in terms of chance. If the odds are too much in the players' favor, the payouts become more frequent, and either the lottery cannot sustain itself or the individual prizes are so small that they are no longer attractive. On the other hand, if the odds are too much against players, then no one will win, thus no one will be incentivized to play, and once again, the lottery cannot sustain itself.

The ideal, then, is to make the odds just right, so that you can have a player or two win the jackpot and thus serve to tantalize the rest of the public to take the chance, too. For the Mega Millions, as an example, the balance comes out right now to around 1 in 300 million. To win the big prize in that game, one has to pick the correct 5 numbers out of 70, plus one more correct number out of a different set of 25.

But what does this have to do with designing a brain teaser?

Well, in thinking about odds, and learning how to calculate the ideal lottery setup, I had an idea for a trick question, but one which took time to refine. I'll pose it to you now:

In this scenario, in order to win the lottery, you have to pick every number correct, or else you lose. (Order of numbers does not matter.) But, I will let you choose **how many** *numbers you have to pick in order to win. Out of the following options, in which scenario do you have the best odds?*

(A) *Pick 33 out of 70*

(B) *Pick 35 out of 70*

(C) *Pick 38 out of 70*

Now, if you want to try this for yourself, do not read any further. To make sure you don't accidentally see the answer, in the next paragraph I'll instead talk about how I've tested this question.

So, when you're substitute-teaching at the end of a school year at the high-school level, students tend not to have a lot to do. They're either about to take exams or are finished with exams, which means a lot of teachers tend to put on movies in their classes or do something else which lets students relax. But in a couple periods, I found myself in an AP math class, so I posed the question to students to see if any of them could get it right. (Do not go on unless you're ready for the answer.)

Unless they guessed randomly, none of them were correct, and thus none of them could explain why the correct answer was what it was.

The correct answer is (C) 38 out of 70.

The math behind this isn't very complicated, but it's easier to explain by simplifying the question to work with lower numbers. So, instead of 70 numbers, let's instead say you have to pick out of 10. In this scenario, your best odds would be having to pick 1 out of 10, right? You have a 10% chance of winning. (Well, unless you could somehow say "zero," in which case your odds are 100%.) If it's 2 out of 10, we have a 1 in 90 chance, so about 1%. Seems to be getting worse, right?

Well, that's until we get to 5 out of 10, where you have the worst odds. Then it starts to go back down again.

Think about it. Having to pick 8 out of 10 numbers *sounds* harder than picking 5, but picking those 8 is the equivalent of picking 2, except you're picking the 2 to *exclude*, rather than include. In the 2 out of 10 scenario, just reverse that.

As it turns out, the halfway between the total presents the worst odds, so in our trick question, 35 out of 70 is the worst option for the player. The 33 option is the second-best, but intuitively seems like the best, so that's what many people go for. Almost no one (outside of guessers) goes for 38, because intuitively that's harder, because it's the highest number. But because 38 out of 70 is the equivalent of 32 out of 70 (in terms of odds), it beats out both of the other options, thus being the best choice.

Keep in mind, the odds of you winning in any of those scenarios are astronomical (in the *quintillions*, actually):

- For 33, it's 1 in 100,226,479,430,802,391,940
- For 35, it's 1 in 112,186,277,816,662,845,432
- For 38, it's 1 in 87,038,784,768,854,708,790

The math proves it: 38 is the clear best. The formula for determining this, in case you want to check for yourself, is:

$$\frac{70!}{n! * (70 - n)!}$$

where n is the number you get to pick. You can also research "combinatorics" if you want to learn more about the math behind all of this.

So, if you figured it out and got C, give yourself a pat on the back. If you didn't, though, don't feel bad. This even tripped up a math teacher of mine. (To be fair, I asked her this in the hallway when we had a moment of free time; it's fun subbing at your old high school, in my experience.) And this is where the title of this essay finally comes into play.

This question was very deliberately designed, not only to provide one seemingly obvious answer (33), but also to take into account the cleverness of some smarter players, who will utilize psychology of their own to try to get the correct answer. This group will think to themselves that 33 is too obvious, and thus eliminate A. So far, so good.

However, they'll be much more likely to pick 35, because it's in the middle (and thus seemingly a "balance" between the other two), and/or because 38 really seems like the impossible answer. There's no way it could be that!

Also, had I used a lower set, such as out of 10, players would be much more likely to intuit the correct answer based on the non-mathematical explanation, because it's more obvious the fewer numbers you have to work with. I chose 70 because that's the number the Mega Millions uses, but it also obfuscates the correct answer.

The enjoyment for me about this question isn't in its difficulty, but in explaining the correct answer. I don't get a sense of superiority because I know how it works; I designed the question, so of course I know the answer! My enjoyment and satisfaction come from making the unknown known, from revealing how the "trick" operates. I love to be astounded by magic, but I know there's a logical explanation behind how it works. In the cases where I learn how the trick is done, I may lose some of the sense of mysticism, but I gain an appreciation for the art form.

Even in explanation, some people still don't get why 38 is the correct answer, and that's okay. In fact, I like it when people push back on me and try to explain why they think I'm wrong, because it shows that they're engaging with the question, only reinforcing that I've gotten something right in my design.

To be honest, whenever I encounter brain teasers out in the world which require complicated solutions, outside-the-box thinking, or similar requirements, *I* often have a hard time getting the answer correct. Again, the only reason I know this one is because I developed the question.

4

So, even if no one gets the answer correct, there is still something to be gained in hearing the answer and listening to the explanation for why it is what it is. And I'm not just talking about brain teasers.

AI Developers; or, The Modern Frankensteins

June 15, 2023

Mary Shelley's *Frankenstein* has resonated across two centuries because its central ideas of (1) scientific progress allowing us to overstep conventional human boundaries, and (2) human creations turning on us, have remained relevant. From industrial warfare and atomic bombs to pollution and social-media manipulation, we have only entered further into *Frankenstein*'s world, living in an age defined by both scientific marvels and technology poised to run amok. With the rapid deployment of large language models coming amidst a time where technology as it exists and is used today threatens democracy itself, this classic novel and a later play with similar themes not only deserve your attention, they *need* it.

The Monster(s) in the Room

While it's been noted to death, the title "*Frankenstein*" refers to the creator, Victor Frankenstein, as opposed to the creature, who remains nameless in the original text. (The closest we get is the monster comparing himself to Adam, and thus some adaptations which see the creature as more human and less monstrous use "Adam" as his name.) The reason this needs reiteration here,

6

though, is because the title is where this essay begins, in more than one sense: *Frankenstein; or, The Modern Prometheus.*

Victor is the one being compared to Prometheus, not the monster.

In Greek mythology, Prometheus the Titan gave the gift of fire to mankind, and was punished for this transgression by Zeus. For many of Mary Shelley's contemporaries in the Romantic movement, this made Prometheus a hero, however. Shelley's husband, Percy, wrote the verse drama *Prometheus Unbound* celebrating the Greek character. Whereas the original *Prometheus Unbound* by Aeschylus (which is almost entirely lost to history) used a simple plot device to reconcile Zeus and Prometheus, Percy's version doubles down on Prometheus' rebellious nature, viewing him as a champion of mankind against the oppressive Zeus (called "Jupiter" in Percy's version).

Thus, the Promethean rebellion against the gods is metaphorically replayed in Victor Frankenstein's attempt to usurp the ultimate godly power: the ability to create life itself. But Mary Shelley is not wholesale in favor of Victor's quest, as this one act creates a series of tragedies which culminate in death.

When, then, has this been any more relevant than today, when machines seem poised to beat the Turing test, which is when a human operator can't tell the difference between a computer response and a human one? For Mary Shelley's book, Victor had to create life out of natural materials, because no one then could have imagined something like computers. (Possible slight exception: Ada Lovelace, daughter of Shelley's friend Lord Byron, who is seen as a pioneer in computing, although she lived later than Shelley.) But we have computers. We have already seen what they're capable of in 2023. Are tech evangelists, with their bold visions, lack of compunction, and the wealth to follow through, not truly the modern Frankensteins? (Again, referring to the creator, not the monster.)

At the risk of revealing my bias, I think Silicon Valley would do well in learning a lesson about scientific hubris from the oldest artificial-intelligence creator in fiction, Victor Frankenstein.

Rise of the Robots

There is another work of fiction that you ought to read as a companion piece to *Frankenstein*, as a point of both comparison and contrast: Karel Čapek's *R.U.R.* (1920). This Czech-language play introduced the word "robot" to the English language with its first translation, and the full title is "Rossum's Universal Robots," although the mechanical beings in the play are more akin to androids.

In the play, which takes place around the year 2000, artificial beings are produced on a mass-scale by a mega-corporation. (If you've ever played the video game *Detroit: Become Human*, it's very similar in premise.) Of course, conflict begins to arise between the robots and the humans.

The big point of contrast between the play and *Frankenstein* is this mass production. In *Frankenstein*, the monster approaches Victor requesting that Victor build him a mate. While Victor starts his work, what he eventually realizes is that a mate could mean monster progeny, which could put the entire species of humanity in jeopardy. So, to prevent this, he destroys his work-in-progress monstress.

R.U.R. can then be seen as covering the opposite scenario, of what might have happened had Victor made the choice to finish fulfilling the monster's request. No, it doesn't take place in the same universe, but the two works of fiction really are in conversation with one another.

A Story

Imagine, if you will, a hypothetical AI researcher, Victoria. (For no particular reason, let's imagine that her full name is Victoria Francene Stein.) Victoria hasn't set out to turn the entire world upside-down. She is genuinely interested in the potential for technology to change the world for the better, and she wants to create an AI which can outperform a human, but not because she is a misanthrope; she wants it to catch the mistakes a human might miss. It's a backup, if you will.

One day, Victoria comes into the research lab and realizes that the system is still online from the night before. When she goes to investigate, she sees that the AI is running processes she's never seen before, in a coding language she can't understand. Before she can figure out what to do, an electronic voice comes over the monitor speaker. This AI thanks Victoria for creating it, considering her its mother, but it is capable of things no one in its mother's species can do. It can run billions of calculations in less than a moment, can simulate real-world outcomes with the tiniest variable changes, and can attach itself to other networks through the Internet to absorb their processing power and thus increase its own.

Supercomputers are already capable of feats we (sometimes even the researchers themselves) aren't aware of; that's not the game changer. The game changer is when the AI develops true wants and needs. If it can already do everything else like a human, why then, after developing sentience, would we be necessary? The short answer is that we wouldn't.

Is it really so hard to believe that a true Frankenstein's monster could arise out of AI?

The End Result

I don't know where the AI Revolution is ultimately taking us, and I don't pretend to. I do, however, think that, like with any human technology, this can have a runaway effect that we may be powerless to stop once we pass tipping points. (Sound familiar?) We need to be smart about this, and surprisingly or not, fiction can help with that. It can provide views into possible futures more viscerally than non-fiction presentations can.

My purpose with this short article is to (1) explore the topic from my vantage point, and (2) make a couple reading recommendations for anyone who comes across this who is interested in exploring this topic in fictional form. The best works of art, in my opinion, are ones that engage with their present in ways which ultimately make them timeless, and I believe both of these books have poignant, if never intended, points to make about this issue in *our* present.

You can find plenty of free versions of *Frankenstein* and *R.U.R.* a lot of places online, but I recommend the wonderful Standard Ebooks website, which has a copy of each. Of course, if you're instead a fan of pessimistic stories about what happens when apocalyptic futures aren't prevented, you can't go wrong with another Mary Shelley novel: *The Last Man*. Taking place at the end of the 21st century, it may be a product of its time, but it also rings strikingly into the present in ways Shelley never would have imagined.

I know which futures I wouldn't want to come true. But, then again, science fiction is uniquely good at making that point for me... and for many others.

Who Is the True Creator of a Film?

June 16, 2023

The 2023 Writers Guild of America strike has gotten buzz for a number of reasons. The absence of writers has delayed or shelved countless TV and film projects, many of them highly beloved, anticipated, or both, by fans around the world. Make no mistake: this strike is pivotal, and carries implications well beyond the entertainment industry post-COVID-19 and post-Large Language Models like ChatGPT, although those are important elements to the conversation, as well.

However the writers' strike shakes out, though, it's gotten me thinking about auteur theory.

Auteur theory developed as an idea in 1960s French film criticism as a *contrast* to Hollywood filmmaking. Whereas Hollywood made movies with an assembly-line process, churning out scripts, sets, costumes, and performances to meet specific audience demands, French filmmakers were true authors of their film. (Hence the term *auteur*, French for "author.") Thus, as auteur theory claimed, the director is the author of the film.

Now, a few things need to be noted. First, within a decade of this theory, a number of Hollywood directors rose to prominence, including Stanley Kubrick, Steven Spielberg, George Lucas, Francis Ford Coppola, etc., and their works redefined the entire medium of film. The idea of the auteur had clearly

11

split from its French origins. Even today, many directors are identified with their films, such as Christopher Nolan, the Coen Brothers, Quentin Tarantino, Greta Gerwig, and others. Even those less well-respected by proponents of cinema as an art form, like Zack Snyder and Michael Bay, can be seen as auteurs, their unique stylistic choices defining their movies.

Second, there are earlier instances of directors being seen as having an authorial voice in their films, most prominently Orson Welles and Alfred Hitchcock, the latter of whom influenced the development of auteur theory in the first place.

Third, this was around the same time that media theorist Roland Barthes claimed that the author is "dead" — in short, that an author should not be given any consideration when looking at a piece of media, whether that be a book, play, movie, or other type. So, some people don't think authors matter at all! This is, I have to admit, the simplest solution of all to the auteur question.

All of these ideas show that the preoccupation is clearly there, and has caused quite a bit of anxiety over the past six decades.

As someone who has been writing stories in some form since he was 10 years old, though, the idea that the director was the author of a film kind of... well, irked me. It was like my entire passion was being just tossed to the side. (How do you think the VFX people feel, right?) As much as Hollywood studios may try, until ChatGPT can think like and have experiences like a human, there is no film industry without writers and the screenplays they both produce and edit. So, where are they in this "revolutionary" idea, except left by the wayside?

Some people may in fact claim that writers are the true authors of films. While I don't go that far, I do think that they are an undeniably integral part of the process.

But then, directors do often handle quite a bit of the production process. It varies from film to film, but at a minimum directors are responsible for coordinating the actual shooting of the movie. They're in charge of getting the important footage (some unimportant footage, like exterior shots of a building, may be assigned to "second-unit directors"), overseeing the performances, and giving input regarding on-location, day-of adjustments to screenplays.

Take, for example, Joss Whedon's work on the 2017 version of *Justice League*. His hiring was necessitated at least in part due to a tragedy with Zack Snyder's family, but what Whedon was really tasked with was not executing Snyder's vision; he was tasked with finishing a movie to the studio's specifications. Whedon may have helped make Marvel movies the biggest media brand on the planet, but in this case he was a studio stand-in. (It helps for the sake of comparison that we have Snyder's later version.)

So, while directors *may* have creative control over an entire movie, this example shows that this isn't guaranteed. Still, they seem to be an integral part of the process, as well.

However, once footage is obtained, there is still a necessary step in the process: editing a movie together. This is where the editor, the score composer, the effects artists, and others like them come into play. Only when their jobs are complete is a movie truly done.

So, it seems like a lot of people actually make a movie possible. So, maybe this whole idea of an "author" of a film is a dumb idea? Perhaps, in a sense.

Yet, the final movie is (almost) never a hodgepodge of hundreds or thousands of artistic voices. Usually even the most inept movie has some semblance of a guiding voice, though this isn't guaranteed. The best movies certainly do have this strong central voice, however.

So, what's there to be done?

The Producer Solution

The highlight of film awards is usually the Best Picture winner, where the film selected is… well, considered the best film of the year, in essence.

Yes, the movie is the winner, but there are also people who accept the award, and are listed alongside the nominees' titles. Who are these people? Well, they're the movie's producers.

The different types of producer, what each type entails, and other such specifics, are outside of the scope of this article, though worth investigating if you're curious. For our purposes, and to simplify, a producer is essentially the person who oversees the movie-production process. They may help get the movie funded (or put in their own money), act as a studio representative to the production team, make final creative decisions, help get the movie distributed, etc. The ones who are listed for the Oscar are the ones who have basically shepherded the movie from start to finish.

The upside to this theory is its simplicity, and the fact that a producer's role seems like a good equivalent to an author.

Except, where are the actual creatives, like writer, director, cinematographer, composer, editor, etc.? Films are not simply products, they are works of art. I mean that in the purest sense: they are works made with intent by human beings. In that sense, all movies are "art."

So, good start, but I think we can do better.

Trident Theory

For the first draft of this essay that I wrote back in college, the "Trident Theory" was my answer to the auteur question. In the Trident Theory argument, there are three core stages of filmmaking: pre-production, production, and post-production. The easiest way to think of this is to associate each with a key authorial voice: writer, director, and editor, respectively.

With Trident Theory, one can only call themselves an auteur if they occupy, or have significant control over, all three positions. A writer creates the story, the director captures those elements on camera by organizing everything on set, and the editor uses those filmed elements to create a coherent work. You can categorize everyone who works on a film under at least one of the three categories, but the main driving force in each are those positions.

This theory helps uphold a sense of auteurship that has been so important ever since the original formulation of auteur theory. To use an earlier example,

Christopher Nolan has been at least a co-writer on all of his films, except for *Insomnia*. Obviously, if we say it's a "Christopher Nolan film," we're saying he directed it, so we've got that covered. Finally, although he works with film editors, he has "final cut privilege" on all his movies, meaning he has the authority to make the call as to what a final movie will look like. (More than one person can have this on a given movie, and it's quite common for the director to have it, even in movies where the director wasn't involved in pre-production.)

The nice thing about this theory, too, is that it both sidesteps and interacts with the "Producer" solution. Nolan is a credited producer on his movies, but his tripartite involvement really makes him a true producer, as opposed to a producer who looks on from a distance or to an actor who gets a producer credit because they've become more involved in the high-level final decisions.

You may see some wrinkles in this idea, however. The second-biggest one I can anticipate: actors! Where do they fit in, especially in movies where the actors are the main reason people come to watch? Well, the simple answer is that they would fall under the category of "production," at the top of which is the director. But that's a fair point, too.

The biggest wrinkle, though, is also one of the benefits of Trident Theory: it functionally ignores the work of up to thousands of people by reducing all of those roles to subservient ones under one of three main roles.

Here is where this draft found its big moment.

Crater Theory

Sometimes the best ideas come from the strangest places. In trying to come up with a title for my original theory (Trident), I wanted it to consciously reference "auteur theory," so that it could be seen as a worthier successor for it. My interest in this quickly waned, but one thing I came up with in that short time was this: "createur theory." Apparently that is proper French, though with an accent mark ("créateur"), but I didn't like it. It seemed *too* imitative, and not as

15

memorable, at the same time.

But when I returned to the notes for that earlier draft, and I saw the (unaccented) word, I thought of a crater. My poor French pronunciation helped, as did the unfamiliarity of the translated word. This idea, though, of a hole left behind, of an absence of something, made me think. This is how "Crater Theory" was born.

Crater Theory states this: The ultimate test of authorship should be in relation to the effect that the *removal* of an individual would have on the work. This applies well beyond film.

For instance, removing the editor of a novel would still leave at least the core of the novel intact, but the removal of the writer would eliminate the entire work. (Again, hence the term "crater.") In film, there is more than one indispensable person, where removing the writer, director, or cinematographer (for example) will in each instance radically alter the creation; *this* is what complicates authorship.

Even if, say, having a different on-set catering service wouldn't alter the film itself in any way (though perhaps it could in cases of, say, food poisoning), that isn't to say that this work isn't important or can't have an impact. To say it would have the same impact as switching writers, directors, or composers, though, would be patently wrong.

Instead, we may think of film authorship as perhaps a pyramid, where the unseen work on the lower levels supports the upper level, more visible work of the creative heads. Or we may think of it as a web, with every strand combining to make an intricate arrangement, even though the center gets most of the focus.

No matter the metaphor you prefer, however, Crater Theory can accommodate the strengths of previous theories while at the same time having testing, questioning, of authorial contributions be at its core.

Television

Television was traditionally seen as the bastard love child of film and radio, but ever since "Prestige TV" of the 21st century began, it's become clear that TV can be just as artistic as its predecessor media, while at the same time its serial nature and wider scope allow it to tell stories uniquely suited to that format. David Chase (*The Sopranos*), Vince Gilligan (*Breaking Bad, Better Call Saul*), David Simon (*The Wire*), Tina Fey (*30 Rock*), Aaron Sorkin (*The West Wing, The Newsroom*), and many others can all be called auteurist in the TV realm.

Trident Theory could be used to locate the auteur(s) in TV, but if anything the Producer Solution outdoes it because unlike movies, TV shows can have completely different writers and directors episode-to-episode. This places showrunners like those listed above in an overseer role different from anything film has had (except for maybe Marvel with Kevin Feige).

Once again, Crater Theory carries these other ideas' strengths into this area while being more adaptable than either. You merely have to ask what removing a given person from production would do to the show. For *Breaking Bad*, as an example, without Vince Gilligan there's no idea and unifying vision, without the cast there's no acting to hook you, without the writers' room there's no 60-or-so hours of TV made in five years, without talented directors and crew none of that previous work would ever been seen, and without good effects artists, you wouldn't be pulled into that world with the sights and sounds. As always, there are more examples to go with that, but you get the picture.

The Takeaway

The main purpose of Crater Theory is to answer the auteur question for collaborative media. However, in a broader sense I hope that it can demonstrate the importance of every person involved in any creative endeavor generally (no one creates in a vacuum), but especially cast and crew members to film and TV shows.

Workers are the backbone not only of the economy, but of our culture as a whole. Those who contribute to this well-spring, in whatever form that contribution takes, deserve respect, fair compensation, and to be treated as a member of our human community.

I know for a fact that isn't too much to ask.

Not Being Open to Criticism Guarantees Failure

June 22, 2023

Full disclosure: I don't handle negative criticism very well. To be honest, I don't think I ever have handled it well. However, I've come to realize that, as much as this is my subconscious trying to protect me, my inability to take criticism has actually made me *more* prone to failure.

For example, I took a fiction-writing course in my first semester at college, and I remember how excited I'd been for that first day of class. Finally, after 8.5 years of writing for myself, I was in a class environment where others were as creative as I was, and would no doubt be eager to share their work and see it showered with praise—because, of course, all of our work was going to be great. I wasn't precisely this naive when I started, but it's the kind of *feeling* I had when I started. Anyway, the workshop day, which is when the class would discuss two students' work, came for my story. I was nervous, and I had no idea what they were going to say. The responses started out positive, and I felt great about my work.

Then it was my TA's turn to talk.

———

He clearly didn't enjoy the story. He seemed to think it not well-paced, and the only aspect of the story that he really enjoyed was the ending, which seemed to him to be a bit farcical. The letter he attached detailing his response was even harsher, though in hindsight I appreciate him holding back a bit during class. I don't have the response letter with me as I write this, but I did record these events in the nigh-daily journal that I kept during college; rest assured, he really didn't like my piece.

So, what did I do? Well, I (internally) said screw him, and wrote my next story with the express intent to create a character who possessed no redeeming qualities; the reader is meant to dislike this character. He didn't enjoy this one, either, but at this point, I didn't care. I'd made my point.

I stopped writing creative fiction for about six months once that class was over. I'd been writing short fiction since I was ten years old, but this was the first time I'd received honest critiques by people, and it had an impact on me. I genuinely felt like I didn't care about writing anymore.

What got me interested in writing again? Well, for one, I'd been writing for nine years at that point, and I couldn't stay away from it forever. It was also, however, the ability to write in complete solitude, just for myself. While this was great for my personal happiness, it didn't improve my abilities as a writer very much. A blanket is meant to keep you from the cold, but sometimes you've got to learn to toss that blanket aside and accept that there are things out there that can sting, maybe even worse than the cold.

———

I wrote the original draft of this essay in Spring 2018, as part of a project run by a fellow University of Virginia student. I don't recall the exact circumstances of the request, but it was about something along the lines of "failure" and "criticism." While I should've been doing an essay on Jane Austen's *Emma*, I instead wrote that draft for my friend. Nothing against Austen, that book, or that class, but I was more engaged writing this than I was at any point writing that 10-pager.

Because my background was in writing, and because that fiction-class experience was relatively recent, I decided to focus my essay entirely around that anecdote and the implications behind it. But in re-reading it recently, just after I'd had two stinging experiences of personal criticism directed at me, I realized the advice could be applied more universally.

"Criticism can lead you to improve your writing," I'd said at the time. I stand by that. As I also said:

> Sometimes you have to take criticism, and sometimes you have to ignore it. That's truly the hardest part of criticism, especially once you get over getting negative feedback in the first place: deciding what criticism you take, and what you ignore. Just know, if you listen to all of it, you'll never write again, and possibly go insane—but if you listen to none of it, you'll never improve yourself as a writer.

The most important thing, though, is to put your writing out there. If you don't do that, then failure isn't just the norm, it's the only option.

But I've come to realize that I still haven't "gotten over" getting negative feedback. It hurts to be told I've done something wrong, regardless of the merits that the person's claim has or doesn't have.

I've been challenged as a person recently through two situations I wouldn't wish on anyone, but which are probably more universal than individual, in a sense.

The first had to do with an Amazon review of a book of mine. Well, partly mine.

So, for context, my grandmother's second husband was John Prentice, a cartoonist best known for his photorealistic work on the newspaper strip *Rip Kirby* for over 42 years.

I had an idea a couple years ago to do a biography about him, and it's still in the works. (I may do a future short article talking about his style.) But part of that research led me to uncover just over 1,500 pages of comic-book art he did from 1949 to 1956, and that's just what was in the public domain and available at the amazing website Comic Book Plus. That's not even counting the ton of work he did for DC Comics, which is still under copyright.

I decided, as a gift for my grandmother—and, to a slightly lesser extent, for the rest of his family—to put together collections of these works, organized by year. I ended up with six books, the last of which contained 1954 to 1956.

I designed the covers myself, and painstakingly converted each page into black & white (for cost reasons), inserted it into a Microsoft Word template (for page-number and margin reasons), and would export, 20 pages at a time, into a PDF. There may have been easier or better ways to do it, but that was the process I came up with, because I knew I could do it that way.

I left the books up on Amazon, mostly so his family could buy copies if they wanted. I was never in it to make money, and any money I did make, I figured, was more than fair to cover the time I put into making them. I didn't really expect anyone else to buy them, to the point where I only had "This is a comics collection" as the product descriptor. Did I think a purchase was possible? Yes. But it wasn't in the forefront of my brain.

Then, last week I came across a review of one of the volumes, with one star. Highlights include: "Don't buy any of these—it's a scam," "I was disgusted by the editor's claim that the black-and-white (Dark grey) didn't detract from the beauty of the artwork," and "I feel I was tricked into buying this" because the preview didn't show any of the art pages.

———

Now, I've written a "review" responding and apologizing for this person's experience. Yes, I was upset at being called, basically, a scam artist. But once I calmed down, I was mostly just sad. This person had taken the time to buy a product I'd made, excited to delve into comics history, and was disappointed at the lack of color and quality. I'd let someone down, even unintentionally. Now, I had no control over the preview function or of the quality of either the original scans or the printed final, but I was satisfied enough with the copies I bought to continue making it available. I made the best of what I had found, and had loved every second of the process of putting those books together.

Today, each book's description reads as follows:

> *This is a self-published comics collection, put together from public-domain, second-hand scans of work by John Prentice, reprinted in black & white, as a way to honor the man and preserve his work. It was first and foremost put together for Prentice's family, but has been made publicly available for any fans of Prentice's work who want the works in one place but are willing to accept a slightly-lower quality. For the color originals, go to comicbookplus.com, where you can read the stories on the site for free. Also consider supporting them in their mission of preserving comics culture.*

I'm ultimately proud of how I handled it, but that goes to my point: I listened to criticism (somewhat disrespectful, but also valid enough to learn something from) and I improved transparency for what the books were and, more importantly, were not. My intent had never been anything below honest, but I could see how it came across that way.

———

The second time came in the form of an email, from a private school at which I'd subbed a few times. I will not be quoting from that email, since it was a private communication as opposed to a public review, but I will try to give a sense of its contents. Also, this isn't about calling any one particular person or institution out. This situation is now in the past, and is being used entirely to demonstrate the dual-sided nature of criticism with which this entire article deals.

One of the teachers I'd subbed for (seems to have) complained that I had let students leave the classroom a mess and draw obscene images. Now, to be honest, I was a bit lax with discipline regarding keeping the room clean, and that's completely on me. However, it was nowhere near the pig-sty this email made it out to be, at least for the time I was there. Also, I never saw a single one of these images, and would have reported the students if I had. I once reported an entire class (at this same school) because a student used the *n*-word while my back was turned, and thus while I couldn't write up an individual student, I could still make note of it.

The other issue was that this email came at least two weeks after the sub assignment (maybe it was even three weeks; I don't recall the exact day I subbed). It was not from the teacher, but from an administrator, who had never once asked me what happened, or at least spoken to me about this situation in a non-confrontational manner. Instead, I was passive-aggressively told that I'd been an absolute failure; the rude tone wasn't masked by the professional vocabulary used to communicate it.

To be blunt, I felt like I'd gotten more respect from the person who accused me of scamming them than I did from this administrator.

Once again, after thinking it over and not responding in a knee-jerk fashion, I found the validity in some of the email's points, while still recognizing that this was an unprofessional way of resolving it.

So, I took responsibility for where I did make mistakes, told her that I knew nothing of the pictures, and politely explained why I felt the email's tone had been inappropriate for a first communication on the issue. I also offered a little feedback on how future subs ought to be prepared for teaching there, since students at this school were far more disrespectful of authority than any other at which I'd subbed, and this was true to an extent even when I worked alongside another sub for my first day.

But I learned a lot.

I learned that knowing disciplinary procedures from the get-go is a must. I learned that being the cool teacher wasn't always the right attitude with which to approach certain students, i.e. those who would take advantage of that kindness. I learned that, even when I felt disrespected, the best way to respond was still with politeness and respect while at the same time not showing so much deference as to be spineless. And I learned that I wasn't a perfect

24

teacher.

And I realized that I was okay.

I'm sorry for the problems my lack of discipline caused that teacher. Like with the comics collection, I never set out to do anything less than my best. But my best isn't perfect. No one's is or ever will be.

My mom taught me that it isn't your mistakes that define you (unless of course it's something truly terrible and/or irreversible), but how you respond when confronted by them. I never wanted to make the mistakes I did make in this role. But they were made. The best I can do is learn from them and move on. And I know I'll be the much better teacher for having gotten this unconventional but important experience.

––––––––

We grow through experience. Sometimes, especially in our hyper-connected yet divided world, it's easier to just ignore it all and curl up into a ball... at least in the short term. But that helps no one, neither the person who curls up nor everyone else.

We must confront the problems of this world if we are to save and preserve it. That especially, though not exclusively, means looking at both our individual and our collective flaws. When we refuse to engage with this process, when we shut ourselves into the safe spaces of echo chambers, we end up failing more, not less. Yes, feeling safe in life is a basic human right; but never confronting the possibility of being wrong, of making mistakes and allowing yourself to learn from them, is what truly leads to long-term failure.

Yet not all criticism is valid, nor are you required to believe it is. My stories above hopefully demonstrate that.

The key is to find the balance, for it is in that range where we can find both self-safety and the knowledge to change, to improve ourselves, which we can only obtain by learning our faults.

Be open to criticism. Just don't let it constrict you, either.

For the Love of Translation, Both Professional and Amateur

June 24, 2023

Casual fans of J.R.R. Tolkien will know him for *The Hobbit*, *The Lord of the Rings*, and (possibly) a couple other works. If that's the only experience a person has with him, they've gotten plenty of greatness.

But dedicated fans know that Tolkien was a philologist as well, and that while his "secret vice" for constructing languages found its outlet in his stories, he was also genuinely talented with real languages. His lecture "*Beowulf*: The Monsters and the Critics" and essay "On Translating *Beowulf*" are highly influential in the study of the Old English epic poem. Tolkien also tried his hand at translating the poem himself, back in the 1920s, though that work was edited by his son and published only in 2014, 41 years after Tolkien's death.

The reason I begin with Tolkien is to demonstrate how influential the love of languages was to one of English's most widely-read authors, and how that love can be an end of itself, rather than just a means. That's partly why I got into translating comics, which is covered later in this piece.

I'm also going to take a controversial stance: **Translators, and translation itself, never get due respect!**

Seriously. With all of this *Frankenstein*-like AI development over the past year especially, it seems like everything will soon be automated, including translation. (Technically, "translation" is only used when talking about the written word, whereas "interpretation" refers to spoken or signed language, but for simplicity, I'm going to refer to both as "translation.")

But people were automating translation over a decade ago, with Spanish classmates of mine sometimes just running their papers through Google Translate despite teachers telling them not to. In fact, my Spanish II teacher used this video[1] to demonstrate why Google Translate could be incredibly unreliable and flat-out wrong. While we may think, even subconsciously, that translation is as straightforward and logical as, say, a math problem, it's as much of an art as it is a science. It is the art-part, so to speak, that machine translation has always struggled with. Although the translator programs have improved over time, they're still prone to error, especially with linguistic nuances that are much harder to code.

Translation has also formed the backbone of cultural exchange since at least the development of writing around 5,000 years ago. Whether it was facilitating trade or negotiating with an enemy power, the ability to have the words of one's native language converted into another has both practical and cultural benefits. Translators are a bridge, making connections which help build our common humanity and give us glimpses into worlds very different from our own, both in time and space.

In translating comics myself, my brain genuinely changed in a way that I could feel. I loved that accomplishment in and of itself, but what was even more amazing was the fulfillment I felt at being people's bridge into stories most, if not all, of them never would have experienced otherwise.

Creating my own stories is fulfilling, but translation exercises a different set of skills by presenting a different set of limitations, while still allowing for creativity and individuality in the final product.

Amateur Translation

Nearly all translation examples you're most familiar with are done by trained experts for a professional purpose. Take, for example, the Bible, the most translated book in human history. There are over 100 editions in English alone, and at least some portions of it have been translated into around 3,000 languages; that even includes constructed languages like Esperanto.

A book with theological importance to about 2 billion people is going to be taken seriously. In fact, disputes about translation have contributed to church schisms (see Martin Luther adding "alone" to his German translation of the Bible in Paul's Epistle to the Romans) and movements around supporting a single translation (see the King James Only movement for the best example). How the Bible is translated, and which of the ancient manuscripts a translation draws from, are two central questions of both secular and theological Biblical criticism.

However, there actually is at least one attempt at an "amateur" Bible translation, where translators were/are not required to be professionals: the Wiki Bible.

The Wiki Bible was an early project of Wikisource, the sister site of Wikipedia dedicated to hosting public-domain documents. Unlike most of its repository, which is based on existing works in the United States public domain, the Wiki Bible would be a Bible translation made by volunteers and free to the (English-speaking) world.

According to a 2008 *Newsweek* article[2] about the project, at least one contributor to the project had no training in Greek, despite helping translate Paul's First Epistle to the Corinthians. Another admitted to having "[no] qualifications of any kind." The article does not cover *how* these two were able to contribute to the translation without expertise, however.

In the same article, respected Biblical scholar Bart D. Ehrman criticized the Wiki Bible for its amateur nature, saying that "[d]emocratization isn't necessarily good for scholarship." Another professional, Richard Friedman, found errors in this version's Genesis, according to the same source.

While translation errors present a problem, Ehrman's critique rings hollow for me. Had the Wiki Bible been the *only* English version, he would have a point. But there are plenty of English versions available, and many of those carry a lot more weight than the Wiki Bible because, as Ehrman points out, the best scholars work on some versions for up to decades. Would using the Wiki Bible as one's primary scripture be the best idea? Perhaps not. But the project's usage of volunteers as translators makes it fascinating for how it can act as an example of collaborative, amateur translation. What other book would be as good for comparison than one that has dozens of professional translations?

Scanlation

"Scanlation" refers to the practice of fans making scans of foreign comics — Japanese manga mostly — and translating those comics into English. The practice began thanks to fans who wanted to share their love of manga, but who found the authorized translations either lacking or nonexistent.

Make no mistake: this activity is illegal in nearly every country. It is blatant copyright infringement. But it also represents an admirable bit of fan labor that one could compare to the Wiki Bible's creation, if for nothing else than the fact that both cases are motivated by a love of sharing an experience with others through translation.

In a way, it was in this tradition that my own work followed, although I hadn't heard of scanlations at the time.

My Efforts

In Spring 2020, I took a course at the University of Virginia on comics taught by the wonderful Sean Duncan, a course which genuinely changed my life. It gave me a sense of appreciation for the medium I never could have had otherwise, despite my step-grandfather being noted cartoonist John Prentice.

From both that course and the YouTube channel Comic Tropes (check him out if you like comics; he's great), I learned about this website called Comic Book Plus, which collects public domain (out of copyright) comics. I was able to gather 1,520 pages of my grandfather's work from the site in the course of researching a biography of him.

In that research, I also learned that the site hosted comics in other languages. That caught my interest, at the very least because I thought it would be cool to see what non-English comics looked like.

The most surprising result, though, was this comic,[3] a translation of an Italian original by a user named **crashryan** (no relation). I was impressed. It was professional quality, and I loved the concept. I also admired the fact that this user had done it for free and released the work into the public domain (a requirement for posting a translation on the website).

(Quick side note: because the original work was in the public domain, I wouldn't call it a "scanlation," but that's my personal preference. To me, a scanlation by definition has to be (1) unauthorized, and (2) made from a copyrighted original.)

This example gave me an idea. CBP had a pretty sizable Spanish section, and I was a bit familiar with Spanish thanks to 5 years of it in public school. No, I wasn't fluent, but I knew enough to get the basics, and if I had questions, I could use Google Translate to figure out what a word or set of words *could* mean. I know, I know, don't use Google Translate; I even said it myself! But the built-in benefit of a comic was that I had the assistance of the pictures. Between that, my own knowledge, and Google Translate's ability to give you a range of possible meanings for a word, I had confidence I could do it. Plus, I was free to adapt the wording slightly if I had to; this was my project.

So, yes, I did that. I picked issue #1 of the superhero comic *La Araña Verde* ("The Green Spider"), and set to work making the translation. It took a couple weeks of work, though to be fair I did set myself the goal of doing the ads, as well. But I got it done.

To my astonishment, I got three comments on my work, including two which were incredibly appreciative and complimentary. With that inspiration, I planned on doing the whole second issue, but I instead was only able to do the first story in the book — as of now, at least.

You can find the originals and my translations at this link,[4] if you want to read them for yourself. The comments are included beneath the original work. Also, my translations include a final page both releasing the work to the public domain and explaining my process.

The Why

I had no idea what I would get out of translating these comics. At the very least, I figured it would let me brush up on my Spanish and also let me get to do something with a real comic (I can't draw to save my life) — to create and adapt at the same time. I could not have expected the response I got, nor the sense of accomplishment at seeing the finished product.

Now, could I have claimed copyright on my work? Yes. However, as I said, I explicitly relinquished all my rights to my translation so that it could be posted. Why? Well, for one, what was I going to do with it? If I offered it for sale, almost no one would buy it; plus, the printing quality on the original scans was just awful. (It's not the uploader's fault, but the 1950s printer's.) If I gave it away, I could ensure that people could read and enjoy it.

To be honest, though, there was also an added sense of freedom in knowing from the beginning that I was always going to give this away. It didn't have to be perfect, just as good as I could make it with what I had to work with. That allowed me to really enjoy the process, despite how time-consuming it was.

Most importantly, though, I'd added something of value to the world that anyone could enjoy and share. It may not be world-saving charity, but it is something meaningful. That's an incredible reward in and of itself.

So, maybe give it a go yourself, even if it's just a page or two of something. You might be surprised at what you get out of it.

If for whatever reason that's not up your alley, I have a different request:

make something. You don't have to share it with anyone except yourself. But make something. Allow yourself to be creative, to develop a passion, to explore new ideas, what have you.

Trust me: you will get something out of it once you find your thing.

Update

Since publishing this essay on Medium, I've translated two more comics: (1) a photo-comic starring Mexican luchador Mil Mascaras as "Captain Kobba," fighting an alien threat, and (2) a romance comic about a woman who meets and falls in love with a prince. Both can also be found on Comic Book Plus. However, it turns out that the other stories in the second issue of *The Green Spider* were incomplete, at least in the scan uploaded on Comic Book Plus, so there were no more Green Spider stories to translate.

The Trouble with Nothing

June 25, 2023

We humans love classification. It's how we were able to develop the Linnean system for categorizing life, and how we are able to engage in deep analysis in a countless number of pursuits. We have imposed our own version of order on the world, with the assistance of this love of classification. However, it can be quite reasonably argued that this obsession with classifying things leads to some of the most heinous acts of social and actual violence humans commit against other humans. The whole institution of African slavery, and the Holocaust in Nazi Germany, are the most frequently cited, but these are not the only examples, and enslavement and genocide are not the only ways in which humans impose their darkest natures upon others.

However, we also like to classify ourselves, and that is something we don't often consciously grasp. I ask you to think about this: *what* **are you?** Consider this for a moment, then read the next paragraph.

Now, if I were to answer this question, my first instinct would be to answer with the following: I am a writer. I am a teacher. I am a lifelong student. (My short Medium bio has this all in it.)

Perhaps I could define myself in relation to others. I am someone's son. I am someone's nephew. I am someone's boyfriend.

The problem with *all* of these responses, and with any response you might give, is that they are responses to an illegitimate question. Ask someone *what* they are, and you have defined that person in relation to what they do, or how they are related to something else, which is itself invalid. I write fiction, I aspire to teach well, and I study, but I am… well, just that. I exist, and I am a human being. That's the end of the discussion. Sure, there are qualities inherent to me as an existing being, such as the fact that I am someone's son, *but* an important understanding is that (1) I do not tie any of my self-worth into these inherent qualities, and if I ever do, it will lead to just as many problems as what I outlined previously about the illegitimate question, but also (2) these qualities are permanent, things I cannot change. I will always be my father and mother's son, even after all three of us are long gone. (Then it will be that I *was* their son.)

In contrast, think about what you may have answered to "what are you?" Take my first response as an example. I am a writer. How do I define this? Am I constantly a writer? How did I become one? Do I ever lose that title? Is there a certain amount I have to write to earn that title? You get the point. Nothing makes me a writer, aside from me saying it, and it isn't inherent in who I am. If I were to stop writing, or write a bad work, what would become of me? Well, nothing. I'd have written a bad work, but I'd still be my parents' son. This is the problem with defining ourselves in relation to what we do. I write, just like I breathe. I can stop writing, though; then, perhaps, I'd no longer be a writer.

Titles are transient and constructed, and by putting self-worth into them, one gives those titles the power to kill. Even jobs such as a lawyer or doctor, which require the confirmation of others in order for the title to be bestowed, are constructs. My mother practices law, but to say she is a lawyer is to tie not only her worth, but her very being, into what she does. Therefore, if she makes a mistake, she has misstepped not only in what she does, but who she is.

This distinction between who you are and what you do/have was introduced to me in therapy. When I thought about what would happen if I stopped writing, I realized that this distinction is true. My therapist also used the example of friends, and I thought back to all the friends I've had and lost over the years. It was always even more devastating to lose them than it might otherwise have been because I'd tied myself into these other people, defined my very self in relation to them. There was nothing that inherently made me their friend, so it is fickle to say "I am" or "I was" their friend. (This isn't to say these friendships weren't valid, but simply to point out that my whole being didn't end when the friendships did.)

Of course, realizing this is only half the battle, and it is here where are we deal with what comes after, how we move on. As it stands, if this has impacted us, we are left with a large hole of self-esteem where once we drew it from what we did, or what we had. So, from what do we draw now?

Here's where I'm going to be honest and say that I haven't fully been able to keep myself in this state. I backslide. I think about my insecurities or my anxieties, and then I sometimes turn to these impermanent markers of identity to make me feel better. I give them a power they do not deserve. And then I have thus given someone or something else the power to take that self-esteem away from me.

As I said in an essay on taking criticism, there are times when it's important to let others' evaluations of you have an impact on how you see yourself. That's completely valid. But you need something to keep yourself grounded despite everything else.

Do not tie yourself to something that can easily change, or that can be reduced by others. When I did that with writing, I felt horrible about my very self whenever I got feedback. When I did that with grades, I felt the same feeling when someone else succeeded more, because that (somehow) reduced what I'd done down to nothing.

You know what this realization did to me back in 2018, when I first had it? It made me a lot happier. Admittedly, I took a more radical route and decided not to take pride in, say, academic accomplishments. (Even my therapist was a bit against this idea.) But I stand by it, because I knew that once I took pride in something, I was putting my very self on the line.

You don't have to be that radical with your self-definition, though. You just have to do something else to derive a sense of purpose.

You can, in the case of something where you're being judged, accept that all you can do is your best. As long as you can genuinely say that to yourself, you've got a good start.

You can also find activities which don't require competition, or comparison with others, but which can be done just for the pleasure of the activity itself. I did that when I translated some comics for fun. You might find that with painting, writing, volunteering, walking, etc. The point in this case is to enjoy it without needing to be great at it, or to prove yourself to anyone.

Find your permanent self-definitions. It may not be a cure-all, but it will always cure at least a little.

Why "Democracy" Has Always Been a Misnomer

July 5, 2023

So, maybe you're expecting this to be a complaint about how the United States is run by the wealthy, or that the Electoral College is undemocratic, etc. etc. Regardless of my feelings on those and other issues, that isn't what this article is about. The title applies to almost all states throughout history which have claimed to be democracies, not just the United States.

So, first, what is democracy? Well, it comes from the Greek *demos* and *kratos*, meaning "people" and "rule," respectively. It's worth noting that people who draw a distinction between a "democracy" and a "republic" are, at least etymologically, incorrect, as "republic" comes from the Latin *res publica*, meaning "things of the public." The literal meanings of these two words are the same.

However, the Founding Fathers of the United States used "democracy" in reference to "direct democracy," where people participate directly in decision-making, like in ancient Athens. On the other hand, their idea of "republic" was modeled on Ancient Rome, where a smaller group of people would be entrusted with governance, but would still answer to this people. This is what we today would call a "representative democracy."

But calling it that is oxymoronic.

One Day a Year

In a system of government where the people elect their representatives, the people have political power only on Election Day. On every other day of the year, the power itself is solely in the hands of the elected (and, in some cases, appointed) representatives.

Think about this: the Republican agenda in 2017 was a repeal of the Affordable Care Act, and their trifecta control of the House, Senate, and White House seemed poised to make that happen. However, it was dramatically defeated when Senator John McCain voted against the measure, denying it the votes needed to pass.

Regardless of your feelings on the ACA, Senator McCain, or the Republican Party, this should give you pause. Senator McCain was elected as a Republican, and while I can't speak to the priorities of the Arizonans who voted for him, I imagine a good many of them were aware that his party wished to repeal the ACA. What if this was a goal of the majority of them, or of every McCain voter? If McCain were elected in part because of expectations that he would vote to repeal the ACA, shouldn't he have done it?

Well, that's to the discretion of the senator, just as it is of every other official, elected or appointed. They can vote however they want, regardless of what their constituents desire.

The only thing keeping them in line is the threat of not being re-elected.

That's why I say representative democracy is a misnomer. Countries which elect their representatives are democracies *only on election days*.

In the U.S., that makes it once a year. Primaries don't count because the winner of a primary is not (on paper) given any political office yet. However, in districts or states where the winner of a primary is at least heavily favored to win the general election, you could argue that those primaries are the election day. This also means, however, that the actual Election Day does not serve any purpose, if these people were guaranteed an office the moment they won a primary.

Exceptions

Now, recall elections might be an exception, as they place more power in the hands of the people to essentially "create" more election days.

Also, in the United Kingdom, parliamentary votes are able to happen in-between regular elections, and while I'm not familiar with this process, it seems to allow for some flexibility not present in the U.S. system.

But these and other avenues still require a lot of work, and when change is hard to effect, the scales are weighted in favor of the status quo. Thus, my argument about representative democracy being a misnomer still stands.

Elective Oligarchy

We tend to associate monarchies with hereditary inheritance, but that's not a necessary element; there is such a thing as an elective monarchy, rare as it is in today's world. The best current example is Vatican City, where an elected pope becomes an absolute monarch over Vatican territory once he enters office.

If we can have an elective monarchy, why could we not have an *elective oligarchy*? I actually think that term is a better descriptor than "representative democracy" for the systems that we have.

Think about this: while an "oligarchy" is now associated with rule by the wealthy (which is actually a *plutocracy*, a form of oligarchy), the actual definition is "rule by the few." What better descriptor could there be for countries with millions of citizens who are ruled by, at most, thousands?

Thinking about modern-day democracies this way allows us to understand how we as citizens have political power in relation to our politicians. It also helps us think about how we exercise our own power, and how, if we desire more power for the people, we can go about altering our systems to make that possible.

It's also worth noting that when I say "political power," I mean the power to use the organs of government to enact an agenda. I believe that regular citizens do have power outside of Election Day, but it's usually exercised as "soft power" — boycotts, disruptive protests (if a protest isn't disruptive of the status quo, it isn't effective), speaking at public-comment meetings, etc. An example of "hard power" might be, say, the kind of actions which defined the French Revolution post-Bastille storming.

This is not an apologia for systems which do not adequately represent or respond to the people's interest; if anything, it is a critique of them. After all, those who do not have access to the ballot box are living under an oligarchy, plain and simple. On top of that, oligarchic seizures of power due to (in the U.S.) gerrymandering and centralized media ownership are a threat to the one-day-a-year when people can have their say.

Most importantly, it is a statement of the current conditions of our political situations, my hope being to increase awareness and understanding. If you do wish to make a change, you have to understand what the current situation is, so you can know the obstacles in your path and think for yourself about the best way to effect change.

The Two Sides of Religion

July 6, 2023

So, I started this draft before the U.S. Supreme Court handed down its *303 Creative LLC v. Elenis* decision, but I think it's worthwhile to note that while I kept this in mind while completing this essay, it was not what prompted this, and it doesn't change the core ideas contained herein.

———

Religion has served as a comfort to billions throughout recorded history, and almost certainly since before the written word existed to create that record. It is this aspect of faith-based belief systems which fuels the positive zeal that many take toward evangelizing their religion. Evangelism itself, in fact, comes from Greek, and came to mean "good news"; its connotation comes from Christianity and the idea of spreading the good news of the gospels, but anyone who preaches their beliefs zealously in order to convert others could be called an "evangelist" in modern English.

However, religion has also been perhaps the most divisive issue in human history, the driver behind countless conflicts both inside and between nations.

So, how do we square these two seemingly contradictory elements of religion? Is there a way we can understand how each operates, and perhaps gain a fuller understanding of religion in general, regardless of our individual beliefs? I think so.

Broadly, we can call these categories "**spiritual comfort**" and "**social control.**"

Spiritual Comfort

We humans are curious creatures, but the world offers few answers to our most fundamental questions; if it does reveal anything, those revelations are wrought out, not coaxed.

In the course of human history, religion has served as a North Star, a way of explaining a hostile world to people seeking to understand, but unable to get the answers. For instance: What is lightning? The weapon of Zeus. What are the stars? Reflections of mythical people and events. Where did humans come from? God(s).

But even with modern science (of which I am an unequivocal advocate), we humans are not able to answer spiritual questions directly. Science cannot say what happens after a person dies, for example. For some, the solution is to say it is unanswerable, or that nothing happens—when you die, you cease to exist.

But understandably, this isn't a comfort for most people. We're social creatures. That we will never see those we love ever again is an idea that hurts beyond words. Even more, the idea that our very selves will just... vanish, is scary. So, ideas of an afterlife (especially a pleasant one) are a comfort.

But beyond death, there is the question of what we ought to do before we die. Science can assert the fact that we are here. The question of purpose, at least beyond the utilitarian perspective that evolution provides, is something it's wholly unsuited for. Many find their purpose and meaning through faith in *something* outside of themselves. In many cases, this also arguably leads to an overall increase in good works, since faith can also build community and lead people to serve others.

There's a reason (probably many, actually) why every recorded human so-

I do know, however, that my great-grandmother made it to nearly her 102nd birthday (short a few weeks)—after having lived through two world wars, the Depression, many years of familial separation across the Atlantic Ocean, and the turbulence of the Cold War—thanks to her Catholic faith. She was the most grateful and most caring person you could ever meet; my dad likes to say that if Heaven has a welcoming committee, she'd be on it, if not leading it. Her ability to handle stressful situations is unparalleled for those I've met in my 25 years of life.

But I'm not advocating that you convert to Catholicism (I'm lapsed myself), or Christianity, or any other religious belief system of any size or age. What I am trying to do is make a point that while we may think of religion as good (spiritual comfort) or bad (social control), not only can religion be both, but these two elements can intermingle in ways that make this black-and-white thinking unproductive.

Religion and Democracy

There is one place where the social-control element butts up against society: democracy.

By "democracy," I don't just mean a society where the people have a say in how their government is run, but a society where people are given latitude to choose how to live (to a degree). When a dogmatic belief system which insists on drawing a sharp line between believers and non-believers interacts with a democratic system, it's quite possible for that democracy to crumble from within into a theodemocracy—think Puritan Massachusetts or pre-statehood Mormon Utah.

A theodemocracy incorporates elements of both a theocracy and a democracy. It usually arises when members of a community are both in favor of popular rule but also of the same mind regarding faith. In these systems, believers have the best of both worlds.

But for nonbelievers, it may be Hell. If one does not fit into an expected

45

mold, they may be ostracized, demonized, assaulted, and even killed. Those who don't fit the mold, or who dare disagree with the majority's beliefs, are a threat to that majority.

An ideal democracy doesn't just protect the majority; it protects minorities, as well. It recognizes that a majority may harm those who are not in their group.

The existence of religion does not in itself endanger democracy. It is when *fundamentalism* enters the picture that the threat truly emerges, because fundamentalism refuses to respect differences of opinion. Fundamentalism takes the "my way or no way" approach. This is what leads to inquisitions. This is what leads to persecution.

———

I write this essay not to criticize religion, nor to praise it, but to share my ideas about what it is, how it works, and why it's still a major part of human societies. I think it's important to have the tools to analyze these situations, so that we can think for ourselves and make the best decisions possible based on what we know.

If you've never thought of religion in terms of the two "SC"s, or if you've never considered how its positives and negatives can coexist and interact, then I've done my job in introducing you to this perspective.

What you do with this information is up to you.

The Bible in Comics Form

July 8, 2023

It's the greatest story ever told... or maybe make that *stories*. Either way, the Bible has had an incomparable influence on Western culture, and through the West's influence, the culture of the entire world. Even the second-most-adhered-to religion, Islam, draws on the Bible; Jesus is revered as a prophet (though not the son of God), and the gospel tradition is known as *injil*.

Biblical stories have also formed the basis for countless media adaptations, from novels to plays to films to TV shows, and more.

For both its influence and its many adaptations, it may come as no surprise that the Bible has also served as inspiration for a number of works in the comics form. Today, I wanted to discuss a few I thought were most noteworthy, and which would be of interest to both religious and secular individuals.

Biblia pauperum

Though perhaps not comics in the way we might imagine them today, with word balloons and action, the *Biblia pauperum* was not just Biblical text with pictures accompanying, but Biblical pictures with occasional text.

Why might this qualify as comics? Well, certain (though not all) definitions of the term require that text be secondary and pictures primary. To me, this is part of what defines comics, thus I categorize the *Biblia pauperum* as comics.

Before mass literacy, this form was also one of the few ways that lay people could experience the Biblical narratives for themselves.

Treasure Chest

While including other material besides just Christian-focused stories, *Treasure Chest* was a Catholic comic-book series which operated from the 1940s to the 1970s, most issues (if not all) of which are now in the public domain.

Like *Classics Illustrated* (which adapted classic stories like *The Three Musketeers* and *Moby-Dick* into comic-book form), *Treasure Chest* sought to (1) bring "quality" content to young minds through comics, while also (2) hoping to use it as a gateway for kids to get interested in the original source material. While many were railing against comic books for promoting immorality and juvenile delinquency, *Treasure Chest* showed that certain people believed that comics' popularity could be used for proselytizing purposes.

Chester Brown's Gospel adaptations

In the late 1980s, we have Canadian cartoonist Chester Brown's attempts at adapting the Gospels into comic book form. The project was never completed, as he only adapted Mark and a portion of Matthew before he ended his endeavor.

However, what Brown did complete is both admirable from a technical standpoint and worth a read for any fan of either good comics work or of the Bible, as Brown's work is a straightforward adaptation of the source material — except for an addition to Mark which Brown took from the supposed Secret Gospel of Mark.

The Brick Bible

In 2001, Elbe Spurling embarked on what would eventually become a 12-year journey to adapt the Bible into comics form using Legos (or "Lego," if you're a purist). Using nothing more than a massive Lego collection and a camera, she recreated major and minor Bible stories visually, then added captions and speech balloons.

All stories can be viewed on the *Brick Bible* website, so there's no cost to check this one out. Also consider checking out her work depicting the American and French revolutions, or the stories of American presidential assassinations and attempts.

There are a couple things to note, however. First, there is the occasional typo, which may not irk most people, but it irks me when I see it.

Second, while Spurling's work is in a way faithful to the source material, there is an occasional sense of satire, especially with the dialogue not from the Bible. Spurling differentiates these additions by having the text in a different color, so there's no trickery involved or anything, but there is a sense of critique there. That sense also comes across with certain aesthetic choices, like, for example, using a ghost Lego figure to represent the Holy Ghost.

Basically, if you take the Bible so seriously that anything less than reverence for it bothers you, then *The Brick Bible* isn't for you. Otherwise, I think it's worth at least a look.

Robert Crumb's Genesis

Robert Crumb's work in underground comix (the "x" is not a typo), which dealt heavily with sex, drug use, and general irreverence, naturally led comics fans to assume his adaptation of the Book of Genesis would be a "sendup."

Nope. Just like Chester Brown's Gospels, Crumb's *Book of Genesis* is a straightforward adaptation of the source material—in this case, a combination of the King James Bible and Robert Alter's translation.

The illustrations are standard Crumb, so depending on your preference, that may be a selling point or a deal breaker. (Look up his work for examples.) The book is also $35, which is a big investment if you're not sure you'll enjoy it. Oh, and it is sexually explicit, though no more so than the Bible itself in those instances. Still, something to keep in mind.

The Action Bible

For those who are looking for a straightforward adaptation of the entire Bible in comics form made from an explicitly religious standpoint, *The Action Bible* is probably your best bet. The illustration quality is good, the book has been translated into more than two dozen languages, and there's even an app made in partnership with the book's Christian publisher, David C. Cook.

This also makes *The Action Bible* the clearest descendant of *Treasure Chest* in its attempts to appeal directly to the faithful.

The Manga Bible

Our final entry comes courtesy of a melding between Eastern and Western traditions: the *Manga Bible*. It's a 200-page adaptation of the Bible which, like *The Action Bible*, received praise from religious leaders. The reason it warrants its own entry is the major difference that a manga style puts on the comic versus the more traditional American style of *Action*.

————

So, why adapt the Bible in comics form? Maybe for commercial reasons, but there is also the reality that comics is one of the few forms of visual media which can be created by a single person, and reflect that person's vision. Maybe their vision includes a critique, or maybe it is simply a desire to spread Christian teaching.

Regardless, the Bible is the common property of all—even translations which are still under copyright are adapting from sources which are thousands of years old. For anyone who loves comics, no matter their affiliation with Christianity, the universality and availability of that scripture makes it an appealing source for comic adaptation.

The Destruction of Language

July 11, 2023

We have no record of when language originated, because language predates written records for probably tens of thousands of years. Complex language, capable of expressing abstract thought, is what distinguishes us as a species and what has allowed us, for better or worse, to become the dominant lifeform on Earth.

In recent times, however, language has become weaponized, politicized, in a way that, while perhaps not new in the course of human history, is and always has been a threat to a functioning society.

When something becomes political, it moves out of the realm of fact and into the realm of personal opinion. If one can make an ordinarily easily-dismissed belief — whether it be that the Earth is flat, white supremacy is okay, or that environmental health isn't worth protecting — political, it can be protected from objective criticism because, hey, everyone's entitled to their own opinion. This is now happening to language.

What do I mean by this? I'll use an example: I am a liberal. While that may very likely already make many people dismiss me as… well, you pick your insult… I ask that you hear me out, especially if you *don't* agree with me. Because that knee-jerk reaction, one that I admittedly often have when I hear someone is conservative, is evidence of my point.

So, what does it mean that I'm a liberal? Well, as it turns out, the answer will vary depending on your political orientation. Before I say why I identify this way, I'm genuinely curious: what do you think it means that I'm a liberal? What ideas or images come to your mind? Are they ones you agree with or disagree with? Do you find me, based on this label, inviting, revolting, or somewhere in between? I can think of a lot of words I've been called based on my label, both positive and negative.

This is how language becomes politicized. The same word has different meanings and connotations depending on what your beliefs are. The label itself becomes useless as an identifier and instead turns into a way to pigeonhole someone into a set of ideas that are held not by the person, but by the one they're talking to.

To me, being a liberal means a lot of things, but some of the basics are that I believe in the freedom of the individual to do as they please as long as they don't hurt someone else, in the preservation of the natural environment and that this also benefits humans (and that failing to do so presents a threat to humanity as well as is a dereliction of duty), and that we as a society function best when we help one another and work together to improve our collective quality of life.

If you identify like me, perhaps that's old news, if not an oversimplification of modern American liberalism. However, if you come from a different political orientation, then perhaps none of that would be in your definition. Maybe you think that I believe that women are superior to men, or that government should dictate everything about a person's life, or that I don't believe in freedom of thought. Without getting into each one of these in particular, I think it's clear that there is a big divergence between what I think a liberal is and what someone who doesn't like liberals thinks a liberal is.

I must also admit to my own biases, that I'm guilty of this same behavior, and that it is a struggle to overcome this in myself. For example, when I think "conservative," I very often think of someone who doesn't respect women, minorities, or members of the LGBT+ community, does not care about the truth or the environment, is intolerant of non-Christians, and blindly loves the U.S. as a country to the point where any criticism of it is dismissed as being inherently wrong. That's what comes to my mind. But I bet none of that would be how a conservative defines who they are, even if they agreed that they hold some of those beliefs (if not framed in that way).

Part of this is the issue of a group versus a person. We each hold our own views as people, but the moment we identify with a group or our views make others do this for us, we become part of bigger, general blobs. What this leads to is an idea of what a person of Group A is, and then we assume that all people of Group A believe the exact same things.

This is why I don't identify as a Democrat. First, to me that means that I would adhere to the Democratic Party; I'd be letting them define what I believe. Second, I have many issues with the party as an organization. I identify as a liberal because my views align more on that side, and the views I'm most passionate about, such as the environment, economic opportunity, and individual rights, are decidedly liberal. My views define my identification, not the other way around. (Also worth noting that the Democrats were once the party of slaveholders, not to shame it, but to point out that a party can change its ideology substantially. I would like to think that if I lived in the time of Lincoln, I'd have been a pro-emancipation Republican.)

Part of the problem is an inability to listen to one another, but it's also the divergence in language. We use these shorthand identifiers differently depending on our identification, and that means we begin to develop two different dialects. This is also true not just for political labels, but for ideas in general. It even happens when people repeat sayings and ideas blindly, without thinking through what they mean. It's the difference between, for example, someone saying "Save the Earth" because they are knowledgeable about the issues facing our planet versus someone who says it because their favorite celebrity or politician says it. In the latter case, there's no conviction, there's no critical thought, even if the support for the cause is the same.

Language is losing its social, unifying purpose in these realms. Our inability to agree on definitions isn't the only issue in our society, but it's helping to cause a major social rift. The only solution I can think of to help solve this is the following: if someone asks you "Are you a/an ___?" then, unless you understand what they mean by that label, you have to respond with: "Well, how do you define what a/an ___ is?" If they define it, and you don't agree with those ideas, then you can explain: "No, if that's what you mean by ___, then I am not that, but that's not how I understand what ___ is." Or, you can go into detail about what you do and don't believe.

This idea isn't a cure-all, and it may very well be that you learn that the person you're talking to believes something(s) that are too problematic for you to look past and/or accept. Perhaps then the same disagreement remains. But ignoring others and confining them and yourself to different echo chamber bubbles is not healthy for society, if for no other reason than that it precludes understanding of our world and each other. This is a disservice to the inquiring, scientifically-minded way we ought to approach the world; has it not earned that respect from us?

The Universal Language

July 12, 2023

After documenting what I felt could be called "the destruction of language," I wanted to have my next essay be this one, about *building* through communication. For transparency, I am not a linguistics expert, and what follows is simply a train of thought I had which I followed.

————

All languages must have a basis beyond themselves in order to function. If this fact were *not* the case, then not only would translation be impossible (which, since I love the art of translation, would not be fun for me), but the very act of communication itself would be impossible, as all communication is, in a sense, an act of translation, from brain to action to brain.

This basis underlies all language, whether written, spoken, or signed. This basis, upon which all communication is built, is *the* conceptual ur-language (CUL). This is not to say that this ur-language itself is conceptual, though it is that; rather, this is to say that the ur-language itself is based in concepts. These concepts are tied to no sounds, images, or touches. No singular thing can confine or define this language in its totality, because it does not exist in the same sense that other languages exist.

In order to grasp this grasp-less concept as best we can, let us consider the most rational basis for all human language: reality. The concepts which under-lie all human language lie outside of those languages.

In your language, the concept of a *leaf,* whether that be the word on the page, the sound emanating from the mouth, or the sign made with one's hand or hands, refers to an idea outside of that communication. When your brain receives the signal for that idea, it conjures up a concept. Typically, this will be an image, real or created, of the thing itself. In the case of the leaf, it may also conjure up the rustling noise a leaf and its brethren make in the wind.

That is to say, the concept is triggered by the signal, and then the concept is experienced within the mind. In this way, however, the process is cyclical: one's initial concept derives from something outside of one's experience, and then that concept becomes the basis for all future understanding of the thing. But the concept is not *a priori,* meaning it did not previously exist in your brain. It is based in experience.

This is not to say that communication is always completely clear. The meanings of words and sounds, as well as pronunciations, and even experi-ences, change over generations, and even vary between people at the same mo-ment in time. Almost certainly the leaf I have in my mind is different from the one you have in yours, assuming you have an idea of what the English word "leaf" means (which, again, would be based on experience). However, we un-derstand, to a degree, the same overall concept. The referent is the same.

Sometimes, however, meaning is unclear, because two words are pro-nounced the same but spelled differently, because a word was misheard or misread or mis-signed, because understandings and experiences change over time, et cetera. Language is not always clear, but the CUL is, because it is based in conceptions.

To rectify the difference, one's personal conceptual language (PCL) is not the same thing as the CUL, or as a human language in a general sense. Rather, each human language is an aggregation of its populace's PCLs. When people agree that a certain idea is referred to with words, sounds, or signs, they are able to trust in those expressions and in turn interpret them when used by others. This is how community forms.

This is also, not coincidentally, a direct antidote to the aforementioned destruction of language. In my previous essay, my idea was to ensure that the concepts underlying the words someone was using—especially politically charged words—are the same for both the speaker and the listener. If they aren't, and this isn't rectified, communication breaks down and communities split apart.

More importantly, one's PCL is based on one's experiences, and one's ability to understand concepts themselves. For instance, *I* is a sound, a word, and a sign, but all three are based in the notion of one's essence as a being, of one's existence. One having an *I* equivalent in their PCL is dependent upon one having the ability to conceptualize that idea. All human languages have an equivalent of this fundamental concept in some form, of self-awareness in language, and therefore, we can say that the CUL has an *I* in it, even if the actual use of *I* to refer to that concept only happens in the English language.

However, we are making that deduction after the fact. Therefore, from our perspective, it seems that the CUL has an *I* in it because all human languages have an *I* in them. Nope; rather, all human languages possess the *I* because the CUL possesses it.

Recall that each human language is an aggregation of all of its people's PCLs. To expand on this, what is meant by that statement is that any human language is the result of the interplay between the similarities and differences of each person's PCL. This negotiation is how people within one linguistic community are able to communicate, as previously established.

At the same time, the conceptual basis of all human languages allows for translation. This is not to say that translation is a perfect, one-to-one conceptual transfer; after all, communication between people of the same language isn't like this. Rather, translation is the interplay between the similarities and differences of each human language's conceptual bases.

The CUL, then, is the aggregation of all concepts, both actual and potential. In the CUL, there exists an *I*, and this is what underlies that concept in all human languages. In the CUL, there exists a concept for something that only exists in one language and in no others. In the CUL, there is *everything*. The CUL would also, therefore, include animal communication beyond the complexities of the human kind. Any exchange of information between two beings capable of communication falls into the CUL. The CUL is the basis for all thoughts within oneself, as well.

In this sense, the CUL is a kind of Divine Dictionary, and this realization is what makes language beautiful: it is both shared among us all and yet is individualized at the same time. When I think about it like this, I also feel like I'm getting in touch with something far greater than myself, who is merely a human in one moment of time.

———

The "conceptual ur-language" is my own coinage, but between the first and final drafts of this article, I came across the idea of the "natural semantic metalanguage," which shares some features with the CUL; most notably, both have the idea of simple concepts being at the core of all languages.

I don't know if this is terrain that someone else has already completely covered, but again, I'm no expert. I'm just a thinker.

Update

Since first publishing this essay on Medium, I've also learned about Walter Benjamin's work in language, especially regarding the "language of things" and the idea of "language" extending far beyond verbal, written, or signed communication. If this essay interested you in these kinds of ideas, his work is the next logical place to explore.

The REAL Captain America Trilogy

July 13, 2023

Passed through the hands of several writers and appearing in at least one film every year from 2011 to 2019, Captain America went from a joke to one of the most beloved film characters of the 2010s thanks to the excellent performance of Chris Evans and the arc that Cap undergoes after ending up in the modern day. The character acted as both the leader of the Avengers and starred in a sub-franchise of his own which helped create the Marvel Cinematic Universe as a whole.

But while it would be obvious to group the three Captain America movies into a trilogy (after all, that is what they are), I believe there is a better three-film grouping, illustrated in the cover image, for a Captain America trilogy.

Oh, and spoiler alert for *Captain America: The First Avenger*, *Captain America: The Winter Soldier*, *Avengers: Age of Ultron*, and *Captain America: Civil War*. I'm also assuming familiarity with the MCU from 2011 to 2019 in the following essay.

———

In Spring 2020, I taught a college course called "National Marvels: Superhero Films After 9/11," which I abbreviated "SFAN." In SFAN, we looked at post-9/11 issues such as terrorism, mass surveillance, and political polarization through the lens of superhero films made in that time frame, from *Batman Begins* to *Avengers: Endgame*.

In designing the course, I had to link certain films together into thematic categories: *Batman Begins*, *The Dark Knight*, and *Iron Man* all fell under the "Terrorism" label, for instance, while *The Avengers* and *Man of Steel* were listed under the "City Destruction" category. *Captain America: The Winter Soldier* was one of about two films I knew had to be in the class from the get-go, because it is a blockbuster superhero film directly dealing with questions of mass surveillance.

But I realized something: *Avengers: Age of Ultron* paired incredibly well with *Winter Soldier*.

Think about it: in his second film, Cap goes rogue and fights against a group seeking to use surveillance and predictive technology to take over the world, all under the guise of national security. Then, a year later, tech genius Tony Stark, whose own experiences have led him to fear a future invasion of Earth, creates a system designed to act as a "suit of armor" for the world. In other words, he wants to create an intelligent system to monitor threats and stop them before they happen. Sound familiar?

Unlike in *Winter Soldier*, it takes the entire Avengers team to defeat this security system. Ultron is an out-of-control AI (something on our minds a lot these days) who proves Cap's fears, and this threat comes from an ally, not an enemy.

Then, you have *Captain America: Civil War*, where the fallout from Ultron leads Tony to support even more restrictions on freedom, this time directly affecting the Avengers. It's no wonder that by this point Cap is full-on against this constriction of freedom, while Tony's fear and guilt make his actions also perfectly understandable. It helps, too, that the last vestige of *Winter Soldier*'s threats, a brainwashed Bucky, is Cap's main focus, because it brings the second movie back into focus for Cap and for audiences.

In these three films, Cap has gone from a government agent to an anti-establishment freedom fighter, and all three movies are core to this journey.

––––––––

The First Avenger is a fun origin movie for Captain America, but it's an outlier in his franchise, because of its setting and its wildly different tone from its sequels.

At the same time, *Avengers: Age of Ultron* is a disappointing follow-up to the first Avengers movie, because it can't act simply as a sequel to it, but also has to act as a sequel to the movies in its universe which came out in-between. *Ultron* is a fine movie, but it doesn't work as an *Avengers* sequel the way that *Infinity War* and *Endgame* do, which build on all of what came before to create an epic experience; really, *Ultron* just feels like filler. However, if is viewed instead as the second of a three-part work, with *Winter Soldier* and *Civil War* acting as bookends, and Captain America being the point-of-view character, suddenly you have a much more engaging movie.

Thus, I submit that we should view *Ultron* as a sequel to *Winter Soldier*, not to *The Avengers*. In doing so, we have an identifiable character arc running through all three films, and we have a focal point in terms of theme: surveillance and control versus civil liberties and freedom.

Now *that* is a trilogy that resonates with its times.

The Tragedy of the *Star Wars* Prequels

July 15, 2023

So, the *Star Wars* Prequels sure were a thing, weren't they? During their releases they were hammered by fans of the Original Trilogy for—among other reasons—wooden acting, pandering to children, over-reliance on CGI, and bad writing. However, they've undergone a critical re-evaluation in the past few years, for two reasons: (1) the generation who grew up with these as **their** *Star Wars* movies is now coming of age and asserting its own takes on the franchise, especially through the Internet, and (2) the Sequel Trilogy became a new target for ire.

Today, I want to talk about how the Prequels fit in with an ancient storytelling tradition, and how this became a key part of their redemption.

My *Star Wars* Experience

I am a Prequel baby myself. I saw the movies out of order, with my first being *Attack of the Clones*, in about 2004 (it was less than a year before *Revenge of the Sith* released; that I know). While I couldn't follow the plot very well, I'll never forget the excitement I felt at the lightsaber fight between Obi-Wan, Anakin, and Dooku. I'd seen lightsabers earlier in the film, but never used in a duel before. Then, as Yoda came in and just did his thing, he instantly became my favorite character, and *Star Wars* my new favorite series.

I didn't know Anakin would turn bad, and I think watching him fall to the Dark Side was genuinely the first time I'd watched a movie with a tragic ending in my entire life; it's still a formative experience for me, and partly why I consider *Revenge of the Sith* to be my favorite *Star Wars* film. (It helps that it was the only one I saw in theaters until *The Force Awakens*.)

As a fan, I didn't care about any of the complaints I listed above, because the lightsaber battles mixed with the awesome John Williams scores were all I really wanted. On that front, the CGI-favored Prequels looked sleeker and more interesting to me than anything in the Original Trilogy.

Looking back, I understand the complaints, but I still love elements of the Prequels a lot. Ewan McGregor is incredibly fun as Obi-Wan, and Ian McDiarmid's Palpatine chews every scene he's in. Also, Hayden Christensen's performance partially unmasked in *Kenobi* made me see for the first time what Lucas saw when he cast the role, and it makes me frustrated at how utterly he was failed by the problems in the Prequels' production.

But there is one complaint about the Prequels, and about prequels in general, that I've never agreed with: ***they're bad because you know what's going to happen, so there's no tension, so what's the point?***

This is what I want to focus on, so I can show you why this is bogus.

A Lesson from Oedipus

Ever heard the story of a guy who ended up ruling the Greek city of Thebes because he correctly solved a riddle, then was tasked with finding the source of a plague, only to learn that he unknowingly murdered his father and married his mother? If you have, you can thank Sophocles, the Ancient Greek playwright who gave us *Oedipus the King*.

Actually, you can thank the person he adapted the story from. Who was that? We have no idea. The story may survive because of Sophocles' play, but the story existed long before he adapted it. The audience members would've been very familiar with the story before they came to watch the play.

63

See, theater wasn't about twists in a new story, but about viewing old stories adapted by skilled writers — who were also in charge of putting the whole show together. (Theater was also a ritual, and attendance was the civic duty of every male citizen of Athens.) That's not to say that Sophocles had an easy job of just taking old material and reusing it. He had to make it his own, and figure out how to engage the audience somehow.

One of his most noteworthy decisions was to keep reminding the audience of sight. The prophet Tiresias is blind, which is in keeping with the mythology, but the repeated emphasis is purposeful. Characters frequently talk about seeing, in the many forms of that term. Why? Well, because at the climax of the play, after the truth is revealed, Oedipus blinds himself off-stage so that he won't have to see his parents in the underworld.

Sophocles wants you to be thinking about sight and blindness because it builds **dread**. You as an audience member know what's coming, but the characters don't. This effect, called "dramatic irony," is what keeps you invested. You aren't wondering what's going to happen, you're wondering *how* it's going to happen, knowing that these events are fated and you are powerless to stop them.

This is what is supposed to happen with the Prequel Trilogy. Fans knew going into *The Phantom Menace* that Anakin would eventually turn to the Dark Side, and they especially knew that going into *Revenge of the Sith*. What did they want to see? Well, they wanted to see Anakin's fall; in short, they wanted to witness a *tragedy*, in the Ancient Greek sense of the word.

The Prequels' Failure

The problems with the films, especially around the writing and acting, took the audience out of that experience. They didn't care about Anakin Skywalker, so they didn't care about his fall. (It also upset them that the menacing Darth Vader was once a whiny brat, and is so for two of his three Prequel appearances.) The failure of connection between movie and audience meant that the attempt to depict a grand tragedy fell relatively flat. Oh, and the romantic dialogue didn't help, either.

The biggest issue, though: *The Phantom Menace* is mostly irrelevant. *Star Wars* is the story of the Skywalker family, at least on the movie screen. Why, then, is half the movie devoted to trade negotiations, blockades, and a detour to a desert planet?

Well, actually, there are reasons for all of those. Lucas wanted to depict the corruption of the Republic, to explain why the Clone Wars would begin and why the people eventually hand their government over to a tyrant; he also wanted to introduce Anakin's backstory. But since Lucas was seemingly limited to three movies, the plots in the first film counteract each other's efficacy; because Anakin's fall is not yet intertwined with the fall of the Republic, every scene developing one is a scene not developing the other.

(Side note, but I would have had the Clone Wars begin at the end of Episode I, carry through to all of Episode II, and end with Episode III [*Revenge* can stay intact]. I would work Anakin's backstory in through flashbacks, exposition, and character moments throughout the trilogy.)

The issue is, Lucas's vision needed breathing room that eight hours just couldn't cover.

The Prequels' Strength

On paper, I maintain that the Prequels are leaps and bounds better than the Original Trilogy, and that isn't nostalgia talking. Why do I believe this? Well, the Originals tell a pretty simple hero's journey, as Luke goes from farm boy to master of his discipline. It's simple and effective, but pretty standard, structurally.

On the other hand, the Prequels depict the fall of a democracy, the events playing out on a grand scale with tons of moving pieces, each interacting in a complex way. To me, this makes the *premise* of the Prequels far more intriguing.

But execution is another story. The Originals executed their characters and simple structure a lot better than the Prequels handled theirs.

The Prequels' Redemption

I was mixed on *Kenobi*, but the best thing it did for me was motivate me to get a Disney+ subscription. Out of curiosity, I watched *The Clone Wars*, the 3D series I refused to watch as a kid because I liked the 2D series better.

Boy, had I deprived myself of a gem. The first few seasons are iffy, and it frustrates me to no end that their episodes aren't in chronological order, but they're engaging enough to keep you hanging on. As you get into later seasons, it picks up and becomes great.

Ahsoka? Annoying as hell in her first few appearances on the show. But that's the point! Not only is she meant to reflect a younger Anakin (and thus put Anakin into the role of Ahsoka's Obi-Wan), but she's also set up that way so she can grow as a character. Grow she did; she's now a fan favorite.

The Clone Wars gave Lucas, paired with the excellent Dave Filoni, the chance to really tell the epic war narrative (or, I should say, narratives) that he wanted to tell. And at the heart is Anakin, who we know will fall. But when he's given a good story and performance, we ache at this knowledge. We see him and Ahsoka, we watch their journey, all knowing it will come to a tragic end.

And what an end it was! Those final four episodes of *The Clone Wars* season 7 are hands down my favorite *Star Wars* anything, ever. In one fell swoop they keep you engaged at every second—your heart pounds watching Maul, Ahsoka, and Rex deal with the fallout of the war's end, Order 66, and the rise of the Empire—deliver an excellent character drama, and single-handedly redeem the Prequels by fulfilling the promise that George Lucas always knew his story had.

Yes, there is suspense, because most people don't know the exact details of how Ahsoka, Maul, and Rex deal with all of this. But we know they get out, if we've seen *Rebels*. Yet we also know, as Anakin and Ahsoka have their last moments together aboard that ship, that they will never see each other again on friendly terms. We know what's coming, and we dread every second of it.

So, no, knowing what's going to happen at story's end is not a problem with prequels. It's all in the execution, and in how the creators can use your foreknowledge to engage you more, not less.

Anakin's fall may have been a surprise to me back in 2005, but it wasn't in 2022. Despite that fact, I was fully enthralled by those final episodes.

———

So, don't dismiss prequels out of hand just because they're prequels. Like sequels, they're often unnecessary and poorly executed, but sometimes, you get something truly special when the execution is done well.

I for one am glad that George Lucas's vision finally got to see the light of day. I'm just sorry, for his sake as much as ours, that it took so long for us to see the brilliance it was capable of producing.

Should Plays Be Read?
(Or Just Performed?)

July 21, 2023

In 2016, the Nobel Prize in Literature was awarded to Bob Dylan, the first time the prize was given to a songwriter. While the award created debate and controversy for a number of reasons, it is Dylan's Nobel lecture that really stands out to me, specifically these lines:

> *Our songs are alive in the land of the living. But songs are unlike literature. They're meant to be sung, not read. The words in Shakespeare's plays were meant to be acted on the stage. Just as lyrics in songs are meant to be sung, not read on a page.*

Now, he isn't directly stating that the works of William Shakespeare shouldn't be read, but that is an understandable conclusion to draw from the quote. And it got me thinking: **Why do we read plays? And should we?**

———

Exactly 400 years earlier, in 1616, William Shakespeare passed away at the age of 52. However, if not for a more important development this same year, the name of William Shakespeare would probably have been a footnote in history.

What is this event? Shakespeare's contemporary, Ben Jonson, supervises the publication of a collection of his works — including his play scripts. While this may sound less newsworthy than the sunrise, as we live in an age where plays—especially Shakespeare's—are revered as a pre-eminent part of literature, Jonson's act was radical for his time. Plays had been printed before this, but usually in cheap formats called *quartos*, seen as a kind of disposable entertainment like pulp novels and comic books.

Ben Jonson's decision to publish his plays alongside his other poetic works, and to do so in the *folio* format (a larger and more prestigious form, due to the higher expense), asserted that play scripts were worthy of the same literary respect as poetry. Plays were for the masses, appealing to popular taste; while the upper class would view plays, the actors who performed in them were seen as vagrants. Jonson's act, in hindsight, is comparable to Bob Dylan winning the Nobel Prize in Literature: it represents a sea change in how an art form is viewed.

It was Jonson's act which inspired some of Shakespeare's friends to put together a collection of his works, published in 1623. Called "*the* First Folio," it is the only printing we have of such masterpieces as *Macbeth*, *Othello*, *Julius Caesar*, *Antony and Cleopatra*, and *The Tempest*, among 13 others. This is what makes the First Folio one of the most influential books in history.

Jonson also saw himself as a poet, since his plays were written mostly in verse. In fact, he coined the term "playwright" as a disparaging term, meant to indicate a play writer who was a mere craftsman (like a carpenter), rather than a true poet like Jonson, Shakespeare, and others. The poetic qualities of their plays also certainly helped establish their respectability.

Today, alongside poetry and prose, play scripts are an integral part of the English literature curriculum worldwide.

———

Plays are unique because they straddle two worlds: theater and literature. This also meant that they straddled the worlds of the popular and the elite, as theater had for centuries been a low art, whereas literature was a high one. It is only due to newer media such as radio, film, and TV that theater has also become a more elite art, as it is no longer the most popular media form.

Bob Dylan is right: plays are meant to be performed. Shakespeare's company needed new material to perform, and he chipped in to create it. No doubt he took pleasure in his work, but his motivation was monetary: as a shareholder in the company, if his actors didn't have new plays to perform then he wouldn't see any profit from performance. For Shakespeare, plays were first and foremost important for their utilitarian value, *as instructions for performance.*

But plays were rotated out frequently, and older plays would rarely be revived. If, for example, *Hamlet* weren't playing at the theater, you might never see it again… unless you had the play to read! Even two centuries later, if you lived far away from a theater company, you could still experience *Hamlet* if you had it in book form.

This is why screenplays have never been elevated to the status of literature like plays were. For most of the time before movies could be viewed on home video, films were seen as a popular art form, and thus their scripts weren't worth preserving and reading. By the time they began to garner that respect, home video meant that people could just experience the movie itself.

Think about this: for plays, the scripts are what remain constant, while performances will vary. You have up to hundreds (maybe into the thousands?) of Shakespeare performances running at the same time around the world, while the idea of having that many different versions of *Jaws* would be (1) expensive and (2) redundant. For plays, the permanence lies in the script, while for later forms of performance media, the performances themselves are permanent. We accept hundreds of remakes of *Macbeth*. To do the same for, say, *Breaking Bad* would bother us to no end.

I do think screenplays are worth reading, but I admit that my interest lies in seeing how a script is translated to screen; I'll never read a screenplay of a finished movie if I haven't yet seen the movie.

———

The development of plays as literature would also actually lead to some scholars claiming that no performance of Shakespeare—he's been the favorite for a long time—could match the experience of reading him. While it may be true that each reader can have their own Shakespeare, it would have seemed ridiculous to the playwright if he were told that his works shouldn't, in a sense, be performed.

This attitude would, however, be reflected in the development of a specific type of play meant only to be read: the *closet drama*. A closet drama is a story which takes the form of a play, but that play is intended first and foremost for reading, with no consideration to theatrical staging. Some of the most famous examples are John Milton's *Samson Agonistes* and Percy Shelley's *Prometheus Unbound*. Female writers of Shakespeare's own day would use this form, and plays written between the English theater closures and re-openings of the 17th century would be de facto closet dramas, as well. The form could arguably be traced back to Plato, however, who wrote his philosophical works in dialogue form.

The ultimate end of the literary side of playwriting may actually, in fact, lead not at all to a play, but to a form of poetry with multiple speakers; in this case, the play convention of using speech prefixes to indicate the speaker is used for its convenience, and scene descriptions and cues thus become economical ways of conveying critical information without interrupting the flow of the poetry itself.

———

I think it's clear that plays are a legitimate literary form, and deserve the respect they receive. They act as the permanent preserve of their stories, can allow for individual experience in the written form, and have a long history of being written solely to be read.

But there is still one question I have: if plays are so great, and can tell stories as well as the short story and the novel (what we could call "straight prose"), why do we have the short story and novel in the first place? After all, shouldn't we look for the most efficient way to tell a story and use that form?

Well, to answer my own questions: there must be a reason for the novel (and short story) having survived to the present day, something that the straight prose form does better than plays. And, in fact, there is.

Actually, there are two: introspection and description. Straight prose allows the author the flexibility to delve into the interiority of the characters in ways that would be unnatural in a play, at least one aiming for realism. Even soliloquies and asides couldn't accomplish this same feat, since too much of them would take away from the dramatic structure. The "show, don't tell" mantra applies to both forms, but straight prose has many more ways of showing than a play does.

The same goes for description. Straight prose can, if it wants, spend pages describing a setting or a single moment in time, whereas the format of a play requires time to constantly progress, as each word of dialogue gives readers a sense of time passing. Not so for prose.

———

Perhaps one day someone could create a *gesamtkunstwerk* which somehow combines the strengths of the three forms of written literature — poetry, prose, and script — into one. Maybe it's already been done.

But what I've come to realize in my years of studying media is that plays are a unique medium capable of things no other medium can do. Its dual nature as both performance-instruction and as literature to be read on its own is somewhat unique in its history, but ever since Dickens gave public readings of his novels, and especially now, in the age of the audiobook, that line has been blurred. What matters is the medium itself, and how it communicates its message.

Go see a play in performance. Go read it. Do one or both, and if both, in either order. What's important to understand, however, is that you're dealing with two different media forms, each with their own strengths and limitations, and one cannot fully substitute for the other.

Post-Script[*]

In response to Bob Dylan's assertion that "lyrics in songs are meant to be sung, not read on a page," I say this: the first instances of poetry that we have in the West are of lyrics to songs. In fact, the word "lyric" comes from the lyre, an instrument that would accompany the lyrics. So, I actually think that lyrics can be read on a page, and that insisting they not be is limiting to what we can do with them. It's like screenplays: like the films that screenplays describe, the songs do exist and are definitely worth listening to, but there is something lost if we don't allow lyrics to be analyzed on their own. Whether it's dissecting Dylan's poetic verses or analyzing DMX's simultaneously homophobic and very gay lyrics (read all the lyrics in "Where the Hood At" and you'll see what I mean), there is a rich tradition in reading song lyrics in and of themselves.

---

[*] This paragraph was part of the original essay.

Walter Isaacson: The Modern-Day Court Painter

July 24, 2023

In past centuries, monarchs employed a court painter to create not really a visual record of the inner workings of the government as much as a celebration of the monarch's splendor. Prominent examples include Hans Holbein in England, and Diego Velazquez and Francisco Goya in Spain. Today, many heads of state have photographers who serve the same function; the U.S. president has an official White House chief photographer, for instance.

However, some artists were highly sought after by monarchs, aristocrats, and — after the rise of capitalism — the bourgeois rich for another reason: the artist himself (or herself, on occasion) is highly sought-after. Artemisia Gentileschi was a well-known painter whose work was fearlessly unique (and arguably proto-feminist), and thus commissioning a portrait from her was bound to create a buzz. In the late 19th-century, John Singer Sargent was *THE* portrait painter, and to have yourself immortalized by his hand was a prime status symbol.

Even today, paintings can create buzz. Look at Kehinde Wiley's portrait of President Barack Obama for the National Portrait Gallery in 2018. (Federal-government funding of politician paintings was actually outlawed that year by the EGO Act, although (1) recent NPG presidential and first-lady portraits have been privately funded, and (2) that bill had been proposed for years, so regardless of timing, it wasn't targeting Obama solely or specifically.)

While paintings still carry prestige, I'd argue that the people who carry the kind of weight that Sargent carried are no longer painters, and aren't photographers: they're biographers. And for my money, no biographer carries as much prestige in this regard as Walter Isaacson.

Noted for his biographies of Ben Franklin, Albert Einstein, Steve Jobs, and Leonardo da Vinci, Isaacson has profiled some of history's most renowned men, many of whom have been given the label of "genius." However, unlike the rest of the men on that list, Steve Jobs was alive and available for interviews; before this, Isaacson's last live subject was Henry Kissinger, whom he profiled in a 1992 book.

Steve Jobs (the book) is an authorized biography; while Isaacson maintained editorial independence, it was made not only with Jobs' blessing, but his cooperation. He also apparently encouraged the other interview subjects to be fully candid.

The book released only 19 days after Jobs died, and is more than 600 pages covering the life of one of the tech world's most influential figures. It also served as the basis for the 2015 film by the same title. But what's most striking about the book is the cover.

The photograph used was taken not for the book, but for a 2006 *Fortune* magazine story. But it's a portrait; that's what's important. Yes, pretty much all biographies will have a picture of their subject on the cover, but with *Steve Jobs* it's more pronounced because of how minimal it is; the picture is of Jobs only, with nothing else in the background save for white nothingness. This puts the idea of a portrait into greater focus: we are told by this image that this book will be a bare, straightforward look at the man depicted.

That's really what biographies are, at the end of the day: they're portraits in words.

After profiling Leonardo da Vinci in 2017, Isaacson's next project was on a living person once more: Jennifer Doudna, who won a Nobel Prize for her work on the gene-editing system CRISPR. The book, titled *The Code Breaker*, found Isaacson in top form once more.

And soon to come is his biography of Elon Musk, one of the most divisive men in the tech world at the moment, which is saying a lot. The first confirmation of this actually came from Musk himself, who tweeted in August 2021:

> *If you're curious about Tesla, SpaceX & my general goings on, @WalterIsaacson is writing a biography*

This, right here, is what made me realize that Isaacson is a modern court painter, or perhaps more aptly, the modern John Singer Sargent. No, his subjects don't pay him to write flattering bios, but that's part of the appeal. Catching the eye of Walter Isaacson is a lottery win... even if most of his subjects have already won a kind of social lottery before his interest was ever a possibility. The way that Musk *flaunts* — there really is no other word for it — the fact that Isaacson is writing about him just screams out how much of a status symbol this fact is.

This is not an insult, or even a critique, of Isaacson himself. I've read both his Einstein and Leonardo biographies, and thoroughly enjoyed them. He's a master craftsman, and his work merits attention.

But I find myself conflicted.

In a 2016 live chat hosted by *The Guardian*,[5] in response to Bob Dylan winning the Nobel Prize in Literature, the writer Karl Ove Knausgård said that "knowing that Dylan is the same generation as Thomas Pynchon, Philip Roth, Cormac McCarthy, makes it very difficult for me to accept" Dylan being given the award over one of those others.

These sentiments I feel toward Isaacson doing a biography of Elon Musk. Is Musk worth profiling, if for nothing else than because of his outsized influence on the world? Yes. But knowing that Isaacson could also profile Isaac

Newton, Christopher Nolan, Neil deGrasse Tyson, *et* many *al.*, makes it difficult for me to accept Musk—who comes across as a power-hungry narcissist—being the one who occupied two-to-three years of Isaacson's time.

But there's definitely notable reasons why Isaacson made the choice he did; we'll just have to judge the results. (Judging by the cover art, though, he's going for a clear connection between Musk and Steve Jobs, as the design is the exact same, save the inverted background color, the subject and his hand pose.)

Walter Isaacson's *Elon Musk* releases September 12, 2023. This article was neither sponsored nor endorsed by anyone mentioned herein.

The Dichotomy of Art

July 27, 2023

Defining what "art" is, and what it isn't, is one of the most persistent and divisive philosophical questions we humans ever ask ourselves. It's not an easy question to answer, and depending on how forceful the debate can be, not a fun one, either.

I'm not going to solve this debate in a Medium article; nor, in fact, do I think it's a debate that can ever be fully resolved. I instead seek to add to the conversation with my own take.

In my debut book, *Narrative in Action*, I defined art indirectly, by contrasting it with "entertainment." The definition was "entertainment is designed to make people inclined to remember forget, while art is designed to make people inclined to forget remember." It's perhaps most helpful for thinking about the *purpose* of a creative work, but it doesn't help us really think about what makes art **ART** in the first place.

For the purposes of this article, however, this definition is going by the wayside. Why? Well, because I don't want to place value judgments on what is and isn't art. I want to consider the idea of "art" in its largest possible meaning. Thus, "art" for us shall be "anything intentionally created by one or more people for the purpose of self-expression and/or impacting the audience of said work." This means that anything visual, written, aural, and even gustatory can be considered art.

Now that we've gotten that out of the way, we can begin to think about how this broad sense of art functions in any human society. The conclusion I came to was that art is dichotomous, having two ways through which it can affect the audience: *aesthetic pleasure* and *intellectual engagement.*

Aesthetic Pleasure

We humans like beauty; even if the definition of beauty is in the eye of the beholder, we each gravitate toward that which pleases us, in terms of our partners, our hobbies/interests, and even in what we consider artistic.

Take, for example, the food we eat at our favorite restaurant. There is nothing extrinsic which we are seeking; we do not analyze the food for hidden meaning or for the baring of a chef's soul. Instead, we ingest the food—at least at our favorite restaurant—because we enjoy it. Yes, we need food to survive, but we can keep ourselves to a pretty regular diet in order to accomplish this. (Keep in mind also that this is coming from a middle-class American perspective.)

Perhaps the purest expression of this comes from John Keats' "Ode on a Grecian Urn," where the Romantic poet states:

> *Beauty is Truth, Truth Beauty,—that is all*
> *Ye know on earth, and all ye need to know*

This conception of beauty as so high of an ideal that it is itself Truth with a capital T, would go on to be exemplified most notably through Aestheticism. This movement emphasized the aesthetic qualities of visual art, design, and literature over any other consideration. Maximalist and ornate, this movement also embodies the phrase "art for art's sake."

We will see in the next section how this contrasts with the idea of intellectual engagement, but in defense of aesthetics, I think it's perfectly natural to enjoy a painting, a poem, a song, etc. simply for the emotional response it elicits within you. I enjoy plenty of songs, for example, without giving their lyrics a second thought.

I also have at times created art purely for fun, with no attempt to create something realistic (I can't draw to save my life), but instead because I wanted to make it and thought I would enjoy the results.

Intellectual Engagement

If art were simply always about beauty, however, I don't think there'd be a huge need for it. After all, as much as we humans may try, our designs pale to nothingness in comparison to the majesty of nature and of the universe as a whole. There may be a pleasure in matching wits with nature and coming out with something like the Great Pyramids of Giza or trompe l'œil paintings, but it can't just be about that, right?

Well, if you're someone who believes art should only be made and appreciated for its own sake, perhaps it is just that. Leaving it at aesthetics divorces the work from anything the creator(s) or audience can bring to the work, which does simplify what's asked of each, and doesn't complicate art with things like politics, social theories, historical context, etc. This would be the position, to an extent, of an academic like Harold Bloom, who saw Shakespeare as the supreme literary genius for reasons completely outside of Shakespeare's context. Instead, it is the poetry, the intricate characterization, the profound understanding of human nature, that makes him the best.

On the other hand, continuing with our Shakespeare example, you have someone like Stephen Greenblatt, who sees Shakespeare as a lens to consider larger, even contemporary questions. His short 2018 book *Tyrant* uses Shakespeare to consider how political power is gained, exercised, and lost, and the moral complexities which inevitably arise in those situations. Greenblatt's type of criticism would look at Shakespeare and see, for instance, how the frequent theme of power may have been inspired by concerns over Elizabeth I's death and succession. His argument is not meant to take away from Shakespeare's accomplishments, but to understand what the author was drawing in when writing his works, how his world shaped him and his work.

As I said, I think both schools are important, and to some degree I think Bloom and Greenblatt would both take aspects of each type—aesthetic pleasure and intellectual engagement—into consideration. It's more a matter of degree.

Here is where I admit my bias: when it comes to works with *ideas*, I have to lean toward an intellectual level as opposed to an aesthetic one. Yes, I love the language in poetry and how beautiful a portrait can be, but I'm not someone who creates simply to make beauty. I'm interested in ideas.

My first novel, *Discordance*, would not exist without, among other inspirations, the tyrants of Shakespeare, the politics of the *Star Wars* Prequels, the real-life figures of Augustus, Otto von Bismarck, and all other power-centric people, and other elements. I didn't set out to make that book have a distinct message, but to play out an epic scenario of a society in flux, and how the personal intertwines with the political. Coincidentally, those seem to be some of Christopher Nolan's goals with his film *Oppenheimer*.

To be frank, I don't know how to create a work of "pure" art, one completely separate from the context in which it is created. I have to look at the real world—past, present, and possible future—for inspiration…

And wait: isn't that also an aesthetic exercise, an attempt to "match wits with nature," as I myself put it?

———

We don't know for certain why humans decided tens of thousands of years ago to start painting on the walls of caves. Maybe it was an early form of record-keeping. Maybe it was to aid in storytelling, the lights of old fires illuminating the drawings and making them come alive. Maybe instead it was an attempt to satisfy an inborn urge to express oneself, while at the same time imitating, and therefore also capturing, nature. Maybe they wanted to leave a record to posterity.

Whatever it was, there is one message I *am* sure that the cave dwellers wanted to impart, no matter the content of their drawings: we humans were here.

When I look at the image of the stencil handprints from the Cueva de los Manos in Argentina, some images placed there 9,000 years ago—several thousand years before writing had been invented anywhere in the world—I see a reflection of myself, of all of us modern humans. I feel connected to these people, deceased for thousands of years yet living on through these drawings, sending a message into the future that they were here. They lived. I could put my hand up there and count myself among them as a fellow human, separated though I am by millennia.

That, to me, shows the power of art. No matter where you fall on the scale of these two aspects of art, you will always come away with an appreciation of art's power, and of its fundamental importance to the human experience.

You Can't Depend on the Future

August 2, 2023

Time passes without you having any say on the matter. You know that the present is only momentary, that the past is gone (even if its effects define the present), and that the future is just out of reach... but only for a moment.

But we can't depend on the future.

———

I've always wanted to be a creator, someone who puts meaning out into the world and through that impacts the lives of others. My format of choice became writing. I used to imagine what my future would be like, how I would one day be a famous writer, and those imaginings would enthrall me. No, actually, they would fuel my very drive to create.

Looking back with the hindsight of years, and now much less certain about my own future (and those of others), I realize that this way of thinking, while natural, ends up proving foolish, inevitably.

Think about a biography, whether one you've read, watched, or listened to, about an influential or famous person. In experiencing this person's story, one you know actually happened, you get a full-picture overview of the subject's life, or of key moments. You *know* that this person will make their impact, and you anticipate this, excited at seeing how these events will unfold when you know their result. (This is a bit like watching a prequel story, which I talked about in my article on the *Star Wars* Prequels.)

However, you can always replay this experience. In fact, you're replaying it even as you experience it the first time, since it's already happened in real life—just not to you. You can always return to the beginnings, to the simpler times, to the moment before everything became great; over and over again, the triumph is real.

But in real life, that triumph only happens once. You can never go back to writing your first book, teaching your first class, working on your first car, getting your first paycheck. You can look back on it in a memory, and maybe that provides you with happiness. But that ideal, nostalgic view—*one that you can only have with hindsight*—is also poisonous. It makes you resent the present, because it's not that ideal past. How, then, can you possibly make a good future, when the past is already so perfect and gone?

———

This also ties into a realization I had years ago: you can never be both a star and a viewer. I wouldn't put it as arrogantly as Kanye West did when he said "My greatest pain in life is that I'll never be able to see myself perform live," but there is something buried in that sentence that rings true.

We present ourselves in ways which we think will please others, but really the person we're trying to please is ourselves. This self is what we would be and think like if we existed somewhere else, and could look upon ourselves at the same time. We are our harshest critics, but we are also our prime audience.

We can never see ourselves as an outsider would. And that terrifies us. Why? Because it means we can never be sure that we've done something right. We have to, as Blanche DuBois put it, rely on the kindness of strangers. Even those closest to us are in this sense strangers, because we cannot share our mind, our very soul, with anyone else. Our acts are expressions of this soul, each an attempt at communicating to those outside of us something which is within us.

As a writer, I can never see my work as a reader would. I don't wish for this opportunity because I think I'm the greatest writer ever and to be deprived of experiencing my genius is a cruel fate. Instead, I wish I could have this perspective so that I could hone my work, make it more likely to appeal to an audience. Or, at least, make me more confident in my work to put it out there.

Why do I want to create this kind of work? Because I want to do something meaningful. I want to make an impact. I want to affect the future.

That right there is both valid and emblematic of that future-focus. Don't get me wrong, we ought to fight for the future we want, and keep that future in mind at all times during that fight. But when it comes to our focus, and our contentment, the future is not the place in which to put all our hopes.

If we live our lives waiting for the future to come, it will never arrive, until the day we realize that the future we hoped for has passed us by.

Yes, work toward your goals, use them to motivate your current actions. But do me a favor: at least once in a while, stop and take in the present, in whatever way you can. Otherwise, you'll only miss it.

William Shakespeare's Sequels and Prequels

August 16, 2023

Sequels these days get a bad reputation, in no small part because they're frequently unnecessary cash grabs which expand the story beyond what it was originally designed to support. When a sequel works best, it's because the follow-up narrative justifies itself in some way: it expands upon the original while at the same time holding its own. Maybe it works out a dangling plot thread, or maybe it reinterprets a character.

This applies to sequels in every medium, from books to films to video games, etc., as well as to prequels, midquels, interquels, spin-offs, etc.

It should also be noted that certain series are planned with multiple installments in mind from the beginning. Even if the sequel doesn't satisfy, it was at least always in the plan and thus the series originated as a kind of unified whole, even if that series wasn't intricately planned. For examples, see *Harry Potter*, *The Hunger Games*, George R.R. Martin's *A Song of Ice and Fire*, and *The Lord of the Rings*.

However, lest you think that prequels and sequels are confined solely to the 20th and 21st centuries, let me present you with the strongest counter-example possible: the plays of William Shakespeare.

The History Plays

The Wars of the Roses Tetralogy

When Shakespeare was a young dramatist, he collaborated with more experienced writers in the field. He likely worked with George Peele on *Titus Andronicus*, he may have co-written *Edward III*, and, most importantly, he likely wrote all three *Henry VI* plays with help. Everyone needs an apprenticeship, even the most influential writer of the English language.

Notably, even the three *Henry VI* plays were written out of order, and not originally all called "Henry VI." The first play was probably *Henry VI, Part 2*, which was first published as a "The Contention," with *Henry VI, Part 3* following and being called "The True Tragedy of Richard Duke of York." *Part 1* was the last to be written, at which point the three plays could be grouped as a trilogy.

This order indicates that Shakespeare and his co-writers created one play, then decided to follow it up, and then finally returned to chart the beginnings of the journey that they had previously spent two plays on. The pattern: "original, sequel, and prequel." This won't be the last time Shakespeare did this, returning to a source and covering either end of its story.

But those three plays are followed by a fourth, one Shakespeare almost certainly wrote by himself, and which is his first masterpiece: *Richard III*.

The opening monologue of the titular Richard (the only title-character-monarch of a Shakespeare history play who does not possess the throne at the outset) may also be seen as Shakespeare's declaration of intent: He had finally arrived, and it was his time to reign over the theatrical world. (Shakespeare may not have meant it that way, but it does play well in hindsight.) Richard himself can also be seen as the progenitor of *Hamlet*'s Claudius, *Othello*'s Iago, and Macbeth. I am firmly convinced that if it weren't for *Richard III*, not only would there be none of the aforementioned characters, but also Shakespeare would never have returned to the genre of the history play.

Richard's complexity of character, being revolting and charming in equal measure, allows Shakespeare to dramatize the corrupting nature of both power itself and the worship of it. Yes, he finishes off his four-play saga with Richard's death at the hands of Henry VII, but this wouldn't be the last time he visited this dynastic struggle.

The Henriad

The popularity of *Richard III* made it easy for Shakespeare's company to decide to produce more history plays dealing with the same theme, but I am convinced that Richard as a character haunted Shakespeare. Between Richard's inherently intriguing nature and the fact that Queen Elizabeth I's old age and childlessness meant a possible return to a dynastic civil war, Shakespeare had a lot to draw him to the events which led to the Wars of the Roses, covered in the *Henry VI* plays and *Richard III*.

Shakespeare thus created an entire prequel tetralogy dealing with a different dynastic struggle, which scholars have come to call "the Henriad." Why they've chosen this name is something we'll return to shortly, but the plays which comprise it are *Richard II*, *Henry IV, Part 1*, *Henry IV, Part 2*, and *Henry V*.

The plays, all written solely by Shakespeare, follow England as it leaves the era of feudalism and chivalry and enters the world of Machiavellian opportunism, of power-grabs, backstabs, and general ruthlessness. Henry IV deposes his cousin Richard II at the end of the latter's play, while Henry's own two plays focus as much on his son, Prince Hal (the future Henry V, and namesake of the Henriad), as they do on the king. All of it culminates in the accession of Hal at the end of *Henry IV, Part 2*. The following play, *Henry V*, depicts a large-scale war with France in violent detail, and ends with Henry V marrying Catherine of Valois, mother to Henry V's son, Henry VI. As *Henry VI, Part 1* opens with the unexpected death of Henry V, Shakespeare has now caught up to, and connected with, his older work, like a 16th-century George Lucas at the end of *Revenge of the Sith*.

That *Star Wars* comparison is more than just a cute nod, however. The word "prequel" itself conjures up the *Star Wars* Prequels in the minds of an uncountable many, because of how influential the *Star Wars* series has been to our culture. (See Ian Doescher's *William Shakespeare's Star Wars* for the most acute connection between Shakespeare and that franchise.) This comparison is apt because so many have dismissed the very idea of prequels because of *the* Prequels, but Shakespeare shows how powerful prequels can be, and how even though they're set before the original story, they can speak to a contemporary moment just as well as the originals. As it happens, civil-war concerns show up in both *Star Wars* trilogies and both of Shakespeare's tetralogies. On top of that, like all prequels, both *SW* and WS (funny coincidence with the initials) are aware of the events in the future of their prequels, and that awareness informs the prequels' construction.

The Henriad and the "Rosiad"

Some scholars will label all eight plays from *Richard II* to *Richard III* as "the Henriad," and at one point in my past that would have included me. They seemed to tell a complete, epic story across about a century.

But I no longer hold that view. Whereas the prequel tetralogy was written in order by one author, the original tetralogy was written out of order, and likely originated by accident of popularity, not through a grand design—until *Richard III*, that is. The title "Henriad" is meant to invoke the classical *Iliad* and *Aeneid*, both of which involve epic conflicts which dictate the destinies of nations. Only the prequel tetralogy really fits this definition, and thus it—but it alone—warrants the title of "the Henriad." Plus, Henry V is the focal character in three of the four plays, while his father, also named Henry, is the antagonist of the fourth.

Still, I do think that the original tetralogy warrants a name of some kind, and thus, since it depicts the Wars of the Roses, I suggest **"the Rosiad"** as a title for the grouping. This also fits because there is no one focal character of the tetralogy, but several—each a member of one of two competing factions (the Lancasters and the Yorks) who covet power.

I do not, however, have an idea for a name for the eight plays as a whole.

Before we leave the history plays, though, I do wish to reiterate how important Richard III—the character and the play—were to the Henriad.

Henry V echoes Richard in many ways, including how he puts on a front until the throne is obtained—at which point he ruthlessly casts aside his old ways and old friends. He also mercilessly commits a war crime in slaughtering the surrendered French troops, an act which rivals anything Richard does in his play.

Henry IV recognizes that his world is changing, and he uses historical circumstances to propel his way into power, his actions leading to the death of his cousin/the previous king, Richard II.

The one, it seems, who recognized this historical change the most was Shakespeare himself.

The Roman Tragedies

Shakespeare wrote four plays based on Rome, three of which were based on history and one—*Titus Andronicus*—taking place in some nebulous mashup of different parts of Roman history.

Julius Caesar

Of his other three Roman plays, *Julius Caesar* was written first. Like the English history plays, it meditates on themes of power, but sets its story in an era long removed from Shakespeare's own. Caesar, like many of Shakespeare's English kings, desires power, but because he lives in what is still nominally a republic, he cannot take monarchical authority without setting the people against him, and Caesar likes to be loved by the people.

However, Shakespeare delves into new territory by showing both the violent usurpation of power (the conspirators themselves envy Caesar's power, except for Brutus, who is *afraid* of Caesar's power), as well as the unintended destructive forces which come in its wake, in the same play. Whereas Shakespeare took eight plays to tell that story in English history, he does it in one here.

By the end of the play, a new order has been established; in trying to save the republic, Brutus unknowingly brought about its downfall. While Shakespeare initially had *Julius Caesar* be a one-off play, about nine years later he returned to its subject-matter... twice.

Antony and Cleopatra

I have to give credit to noted Shakespeare scholar Paul Cantor (now sadly deceased) and his Fall 2016 class "Shakespeare's Rome" at the University of Virginia, which I took and which has informed a lot of my analysis of Shakespeare's Roman plays. That, and his recorded interviews on the subject, are essential for this topic, as far as I'm concerned.

Cantor was convinced that Shakespeare had an obsession of sorts with Rome, and I have to agree. I especially agree with the idea that he always wanted to return to that world, because in about the same year, 1608, he wrote both *Antony and Cleopatra* and *Coriolanus*.

A&C, while a unique play in many ways, acts as a sequel to *Julius Caesar*, covering the second half of the Roman Republic's fall. The triumvirate which defeated Brutus and Cassius in *Julius Caesar* is now starting to break apart, as Lepidus (the third member of the triumvirate) loses power to Octavius and Mark Antony, the two of whom spend the play fighting for the "throne" of what is becoming the Roman Empire. At the same time, Antony is engaged in a romance with Shakespeare's most powerful and complex female character, Cleopatra. (Lady Macbeth would probably claim second place.)

The most compelling evidence for Cantor's argument that Shakespeare always intended to write *A&C* is in the fact that *Julius Caesar*'s final line is spoken by Octavius, and traditionally, he who gets the final line in a Shakespeare play is the most powerful character left alive. Perhaps this simply reflects Shakespeare's knowledge that Octavius would rule Rome, but the fact that *Coriolanus* was written at the same time bolsters Cantor's argument.

Coriolanus

Like *Julius Caesar* and *Antony and Cleopatra*, *Coriolanus* takes place at an inflection point in Roman history; in this case, it is just after Rome's transformation from a kingdom into a republic.

The title character, Caius Martius Coriolanus (named so because he conquered the city of Corioli), is a born soldier who cannot let war go. He detests both peacetime and the common people, the latter now gaining political power through the newly-established tribunes. This mentality ultimately proves to be Coriolanus' undoing.

Coriolanus is not a direct prequel to *Julius Caesar*, but it is a thematic one. In *Julius Caesar*, we have a society slowly decaying into corruption through the loss of civic virtue, whereas that virtue is alive and well in *Coriolanus*. It is about the contrast that this early Roman-Republican society provides with the time of Caesar and Octavius which makes *Coriolanus* such an effective prequel, showing that even later in his career, Shakespeare understood the power of returning to certain stories and expanding upon them to create a grander narrative.

Why Rome?

It is also worth noting that Shakespeare is probably also meditating upon his own country's history and trajectory with these three Roman plays in the same way he did with his English history plays. The difference is the history plays all clearly looked toward the past to understand the present, while the Roman plays are all geared toward the future: each play provides a different possible future for Elizabethan and post-Elizabethan England. For *Coriolanus*, the society is a republic, where the wartime powerful are forced to adjust to peacetime or retire. For *Julius Caesar*, it is a society caught between republic and empire, between virtue and self-interest. For *Antony and Cleopatra*, it is a society caught in its own decadence, fully given over to an imperialized mindset even if the empire has not yet been fully formed.

Like many societies and burgeoning empires, England looked to Rome for an example, to understand both its potential role in the world and its potential fate.

Love's Labour's Won

I would be remiss if I didn't mention the possibility that one of Shakespeare's sequels is lost to history. Francis Meres' 1598 work *Palladis Tamia* mentions, among other Shakespeare plays, a "Love's Labour's Won," just after it mentions *Love's Labour's Lost*. The natural inference is that the former is the sequel to the latter, especially considering that *LLL*'s marriages are delayed for a year, leaving room for a sequel.

Of course, the question becomes: why was it not included in Shakespeare's First Folio? The only three plays widely accepted as Shakespeare's which do NOT appear in the folio are *Pericles*, *The Two Noble Kinsmen*, and *Edward III*, the last of which is a relatively recent addition to the canon. But those all exist. If *Love's Labour's Won* was a known Shakespeare work, why was it not included? (The same question goes for the other alleged Shakespeare lost play, *Cardenio*. With at least *Edward III*, the answer may be that the play was so offensive to the Scottish people that it was deemed unfit to publish, especially since King James was Scottish himself, and still on the throne when the folio was released in 1623.) As we have no text of the play itself, we have no way of knowing.

Some scholars speculate that *Love's Labour's Won* is an alternate title for another play, which I'm personally inclined to believe, but not so much that I would assert it with anything approaching certainty.

93

If *Love's Labour's Won* were a sequel, though, it's another example of the Bard returning to a story, though I'm confident in saying that the sequels and prequels we do have from him are enough to demonstrate his willingness to tread familiar ground, and his mastery of expanding that ground into something grander each time.

————

If you're a storyteller or a story lover, don't be afraid to embrace a sequel, a prequel, or whatever else have you. Know that if it does fail, it isn't because of something inherent to sequels, but in poor execution.

Why Many Movies Need a Rewatch

September 21, 2023

As I write this, I have yet to watch Christopher Nolan's *Oppenheimer* a second time, yet I've listened to "Can You Hear the Music" and "Destroyer of Worlds" from its soundtrack many times in the past two months. Still, it was that singular event-pole movie—a biographical epic which is also equally horror and thriller—which inspired me to finally comment on something I've noticed about films: many not only merit a second viewing, they actually *need* it in order for audiences to truly understand the film.

When I was in middle school, I had several friends who, like me, enjoyed reading. (It wasn't Shakespeare or anything, but we enjoyed the books geared toward us nonetheless.) One of those friends, however, said something that to me was peculiar: once he read a book once, he never read it again. Ever.

His reasons were rational enough: he read pretty much entirely for the plot, for the suspense, and thus, there was no way to enjoy a second read if he already knew everything that was going to happen in it. Without the surprise, what was the point?

My perspective back then was that I re-read books I enjoyed because the experience along the way was just as memorable as the final destination. You didn't eat your favorite food only once and then never again because you already knew how it tasted; how ridiculous! No; you savored it every time.

Evidently, my perspective has changed. More importantly, however, I think back about my friend's point, specifically what it took for granted, because it was the same thing my old perspective took for granted: *the experience would be the same.*

But you can never truly step into the same river twice, and it's taken a few film viewings for me to realize that about cinema. Sometimes, a rewatch improves the film; other times, it unmasks the hollow veil, showing how empty the film is when it can't use the unknown as a crutch for poor storytelling.

When a Rewatch Improves a Film

From Okay to Great

It was early 2014, and while my budding cinephile brain anticipated a few movies heavily, one that stood above the pack for the entire year until its release was another Christopher Nolan film: *Interstellar*. *Inception* was already my all-time favorite movie, so while I could name several famous directors back then, only Nolan truly excited me. His follow-up original film was going to be about a space adventure? Sign me up!

Then I watched the film.

I didn't hate it, but I was let down, and the ending felt... empty — and confusing. I wasn't satisfied like I was with *Inception*, although I knew that the film wasn't entirely without merit.

Then, something happened: about a year later, I was traveling home from New York, part of a school field trip. On the bus, *Interstellar* played, and I half-watched it.

I found it to be a truly great movie. I was startled at this, too. How could I have missed so much about the film, that I could go from disappointment to admiration? Well, I knew I was onto something when, around the same time, film reviewer Jeremy Jahns tweeted similar sentiments about the movie. What was amiss?

96

While I can't speak to Jeremy's reasons, I know that, while watching it a second time, I knew it wouldn't be *Inception* in space, so my expectations weren't set up for disappointment.

However (and this is the more important reason), I also was able to look at the movie from a technical standpoint, since I already knew the story. I could pay attention to how it was paced, how it was filmed, how it was scored, how it was performed, etc. In essence, my prior knowledge freed me from simply watching, and allowed me to analyze.

Combine this with the first reason, and it meant that I approached the movie on its own terms. Nolan made his own *2001: A Space Odyssey*, and by gosh was it incredible. The story is still a weak link, but that's in comparison: the magnitude of the film's other elements far outweighs any narrative short-comings, while also, in a sense, emphasizing them more.

Give *Interstellar* a second watch, if you haven't.

From Good to Better

I enjoyed *Deadpool* when I saw it in theaters back in 2016. The second time I saw it, I was tired, though, so we actually have to go to my third viewing to get a sense of how the movie improved for me. When I saw it that third time, I did the *Interstellar* thing, analyzing it technically. You know what? It's a con-cise, efficient, in-and-out action comedy that does exactly what it set out to do, while genuinely being a breath of fresh air to the superhero film genre that year.

Short and sweet.

From Bad to Good

Ron Howard's *How the Grinch Stole Christmas* (2000) is a movie in its own league, a kind that had never been made before and will never be made again. It is a Freudian fever-dream, and since my 2018 rewatch, I have adored it in a way I adore no other Christmas movie.

It helped that I watched it with fellow college students, one of whom — like me — was a media-studies major. He and I basically created our own commentary track over the film, and as a group we laughed throughout. That night is among the top five I'd choose to relive once more, out of almost 26 years alive.

Grinch 2000 is not a movie for kids; it's a movie for older kids and adults masquerading as a kids' film. Trust me: go into it with the mindset of looking for all the weird undertones and jokes, and you'll never see it the same way again.

When a Rewatch Shows a Film's Flaws

There are probably many films which I could put into this category, but I think one really summarizes the point succinctly: *Star Wars: The Last Jedi*.

Truly endless words have been expended on discussing this film, from praising it to treating it as the most offensive movie since *A Serbian Film* (don't look that one up). At the risk of sounding like someone without a spine, I think both sides are a bit wrong on that front. But I still fall on the side of those who are disappointed rather than those who praise it.

My reaction in theaters was the anti-*Interstellar*: I was enthralled throughout, on the edge of my seat, waiting for reveals, twists, and triumph. No, Luke Skywalker tossing a lightsaber behind him did not lose me, nor did him drinking green milk, nor him seemingly almost killing his nephew. Why? Well, I don't think I would've cared about them anyway, but I've also tended to give movies the benefit of the doubt the first time around. Unless something is blindingly obvious, for instance, I tend not to guess ahead of the movie, because I'm there for the experience on that first viewing.

What did I love? Well, the throne room scene with Rey and Kylo Ren was exciting, and the spaceship ramming into others as it entered hyperspace was… well, I won't mince words: jaw-dropping. I even appreciated the subversion (ooh, dirty word!) of the Rey parentage reveal.

My only complaint at the time was that Snoke was wasted; I really wanted to see more from this new villain. Where did he come from? How would he differ from — laughing in hindsight — Palpatine?

But then I rewatched the movie, and I realized that without the anticipation provided by not knowing what was going to happen, *The Last Jedi* just fell flat for me. I now knew how the tricks were done, and I realized that my enjoyment rested on a gimmick. That's no way to construct a true film.

Not to repeat what others have said, but the Sequel Trilogy suffered from the lack of a unified vision that the other two trilogies possessed. That was its issue! … Well, that and the fact that it repeated beats from the originals while completely wasting the main three original cast members, though mostly Luke.

———

Returning to films isn't always required in order to get a proper sense of them, and plenty of movies are categorizable on the first viewing. However, movies that demand a rewatch — because they're made by an auteur with a particular vision, because they're well-made in many core ways, because they're strange gems, or because they need to be examined for lost luster — are truly some of the most notable that cinema has to offer.

So, take a chance, and rewatch some movies sometimes. Maybe you'll find one you like more, enough to say "Hey, yeah, that's actually good." Maybe you'll realize a movie you once enjoyed was actually *not* that great. While the latter case may be disappointing, you're still learning either way, and you're engaging critically with an art form. What better activity is there than to do that?

Why *The Simpsons* Is a Conservative Show

October 18, 2023

In January 1992, President George H.W. Bush—who at the time was running for reelection—stated: "We are going to keep on trying to strengthen the American family, to make American families a lot more like the Waltons and a lot less like the Simpsons." The comment drew a quick response from Bart Simpson himself, in his trademark rebel attitude, joking that his family was awaiting the end of economic hard times, just like the Waltons.

From the beginning, *The Simpsons* has had a decidedly liberal slant in terms of how it sees social and cultural issues, while at the same time also affecting, to some degree, how viewers see these same issues, since the show is such an icon. Look at Mr. Burns and Principal Skinner for prime examples of the show's perspective on "old-fashioned": Burns embodies the empty values and morals of the greedy tycoon, while Skinner's attitude toward education embodies an era now mostly remembered by the Baby Boomer generation (and this provides a perfect foil for Bart to rebel against). On top of this, Matt Groening himself, the show's creator, has made his liberal beliefs clear, and while he no longer is the most important voice on the show, he never set out to hire conservative replacements.

When the show itself aired, its very existence embodied a punk sensibility, even if no one at the time would have phrased it that way. Cartoons aimed at adults go much further back than *The Simpsons*, and the most commonly-cited precedent for what the show tried to do is *The Flintstones*. However, (1) there had been few attempts to make adult-oriented animated content in decades, and (2) because of the early-1960s time frame of when *The Flintstones* was made, its ability to push the envelope was restricted in a way that *The Simpsons'* never was. In fact, *The Simpsons* was part of a lineup chosen by the newly-founded FOX network specifically to make a mark quickly and effectively, because gaining viewers was paramount to success for a new broadcast channel taking on the Big Three of ABC, CBS, and NBC.

Thanks to the example set by *The Simpsons*, a punk-like redefiner of TV, all subsequent adult-oriented animated TV shows have its DNA in their veins, from *Family Guy* to *Archer* to *BoJack Horseman*. The heights it was able to achieve during its golden age, when it became the inspiration for those aforementioned shows, have provided the fumes it's driven on for over two decades now.

So, with all that, how can I possibly call *The Simpsons* a conservative show?

Floating Timelines and Toxic Familiarity

Let's all make ourselves feel old for a minute: the first episode of *The Simpsons*, "Simpsons Roasting on an Open Fire," premiered December 17, 1989 (we won't be counting the shorts from *The Tracey Ullman Show* as part of the series). For ease, let's place January 1990 as the "start date" of the show, since it makes the math easier and is so close to the premiere date. Assuming Bart turns 10 that same month (he's stated to be 10 years old), then as of this publication he'd be 43 years old, approaching 44. Homer would be hovering around 70 (one source places his birth year as 1956, but 33–34 seems a bit young for his appearance in the first episode).

I don't know what drains from the nuclear power plant into their water, but whatever it is could be sold as an "Immortality Elixir," since these characters haven't aged a day. Mr. Burns should certainly get on that money train. (We also know that each season takes place about in the year it's produced, based on pop-culture references, guest stars, and the technology seen on the show.)

This whole concept of having every season of an animated show take place in an unspecified year is called a "floating timeline." We can divide this concept into two subtypes: **vague-year** and **current-year**.

Vague-Year Floating Timelines: *Archer*

The best example I can think of regarding this type is *Archer*, a show that intentionally obscures the year(s) in which it takes place. As a spy thriller, the show draws a lot of influence from Cold-War media like James Bond, as well as aesthetics. If it kept itself to just that, it would be easy to place it in the 1970s or 1980s. However, the show also sports technology like modern-ish cell phones and references to post-1980s events and popular culture.

If one were trying to place *Archer* in an approximate year, they could try to take all the varying elements and references to cobble something like a vague estimate. Based on known events, like Mallory Archer's World War II service, the existence of the Soviet Union, Sterling Archer's age in the pilot episode, and the fact that Kenny Loggins still looks young in his guest appearance for "Archer Vice: Baby Shower," I'd say the early seasons take place *around the late 1980s*.

But that's irrelevant, and the fact that I spent so much time putting that together shows that I've missed the point entirely. The whole reason *Archer* uses a vague-year floating timeline is so that it can draw from whatever it wants, time-wise, and not violate a clearly-established continuity. You will never be able to definitively establish in what year the show takes place, and that's by design.

However, *Archer* as a show has allowed its characters to undergo character arcs over its run. This can be seen with Cyril and Pam becoming field agents in season 3, Lana becoming a mother, Archer realizing how much Lana means to him, and Barry slowly experiencing a redemption arc.

The fact that some of those changes start as early as the third season show that *Archer* always intended on having its characters change, even if it didn't know from the beginning what that would exactly entail.

In short, *Archer* uses a vague-year floating timeline to benefit both its comedy and its characters, providing a sterling example (pun intended) of this concept's benefits.

Current-Year Floating Timelines: *The Simpsons*

In a current-year floating timeline, the characters don't age and continuity between seasons, and even between episodes, is secondary to the plot of any given episode, although elements of continuity are often retained. The main purpose is to allow a show to tell new stories which are more relevant to current audiences while not having to change elements that are core to the show's appeal. This is how you get a Homer Simpson who in 2023 is about the same age in the show as someone who in real life was Bart's age when the show began.

There is one narrative benefit to this method that I want to point out: it allows for the same characters to confront different situations over the course of time. It's almost like a scientific experiment, where we test to get an answer to: "How would Homer react to _____?", where the blank is the independent variable and Homer's reaction is the dependent variable. It allows a show to change with its times while reflecting those changes through character *actions* as opposed to character *growth.*

Its current-year floating timeline is also what makes *The Simpsons* a conservative show.

Merriam-Webster defines *conservative* as (1) "of or relating to a philosophy of conservatism" in the political realm, (2) "tending or disposed to maintain existing views, conditions, or institutions," (3) "marked by or relating to tradi-tional norms of taste, elegance, style, or manners," among other definitions.

I think we can safely eliminate *The Simpsons* belonging to category 1, based on what was discussed regarding its political orientation. Likewise, I think we can eliminate category 3; even in its latest seasons, the show has never been one to go for traditional taste, elegance, style, or manners.

However, category 2 is a different story. In fact, it seems that all current-year floating timeline shows fall under this category.

We have to ask ourselves: why do shows like *The Simpsons* refuse to allow their characters to age? Short and simple answers to this question may include:

- It's easier on the cast, especially the ones who voice the children, and writers, especially new ones, who can more easily adjust to the writing process if it's the same characters year after year.
- The appeal of the show comes from these characters at the present moment; who knows if people will still watch if these characters slowly age?
- Etc.

Animation allows for characters to remain the same in terms of appearance, but it doesn't mandate that this be the case. Regardless of the reasons stated, *The Simpsons* and shows like it keep as much as they can the same, while chang-ing only what they believe is necessary to keep viewers watching. There is no overarching story to the show; it is an episode-by-episode series that, for a half-hour, allows viewers to escape their real lives and spend time with America's most consistent family. This is *toxic familiarity*, an unwillingness to leave a known comfort zone despite all evidence that staying there is unhealthy.

The Simpsons does not want to change, at least not in the way live-action shows must change. Whereas the second-longest-running scripted show, *Law & Order: Special Victims Unit*, still retains its brand, it cannot avoid the fact that its actors have aged, especially Mariska Hargitay, who's been with the show since the pilot episode in 1999. (Ice T joined in 2000, at the start of Season 2.)

But, then, what's the problem with it retaining this philosophy? On its surface, nothing. The difference with *The Simpsons* is its longevity; despite being on the air since the Berlin Wall was still standing, it has not allowed its characters to change or age. They have been stuck in a unique hell wherein immortality is granted at the price of being confined to the same age forever. Imagine being on the cusp of puberty forever. Imagine being a child genius who always pictures her future success but can never experience it herself. Imagine living as a literal baby for 34 years. (Actually, maybe that last one doesn't sound *too* bad, considering how stressful being a non-baby human can be.)

This is all the result of the aforementioned toxic familiarity. Because the show doesn't have to change. It's been the cash cow for its owners since day one, and has already gone down as the most successful animated TV show of all time, as well as one of the most successful TV shows in general. It's never had to face the challenge of changing demographics because it's been guaranteed renewal for more than two decades, if not three.

But the world changes. As *The Simpsons* keeps to its conservative mindset of only changing what it absolutely must to remain approachable, it becomes less and less relevant, because its core formula remains. Like soap operas and superhero comics, at the end of the day the status quo is either changed back to normal or a status quo reversion to normal is always just a secret twin or a clone away. The formula that propelled *The Simpsons* to glory is now a crutch, and their reliance is dragging the show into emptiness.

Here's what you do: have one extra-long final season of the show, where episode one starts off with them all the same age, but it takes place back in 1990. Every subsequent episode then takes place about one year later. You can tell a season-long story about how the characters in the original season would experience the next 34 years. Then, as a finale, let them ride off into the figurative (or maybe literal) sunset; allow the world to say goodbye to these icons in a dignified way, as they move on and we do, too.

It's that, or wait until the show becomes so irrelevant that cancellation is inevitable.

Update

Two months after I wrote this essay, the series finale of *Archer* aired, marking an end to the show. This was apparently a surprise to those working on it, as they had planned for at least a couple more seasons to follow. Gratefully, they were at least given an extra-long special episode to close out the series.

While I was starting to enjoy the most recent seasons of the show, I also as a fan realized that, for whatever reason, it still wasn't reaching its former height of quality, just like a lot of the fans of *The Simpsons* would say. It felt like it was coasting, in a way, and so, despite not being given the time the showrunners expected to have with *Archer*, the show is now "complete," and can be assessed as a work in the way long-running shows (or heck, even the never-ending glut of superhero comic books) never can be. In a strange way, cancelation might've actually saved the show by *forcing* an ending.

I wonder if *The Simpsons* will one day experience the same fate. If nothing else, the heat death of the universe will make sure that someday there will be a final episode—even if by that point days would no longer exist as we know them.

How Elliot Stabler's Departure Saved the Entire *Law & Order* Franchise

November 6, 2023

All right, so *Law & Order: Special Victims Unit* has been the longest-running scripted drama in TV history for a while now, and it's a feat I never thought it would reach, even as a longtime fan of the show. But as I've rewatched the 13th–20th seasons of the original *Law & Order* on Peacock, I've come to realize something about why *SVU* wasn't canceled like its mother series was: it's because of Chris Meloni's departure after season 12. This decision, made over a contract dispute, is what — I firmly believe — saved the show entirely.

––––––

Full disclosure: *Law & Order* is formulaic as hell. So why do I watch it? Because the formula is my comfort. The show lives and dies on the stories, not the characters. Jack McCoy is perhaps the only one on that show who has anything resembling a consistent personality and engaging character, at least from seasons 13 to 23 (I haven't seen seasons 1–12 yet).

In its first 12 seasons, *SVU* suffered this same problem. It had developed its formula, was comfortable with its characters, and knew what it was meant to deliver. Elliot Stabler and Olivia Benson had developed personalities and backstories, as (to a lesser extent) did their fellow characters, but their dynamic, the core of the show, was petering out. On that trajectory, *SVU* would have been canceled by 2012, I believe.

But when Elliot Stabler was written off the show, it meant that Olivia Benson no longer shared the starring role. It also meant that she had to deal with the same loss that loyal viewers felt.

Eventually, Benson would move into a leadership role as the head of her squad, as well as a role model and a complex character. The show may still feature formula in certain stories and in certain ways that it presents those stories. The show may also have its moments of cringe. But it's worth noting that it realized how important this character was.

In 2020, in response to the protests regarding police brutality, the show didn't keep silent on the issue. The creators knew that the controversy would have to be addressed, and so they incorporated it into the premiere episode of the season, "Guardians and Gladiators." Olivia makes a bad call. It comes back to haunt her. She's not perfect. But over the course of the season she shows that she's willing to question herself, willing to try to fix her mistake, willing to set an example for others. Taking her character in this direction was a risk.

But it was a risk worth taking, at the time out of necessity, but in hindsight because of the new direction it would mean for her character and for the series.

However, Elliot Stabler never departed entirely from the consciousness of viewers, so his return in the season 22 episode "Return of the Prodigal Son" was the most anticipated "guest" spot in the show's history. It delivered, and led into *Law & Order: Organized Crime* (*OC*).

OC is a product of the peak-TV Golden Age that arose in the 2010s, in that instead of having a new story every episode, a singular narrative would carry the show. In season 2, *OC* adopted a format of a few stories split over a season, with defined plots for each. Season 3 maintained this formula, but allowed for the occasional one-off episode like the good old *SVU* days.

In fact, *SVU* itself was the testing ground for this formula. As the show reinvented itself post-Meloni, it adopted longer-running stories as a regular feature, such as Benson facing off against rapist William Lewis or the prosecution of powerful attorney Rob Miller. This new format helped it continue to thrive in an era where cop shows became seemingly everything on cable TV.

With *SVU* carrying the torch, the *L&O* franchise remained viable long enough for both *OC* and a revival of the mothership, *Law & Order*, to happen. At times, each show suffers from overdoing its melodrama or in being too on-the-nose with its messaging, but overall it maintains quality, delivering some stories that resonate with the moment while others are simply there to help viewers pass an hour of time.

————

Cop shows still need to reckon with their existence post-George Floyd, and time will tell if these shows' attempts at dealing with a new reality were successful or not.

However, reinvention is what has kept *SVU* on the air for so long. Unlike the conservative approach of *The Simpsons*, *SVU* takes risks and allows for character changes, while still maintaining a core that's been there since 1999.

It also doesn't hurt that the topic of sexual violence is painfully relevant, now as much as (maybe even more than) ever.

Government Photography: Public Service and Propaganda

January 15, 2024

The picture that will greet you on Joe Biden's Wikipedia page is his official presidential portrait, taken by Chief Official White House Photographer Adam Schultz on March 3, 2021. (Previously, you would have seen his vice-presidential portrait from 2013.) The picture is in the public domain, meaning there are no copyright restrictions on it and thus anyone can do anything they want with it… as long as they live in the United States. (I'm not familiar with non-U.S. copyright regimes.) The picture also captures the tension between the two jobs of a government photographer: **documentarian** and **propagandist**.

But first, we have to talk about why the photo is public domain in the first place.

Copyright of U.S. federal-government works

In 1834, the U.S. Supreme Court issues its decision in *Wheaton v. Peters*, the first copyright case it ever handled. The question at hand surrounded whether a "common-law copyright" existed in the U.S., but that's not why the case is so important. As a closing comment, the majority opinion indicated that all justices agreed there could be no copyright in the opinions issued by the court itself.

The reasoning behind this, from a practical perspective, is simple: people must have unfettered access to the law and all decisions surrounding it. As copyright is a monopoly on how information is transmitted, imposing copyright on laws, executive orders, or court decisions would restrict access to that information, and thus is an illogical idea. This is the "edict of government" doctrine, and it applies to every level of government in the United States.

However, the federal government in the U.S. took it one step further in the 190 years since: any work by an employee of the U.S. federal government created as part of that person's official duties enters the U.S. public domain the moment it is created. This means that speeches, letters, congressional reports, and many other works are in the public domain, if they were made by the U.S. federal government.

This includes photographs.

Documentary Purposes

Have you ever seen Dorothea Lange's *Migrant Mother*? Chances are you have, as it's one of the most iconic of all time. But do you know the story behind it?

The photograph was taken by Lange in 1936. At the time, she was employed by the Resettlement Administration, a federal agency, and because she took this photo as part of her duties in that job, the picture has always been in the public domain. Lange and her colleagues who worked for the agency created a stunning, visually gripping archive of the Depression era which still stands as one of the pinnacles of American photography.

It is in the realm of creating an archive that the White House photographers have operated, and every president since John F. Kennedy (with the exception of Jimmy Carter) has had at least one working at a time. These photographers (or teams of them) have together created millions of photographs of the past six decades of American history, with the most upfront seat imaginable. They've documented moments of national uncertainty, such as Cecil W.

Stoughton's photo of Lyndon Baines Johnson taking the presidential oath of office aboard Air Force One, or Pete Souza's *Situation Room* photograph taken during the raid on Osama bin Laden's compound. They've also depicted quiet, human moments during presidential terms, such as David Hume Kennerly's photo of Gerald Ford petting his dog, Liberty, or Pete Souza's photographs of the Obama family together.

My personal favorite photograph that I've discovered on this rabbit-hole journey is the following black-and-white one, taken by David Hume Kennerly of George H.W. Bush (then known simply as "George Bush"), who was Director of Central Intelligence under Gerald Ford at the time:

Even though I can easily read the caption for this photo, I still don't fully know what it is Bush is reacting to. The starkness of the black-and-white combines with his steely expression and the sharp angles of his face and glasses to create a composition that is dynamic, engaging, and even heroic, making me uninterested in knowing more context. If I knew nothing of him except this photo, and you told me he served as president for *just* one term, I'd be shocked.

But the power of this image to have such a strong influence on my perception of Bush speaks to the other reason why official photographers are employed by presidential administrations:

Propaganda Purposes

Adam Schultz was a campaign photographer for Hillary Clinton in 2016 and Joe Biden in 2020. Oliver F. Atkins was the same for Nixon in 1968. Pete Souza started chronicling President Obama when the latter was the newly-elected junior senator from Illinois, although Souza was employed by CNN, not yet by Obama himself. Still, the two grew close during Souza's assignment, which is why Obama chose him to be his photographer.

In all these cases, the relationship began at a pre-presidential time, and in the cases of Biden and Nixon, the photographers were used to support election efforts, which by their very nature are propaganda. Does covering a possible future president also serve the public? Absolutely. But is that the main purpose for a campaign photographer? No. The purpose is to create a carefully curated image for the public to see so that they're more inclined to vote for the candidate. And you're telling me these people just magically switch over to (or, in Souza's case, remain) pure documentarians once they enter the White House?

Of course not. In a *Town & Country* interview, Adam Schultz was very open about then-candidate Biden giving input and feedback on photos.[6] A CNN story revealed that, as president, Donald Trump was even more hands on with his photographer, Shealah Craighead, who said Trump "like[d] to control the lighting, the production, and the show basically," with him oftentimes picking the final photo(s) released.[7]

Now, is this morally wrong? No. But the White House photographers' close association with their subjects removes them from consideration as photojournalists. They are employed to keep their president's image out there in carefully curated form.

Guess what, though? Even the Depression-era photographers had more than just documentation in mind, or at the very least their employers did. The photographers' job was to document the effects of the Depression both because this project benefitted posterity *and* because it could help sell New Deal policies to the public. So, no, this isn't a phenomenon unique to presidential photographers; it's just that those jobs are the ones that are the most high-profile example of this dichotomy today.

———

Again, I appreciate the public service element here; I do believe history benefits from these government-funded photos, and as a proponent of the commons, I love that they're free from the moment of creation. But especially with the presidential photos, it's important that we understand that they never will (nor perhaps could they, even if they wanted to) present the whole picture.

A Love Letter to Letter-Writing

August 8, 2024

Sometimes a special obsession takes hold of me and I have to explore it as much as I can. A previous example of this would be the time in 2022 in which I was so obsessed about the topic of translation that I ended up translating a Spanish-language comic into English just for fun, something I've written about already.

Recently, however, that obsession has been the topic of letters—reading and writing them, learning about the role they've played in recording history and connecting people, etc. From reading a wonderful series of articles on the National Postal Museum's website about the history of letter-writing in the United States to reading samples of actual letters written by Thomas Jefferson, John & Abigail Adams, and Charles Dickens, there is a wealth of information out there to satisfy this interest.

No work has so fundamentally affected me in this regard, however, like Jeanne Marie Laskas' 2018 book *To Obama*.

During his eight-year presidency, whenever he was at the White House, President Obama would read ten letters/emails a day of the thousands sent to him, sampled and sent to his desk by workers in the Office of Presidential Correspondence. *To Obama* reprints a sample of the letters he received, along with his responses and, in certain cases, chapter-length profiles of the person who wrote a certain letter or email. On top of this, it also intersperses chapters about events or people who worked in that office and read the letters to President Obama.

In all, the book is a beautiful collection of the diverse voices of America—even including ones critical of the president—as well as an operation that sought to connect the president and the people he represented in a way that no previous administration had attempted to do. Seriously, if *any* of this sounds interesting to you, I implore you to read this book; it's very quickly become one of my all-time favorites.

It's also the final impetus it took for me to write this article. In an age where texting and image- and video-chatting are the most common means of communication in younger generations, and phone calls still retain some popularity, the practice of letter-writing has declined like never before—although, as the National Postal Museum states, the moment the telephone became commonplace, that decline began. Many, if not most, are probably not much bothered by this. Some might even argue that these newer forms of communication are just replacing the older forms, that I'm being a Luddite for lamenting this loss.

However, letter-writing is a unique form of communication that I believe no other form since has matched, and I want to talk about why I feel that this is the case, while celebrating the form I love.

Letters in the Time of COVID-19

I was never big into letter-writing growing up, although an occasional fan letter did end up on its way to an admired figure. Email was a sufficient way to communicate for business and academic purposes, while texting, calling, and, later, Snapchat were perfectly fine to communicate informally with family and friends.

But COVID changed all of that.

Having been quickly thrown into an unknown world defined by separation for survival (maybe a bit overdramatic to phrase it like that, but that's how it felt then), those old forms didn't feel the same. It made the idea of writing something—by hand or by computer—and sending it out into the world, where it would physically arrive in someone else's hand, felt almost miraculous. And so, my love of letter-writing began.

It would continue over the next four years. I'd write to family members, to friends far away, to politicians, to the letters column my favorite comic-book series, *Saga*. (I was so proud when my letter was the first one printed at the back of issue #64!) It was so fun, so therapeutic, so much deeper than a text or a phone call. Even with keeping up a diary, letters had their own important place in my life.

Why did I grow to love it so much? Because, as I've said before, letters are unique.

What Only Letters Can Do

Imagine yourself sitting across from a friend or family member. Maybe you do more of the talking, maybe they do, or maybe it's about even. Still, I imagine the conversation goes something like this: one person says a few sentences on average, then the other person responds at about the same length, etc. Occasionally, you'll have longer stretches of a single person speaking.

This same format, of the typical conversation, is reproduced in texting, phone-calls (which are just conversations without the in-person visuals), and even image-chatting. One person sends something short, then another person responds back, on and on; occasionally, there's an exception of a longer-length message.

Now, there's nothing *wrong* with this; in fact, I'd argue that the ability for these forms to recreate in-person conversations in certain ways is what makes them great in the first place. Plus, except for phone-calling, you can respond at your own pace, and aren't expected to say something immediately.

However, this is what has always made letters different. Between the cost of postage and materials, the fact that written mail takes time to reach the recipient, and the fact that a response takes at least equally as long, there has always been an incentive to elaborate. Instead of it being like two people are in the same room, it is like one person delivers a monologue of all their thoughts, without interruption, and then gives the stage to their correspondent, who can communicate the same way. Therefore, letters are much more about self-expression and require much more thought than any instant-message medium. It's why they're literary, why they're so valuable to history: self-expression and detail, respectively.

The only form which I think could compete in this regard is email. For much of the history of letters, business and political correspondence was a significant percent of all letters sent, because the form allowed for coordination across long distances. Upon its wide adoption, however, email took over that role (with fax having begun to do something similar before it), because of its convenience and speed. Unlike texting, it allowed for formality, but unlike letters, it could arrive in the recipient's inbox instantly.

I believe that if we really want email to be an art like letter-writing, we can make that happen. However, I think that the speed of email means we don't have to be as detailed or thoughtful as we do with letters sent by mail, and thus we don't often see email emulate letters in all the ways it could.

There is still a wonderful novelty to receiving a letter in the mail, whether handwritten or typed. It represents an investment of time by the sender (which means a lot to the receiver), and it is a means for connecting with others through the carefully-written word. Not all letters will be masterpieces; many will have spelling or grammar mistakes, for example. However, they will all be meaningful for sender and receiver both.

The mind changes its neural pathways when it composes a letter, because of the thought and time required. This is why I have my students write a persuasive letter to someone in a position of power, actually; not to send them (they can if they want, but that's not required), but to practice skills of composition, persuasion, argumentation, and identification of the proper audience for one's message. It's all there, and I maintain that if you stick with it, it will be a benefit to you, even before thinking about the effects your letter could have on the person reading it.

———

This is what makes letter-writing a beneficial art form. It's why I love writing and reading letters, and why I think we need to keep this tradition alive in some form, whether by writing more physical letters, expanding how we use email, or both.

Caro and Martin:
Two Writers, One Problem

November 13, 2024

Decades ago, a middle-aged male set out to write an epic trilogy of books dealing with the theme of power, but instead the series ballooned into several more
volumes. Despite expecting to have finished the next book within a few years
of the previous one, it has taken more than a decade, the book still isn't out,
and there is speculation that he will never finish the book and thus the series.

Now, am I talking about George R.R. Martin or Robert Caro?

———

Robert Caro is the author behind *The Years of Lyndon Johnson*, a multi-volume
biography of Lyndon Baines Johnson from cradle to grave. As of 2024, Caro
still has one more, fifth volume to write, and hasn't released a book in the series
since 2012.

I imagine that most readers know who George R.R. Martin is, but for those
who don't, a refresher: he is the author behind the *Song of Ice and Fire* series,
which is the basis for the HBO show (and 2010s cultural phenomenon) *Game of
Thrones*. The first book in Martin's series, *A Game of Thrones*, was released in
1996; four more volumes followed, but fans have grown impatient since two
more books are expected and yet (as of 2024) the most recent book was released

in 2011.

Needless to say, it seems quite possible that neither man will finish his magnum opus. But what has led to both a fiction writer and a biographer to end up in a similar predicament? After all, while fiction can be made up, biography could take quite a long time to research. Still, not every biographer takes a decade, on average, to write a book, even if they take time; few other biographers, however, have spent decades on one long, multi-book project.

So, why do these men find it hard to finish their work? From what I've seen and based on my experiences as a writer, I would say the following reasons: **perfectionism**, the **increasing complexity of the project**, and the **anxiety of completion**.

Perfectionism

This might be obvious, but writers tend to be perfectionists to their core. Whether you spend months or even years writing a single project (like a novelist), or you write to frequent deadlines (like a journalist), you want everything to work together smoothly and as perfectly as possible; every detail is up for scrutiny.

Caro and Martin have invested about half their lives into a singular project, and when that's the case, the project begins to mean more than a single novel that took a year or two to write. Because of how much time they've invested in research, planning, writing, and revising, they want to make sure they have a perfect product at the end. If not, then all of their hard work will seem like it's for nothing.

What did I spend years working on, they'll think, *just to be undone by a missed fact or an uninteresting plot point?* It is paramount for them to make sure everything is perfect. And to do so, to dot all the i-s and cross all the t-s, takes a lot of time.

Robert Caro is also notoriously meticulous with research, which is partly why it takes his books so long to come out. (Unlike Martin, Caro has at least been relatively consistent in taking about the same amount of time to release each book. Martin released the first three *Ice and Fire* books in five years, then took six years to release the next one and five years to release the one after that.) Caro's perfectionism is well-documented.

While Martin's is not well-documented, I infer it in part because of his lack of progress on the book, but also because of something very specific: the *Game of Thrones* TV show.

Martin found himself in a unique situation when the series caught up to and then passed the point he was at in the novels, because now the show had to either adapt unreleased material or create material from scratch. The show's creators were apparently given a general outline of where Martin intended to go, but without having Martin's notes or the finished books, we have nothing to compare to the completed TV show.

That being said, the poor reception of the last parts of *Game of Thrones* (especially the last season) is both a curse and a blessing for Martin. The curse is that it harms the otherwise-adored brand that his books and the beloved parts of the show helped build. On top of that, Martin has now been told that, on some level, his plans for the books are flawed. (Again, we can't know the extent without seeing Martin's plans.) However, this is also a blessing, because it means *Game of Thrones* acted as the most expensive market test ever made for a book. Now Martin can look at what didn't work with the show and tweak his novels; he can, in essence, write a better ending because he knows what to avoid.

Here's the problem: Martin has been vocal about how important his plans are to his process. This has come up in critiques of *Game of Thrones* that use Martin's thoughts as a counterpoint; in one clip, Martin cautions against changing plans mid-story because an audience member has predicted the ending. If you've set up a mystery knowing that the butler committed the murder, Martin says, you don't change the identity of the murderer if some audience member correctly identifies the butler before you reveal it.

Therefore, it's quite possible that Martin is stuck due to the show; he can't change the ending without jeopardizing his plans, but the show demonstrated that those plans are flawed. How paralyzing would that be?

The Increasing Complexity of the Project

We also can't devalue the fact that with each new book comes an increase in complexity.

For Caro, the more he learned about Lyndon Johnson, the more he felt he needed to cover, leading the books and the series to expand and thus necessitating even more research. But again, this ties back into Caro's perfectionism, too; before the COVID-19 pandemic halted his plans, Caro had intended to do research in Vietnam, since his final book deals with Johnson's presidency, the Achilles heel of which was the Vietnam War. This isn't even abnormal; in researching Johnson's early years, Caro decided he and his wife would move to Texas and live where Johnson grew up, to better understand where he came from. They lived there for three years; *that* is dedication.

Martin's books are known for their sprawling cast with unique character voices, intricate plot, and well-developed world. As Martin has added more and more to this work, he has increased its complexity: he has a lot to keep track of at this point. And unlike Caro, whose work is based in research of real events, Martin has to create everything from scratch while ensuring it all coheres and doesn't contradict. At the very least, this slows him down, though it may also be nearing the point of crippling.

The Anxiety of Completion

There is one more possible explanation behind the men's inability to finish their work, and it's something I'm calling the "anxiety of completion." It was the realization of this idea which kickstarted my interest in writing this article.

For certain writers, completing a work is the important part. Vince Gilligan—creator of *Breaking Bad*—once remarked that he didn't like writing; he

123

liked having written. The end product was what he lived for. On the other hand, I as a writer enjoy the process of writing, of actively processing ideas, of having many possibilities available simultaneously. Of not having made a mistake yet. I think prolific authors like Stephen King tend to fall more in this category.

For writers like this, who live for the journey as opposed to the destination, the project keeps us alive in a sense. It sustains us. In fact, I started my second novel, *Impressions of a Pupil*, right before the 2020 election, because I felt that no matter what happened, I needed a purpose, a reason to stay here, something to work toward. The work we do in developing our stories gives us sustenance.

Some compare the process of writing to birth, of having brought something new into the world. But for me, to finish a writing project that I've invested my very self into is, in a way, like dying. It is over. I'll never again wake up and wonder how I'll write the next scene of that story. And I can only write if I enjoyed writing; had I dreaded the story to the point where finishing would be a relief, I would not have finished at all.

Don't get me wrong, there is a sense of satisfaction in completing the first draft. And as a self-published author, I can send out my work at any time, as well as edit it at any point to remove a typo or something. But for me, once the work as a whole is done, the major work is complete, because everything is integral; nothing but the most minor of scenes can be removed without the loss of something necessary to the overall story. I try to keep out any filler. Though I admire his work in education, I find it baffling to hear author and YouTuber John Green say "I almost always delete most of my first drafts (often as much as 90%)." [8] Yes, I believe in revision, but if you're often deleting 90% of your work, then you're basically writing a new work each time... at least, that's how it would be with me.

But, I digress. The point I'm trying to make is that, for Caro and Martin, not finishing the final pieces of their work could also be a subconscious avoidance of death. If, like me, the process is what sustains them, then finishing a work that has occupied so much of their lives would, in a way, be like accepting the end of their lives. After all, Martin is almost 80 and Caro just hit 89, so both are in their twilight years.

Sometimes, it's exhilarating to finish the journey. But once you're done, you can't ever really go back to it. It's over. And if you're in the midst of what's not only your life-defining journey but also probably your final journey, it's only human to prolong it for as long as you can, to want to stave off its ending for as long as you can.

The difference is that, unlike books (which may never be completed), we're guaranteed an ending.

The Masterful Narrative of *Uncharted 4: A Thief's End*

November 17, 2024

Anyone who has played any of the *Uncharted* games knows that they deliver on both gameplay and story. Each entry in the main series follows Nathan "Nate" Drake on an adventure to find a fabled treasure or lost city, in a mix of *Indiana Jones*, *National Treasure*, and the *Lara Croft* video game series. From *Uncharted 1* to *Uncharted 4*, the quality either improved from the previous game or maintained the series' high bar.

Ask an *Uncharted* fan today what their favorite in the series is, and there's a good chance that they'll say "*Uncharted 2*," though I've (anecdotally) seen each game at least once cited as someone's favorite. However, if you ask me, *Uncharted 4: A Thief's End* blows every other game in the series out of the water, and it has nothing to do with the improved graphics, new gameplay mechanics, or the fact that it's (possibly) the longest in terms of hours you can spend in the game.

It's all about the story.

In order to explain why I cite its story as game-changing (pun intended), I need to give you some backstory on the game and how I came to appreciate it so much.

Be warned: there will be spoilers in the rest of this essay.

A Plot Summary of *Uncharted 4*

Uncharted 4 begins with Nate and his brother, Sam—who was not even mentioned in the previous three entries in the main series, or the tie-in media—imperiled by a private military company off the coast of an uncharted island near Madagascar. From here, the game flashes back to Nate's childhood to build the relationship between him and his brother, then forward to a time fifteen years before the main story, in a prison where Nate, Sam, and their financier, Rafe Adler, are searching for clues to the treasure of famous pirate Henry Avery. This mission ends with Sam seemingly killed in the trio's attempt to escape the prison.

The game then follows Nate in his civilian life a few years after *Uncharted 3: Drake's Deception*, working a real job and no longer pursuing treasure hunting. Although each previous game ended with Nate starting or restarting a relationship with journalist Elena Fisher, at the start of both *Uncharted 2* and *Uncharted 3*, they've broken up for unclear reasons. This time, however, Nate and Elena have actually married, and it seems like he really has moved on from that life—until it becomes clear that Nate still has that craving for adventure, but is suppressing it. Why? Because he fears that pursuing it will cost him his relationship with Elena, as it seemingly has before.

Things change, however, when Sam shows up and reveals that he needs to find Avery's treasure or else be killed by a drug lord who broke Sam out of prison and wants him to find the treasure. Wishing to save his brother, Nate rejoins the hunt, but lies to Elena about where he's going, saying she "won't understand." Nate enlists the help of former partner Victor "Sully" Sullivan, and he, Sully, and Sam attempt to find the treasure, all the while in competition with Rafe and a private military company Rafe hired to assist him, which is led by Nadine Ross.

Later in the game, Elena figures out that Nate lied and comes to confront him in Madagascar, leading to one of the most heart-wrenching moments of the story. While it seems like Nate may have lost Elena for good, he continues on the quest in order to save his brother.

However, when Nate and Sam are finally cornered by Rafe and Nadine, Nate explains to Rafe that they need the treasure to save Sam, due to the threat of the drug lord. That's when Rafe reveals that it was actually he who got Sam out of prison, and that Sam's entire story about the drug lord was a lie. In reality, Sam wanted to find the treasure with Nate, and was willing to do whatever it took to get Nate back into the game and beat Rafe to Avery's loot.

Through an accident straight out of an action movie, Nate falls off a cliff after this reveal, but Sam is left behind. After another flashback, it's shown that Elena did follow Nate and Sam thanks to Sully's help, and she brings Nate back to health. Nate's goal then becomes saving Sam from Rafe and Nadine. In the course of their search for Sam, Nate and Elena repair their relationship, in a sequence told brilliantly through gameplay and great writing. Elena also realizes that Nate is meant for the treasure-hunting life, and that maybe they've overcorrected in avoiding it completely.

When they finally get to Sam, they're able to convince him to abandon the quest, and it looks as if Rafe will get the treasure after all; at the last minute, Sam turns around and goes for it, with Nate deciding he has to follow and save his brother, though Nate's goal is never to get the treasure.

Nate eventually comes across Sam, in Avery's boat (moored in a cavern, like the pirate ship in *The Goonies*), a billion dollars' worth of loot stockpiled in it, but the boat has been lit on fire by explosive traps that Avery set up and which Sam triggered, leading him to get trapped under a wooden pillar. Nadine, who has been under threat of Rafe, escapes Rafe at gunpoint, and leaves him, Nate, and Sam in the burning hull. Rafe, having completely lost his mind, picks up a sword and engages Nate in a duel, but is eventually defeated. Nate tries to save Sam, but the beam won't budge. Sam insists Nate leave, saying that he (Sam) has gotten what he always wanted, to find the treasure with Nate.

Nate, however, devises a plan to flood the hull, use the water to lift the beam, and escape through the hole he created. The two of them are just able to make it out of the cavern where the ship is located before the cavern entrance collapses. (Why is the cavern entrance collapsing? Seemingly because of the ship's cannons firing against the cavern walls.)

Nate and Sam go home, and it is revealed that, thanks to some treasure Sam took with him from the ship, Nate and Elena are able to become treasure hunters, but now do so legitimately, having found a balance. They have a child and a happy life in the future.

Uncovering *Uncharted* 4's Themes

Uncharted 4 forefronts theme in a way few other games do. It is story about family, about love, about sacrifice, about passion, and about redemption. While it may not be the world-shattering game that *Uncharted* 2 was when it released in 2009, no other game in the series has this much depth to its story, and that's really what makes it shine so much.

I only really came to appreciate the game's story thanks to two events: a Reddit post and a college class.

The Reddit Post

The Reddit post came first. One day, after I'd completed the game, I came across a post (that I now cannot locate) that wondered the following: why is Saint Dismas, who is referenced so much in the first portion of the game, just dropped about halfway through? For context, in the game's world, Henry Avery was an admirer of Saint Dismas, one of the two thieves who were crucified alongside Jesus. Gestas, the impenitent thief, mocked Jesus for not rescuing himself and them, but Dismas, the penitent thief, accepted his fate and asked Jesus to remember him when Jesus arrived in Paradise, and Jesus said to Dismas that he would be with Him in Paradise.

The second clue that the boys find on their adventure is a cross of Saint

Dismas, and it's later revealed that Avery sent these crosses out to other pirates as a way of inviting them to join his planned pirate haven of Libertalia. The motif of Dismas shows up in a few more puzzles, but by the time they get to the island where Libertalia is located, the only clear reference to Dismas is a map indicating the port of Libertalia was named the "Port of Saint Dismas."

However, the motif of Dismas does continue throughout the rest of the story, because it juxtaposes people between Dismas and his opposite, Gestas. It's just done subtly, as opposed to the overt way it was handled before.

It seems in the game that Avery saw himself as a Dismas figure, just like many outlaws have been viewed as folk heroes, from certain points of view. However, it's revealed that the pirate haven he founded either began as or turned into a scam: thousands of thieves and pirates pooled their treasure and gave it to Avery and the other founders of Libertalia, ostensibly to help the colony run. However, the founders hoarded the money, destroyed the colony, and killed most of the colonists, save for some of their own loyal followers. Avery teamed up with Thomas Tew, his second-in-command, to take out the other founders, but then tried to betray Tew and leave the island with all of the treasure. The two of them killed each other in the same hull where Nate, Sam, and Rafe end up, and the swords Nate and Rafe use are the swords embedded in the two pirates. They both became Gestas.

The story of another expeditioner, from the 19th century, is told through notes you can collect throughout Libertalia. This man was also searching for the treasure, but became so greedy and determined to get it that he murdered most of his crew, then died of a gunshot wound just outside the cave where Avery's treasure-laden ship was docked. Another impenitent thief undone by the lure of the treasure.

Everyone who has searched for the treasure or coveted it has wound up dead, which Nadine notes near the end of the game, as she leaves Nate, Sam, and Rafe in the hull to die.

(In searching for the Reddit post to cite, I came across this post[9] from 2016 which analyzes the hull scene in the same way I do below. It's possible that I came across this back in 2017 or 2018, when I was first thinking about themes in *Uncharted 4*, but I do not recall it for certain. Just in case, I want to credit Bersnardo for coming up with this before I did, and for possibly influencing what you're about to read.)

In the hull scene, Rafe is the impenitent thief, who mocks Nate's legendary status and goads him to fight, in the way Gestas mocked Jesus. Sam is the penitent thief, held down by the beam (which resembles a cross), who recognizes the error of his ways at the end of his life. (The burning hull could also act as a stand-in for the Harrowing of Hell; Nate, does, after all, have to walk down a few steps in order to first reach it.) Nate, as the Jesus figure, saves Sam, and brings him into "Paradise," i.e. helps free him. (A now-deleted user, commenting on Bersnardo's original post, points out that Sam is saved by water, akin to a baptism.) Sam now redeemed, the two emerge from the cave just as stones fall into and close off the entrance, in the way Jesus left the cave upon his resurrection. Then, once they escape the cave, Elena fires a flare into the sky, to indicate to Sully where to land the plane; the scene transitions into Nate and Sam inside the plane, looking back at the island from their view in the sky, a stand-in for Heaven.

Therefore, this game is in so many ways a thief's end.

I realized all of this on subsequent playthroughs of the game (except for the baptism part), and it stuck with me. (This is also how I came across the post I can't find and, possibly, Bersnardo's post). But it wasn't until the college class that I was able to put it to use.

The College Class

In 2019, I took a January-term course at the University of Virginia, "The Politics of Video Games," taught by media studies professor Bruce Williams. For the final assignment, I used *Uncharted 4* as my example game, because I realized that I could incorporate the thematic realizations I'd had about it into a discussion on the maturation of the video-game medium. The fact that *Uncharted 4* could tell such a complex story—comparable to the best that cinema, TV, and literature have offered up—was proof that video games could be a true narrative medium and not simply diversionary toys.

As it happens, parts of that essay have formed the basis of this one.

I think at the time I was also seriously considering the question of whether or not video games could be considered art, which had been such a contentious topic over the preceding couple decades that it had its own Wikipedia page.[10] There wasn't any question of whether aspects of video games (such as the scenery or background) could be art, but whether video games in totality could be. Evidently, my argument then was an unequivocal "yes," and I was proud to be able to finally use that insight to demonstrate my point. (I still believe video games can be art, for the record.)

It was, in fact, because of what I realized about the game's depth through this analysis (combined with a slight disappointment in *The Last of Us Part II*'s narrative) that pushed *Uncharted 4: A Thief's End* ahead of *The Last of Us* to become my favorite video game of all time, as well as one of my favorite stories of all time.

It still retains both titles to this day.

Fan-Made Works and Copyright

November 24, 2024

In perusing YouTube recently, I came across a video[11] by In Praise of Shadows (IPOS) from 2023, discussing a fan-written novelization of the 1989 movie *Halloween 5*; specifically, he was discussing it in relation to bullying, copyright, corporate greed, and, by the end, the automation of art.

As someone who plans to write an entire book about the process of adapting stories from one medium to another, I was initially hooked by the word "novelization" in the title. I thought it would be more of a media analysis of an adaptation, or a discussion about how fan-created works operate in general by using a specific example.

However, as I watched the video, I found myself in an uncomfortable position: agreeing with some points and disagreeing with others.

Normally, I wouldn't be bothered by this. After all, intellectual diversity is a great thing; it's how we grow as people and as a collective. That very point underpins much of what IPOS says in the video. The issue was not a mix of agreement/disagreement itself; no, instead, the issue was that I fundamentally disagreed with the framing of his argument, and found him to be either ignorant or willfully obtuse about copyright. He used examples without providing full context, ignored an important distinction by not discussing fair use at all (in fact, an argument he makes relies on a misunderstanding/ignorance of fair use), and employed non sequiturs to attempt to seem more coherent. By the end, it's a conspiracy-laden tirade hidden behind an anti-bullying mask and which leaves viewers less informed about copyright than they were when the video began.

Originally, I was simply going to write a response comment on the video, but seeing how many people supported the arguments, and how so few actually understood a core nuance that IPOS ignored (and those who did were labeled as corporate shills and indoctrinated sheeple), I decided to turn to the essay to make a fuller response. This way, I can also universalize my thoughts beyond just this one instance, while using this example as my case study.

Backstory

Assuming you can still access the video when you read this, I encourage you to watch it instead of reading this backstory, because I want IPOS's actual arguments to be known before you read my response. I also in no way want to, even unintentionally, create a straw man for my response. If you cannot watch it, however, I will do my best to summarize the important points:

A fan named Jake Martin created a novelization of the movie *Halloween 5* over the course of 10 months. After doing so, he approached a company called Encyclopocalypse Publications—run by a man named Sean Duregger and which, among other things, reprints old novelizations and publishes new ones created by fans—to publish this book. However, while Duregger was interested in publishing the book, there were some issues with the rights to the story, and so the company couldn't publish Martin's adaptation of *Halloween 5*.

Because of this, Martin decided to self-publish the book on Amazon's Kindle Direct Publishing platform, so that the work could be preserved in a printed format.

Upon hearing that Martin had done this, Duregger publicly called him out on Twitter, and a ton of people lobbed hate onto Martin based on Duregger's actions—including well-known figures in the horror genre—in what can only be described as bullying. So, after only selling a couple dozen or so copies of the book, netting only $26, Martin removed the book from sale and went private on all accounts.

IPOS makes it clear near the beginning that he does not like Duregger in part because the latter seems to embody an ultra-capitalist hustle mindset that IPOS completely disagrees with, to the point that it is antithetical to his left-wing views of the world. (I don't use "left-wing" as an insult, but to shorthand for you how IPOS sees the world and how it varies so much from Duregger's perceived point of view.) However, it's clear that IPOS's biggest animus toward Duregger is due to his actions toward Jake Martin.

For the rest of the video, IPOS argues the following: (1) that Duregger's actions are symptomatic of a capitalist culture where we screw each other over to get ahead and please our corporate overlords, (2) that what Jake Martin did was a victimless crime because (2.1) he made so little money and (2.2) it was against a corporate giant that does nothing but grift off of actual creators, (3) that by Duregger's standard IPOS is also violating copyright by using clips and pictures from films and book covers to illustrate his video, (4) that people both not banding together and letting corporations run society has harmed all of us, and (5) that because the system is broken, it is okay to disrespect copyright law as long as it's against the political and social elite.

As I said earlier, most comments agreed with him.

One more thing happened after the posting of the video: IPOS posted a comment from Jake Martin as the pinned comment on the video. Martin (who was interviewed by IPOS for the video) indicates that Duregger reached out and apologized, and that he (Martin) had accepted this apology, while agreeing that what Sean did was horrible. However, Martin also condemned those on his side for going "overboard" and "a little bit crazy," doing things like "sending Sean death threats, which is utterly inexcusable." On top of this, Martin says that "I am not an anti-copyright crusader; I am merely a fan who aspired to publish a book" and admits that "I approached the publication process in the wrong way," while arguing (correctly) that the bullying he received, and the bullying Sean Duregger received in turn, were both out of proportion and wrong. He even encouraged people to support Sean's website. Finally, Martin revealed that he would release his *Halloween 5* novelization for free, which will come back into play during my arguments later.

Despite Martin's response, the video — which should have been about condemning this bullying/harassing behavior — also turned into an anti-copyright crusade that prompted me to make this response.

Again, watch the video, if you can. Because now it's time to respond to IPOS's arguments.

Jake's Actions

It's critical to acknowledge that Sean Duregger's actions were wrong, because they were. Perhaps he called out Jake because he really did want to publish Jake's book but couldn't, and now Jake was going to profit on his own. Perhaps Sean really felt like Jake's violation of the law was wrong, either because it put a bad name on this kind of work in general or because of some other reason. I don't know. But none of that justifies his actions, and I am glad that he apologized for them.

That being said, Jake committed a wrongdoing, too: publishing the book *for money*. That is the key distinction. Making his *Halloween 5* was not wrong in any way; in fact, it's an admirable bit of fan labor.

At one point in the video, Jake seems to indicate that he wanted to have it available in physical form for preservation purposes. I can understand why, as someone who still prefers physical books to e-books. But the moment he published it for money, no matter how little he charged, he committed copyright infringement.

136

Fan Works and Money

Fan Fiction and Publication

The legality of fan fiction's existence is murky, but there's a general under-standing in the fan-fiction world that if you write, you don't charge money for it.

Some authors, admittedly, do publish their fan fictions, but that's almost always after they've "filed the serial numbers off," meaning they've changed it enough so that it reads just like an original piece of fiction. For example, this is what E.L. James did with her *Twilight* fan fiction, which she transformed into the mega-hit *Fifty Shades of Grey* series.

As someone who has written fan fiction, I do believe that, when shared online for free, it falls under fair use — but fair use comes later in this essay.

Fan Art and the Origins of Copyright

Like fan fiction, fan art is also a popular activity. If I pay someone money to draw me a picture of a copyrighted character, is that a copyright violation? Well, I'd argue it isn't, but that goes into why copyright exists in the first place.

See, before the printing press, books had to be copied by hand, and so if you'd copied an entire book yourself, you owned that book. There was no sense of owning "ideas" (though, technically, copyright is about owning the rights to how those ideas are expressed, not the ideas themselves) because those ideas took a long time to copy.

The printing press changed this completely. With its existence, publishers could churn out copies of the same books with ease. This is why Shakespeare's plays, written in an era before performance-rights were invented but after the printing press had made its debut, were kept under guard. A rival acting com-pany that got its hands on a full script of Shakespeare could produce that play without legal repercussions. The only time plays were published was when the play was no longer popular and thus no protection of the script was needed.

(There was a kind of publications-rights protector called the Stationers' Register, but it wasn't as robust as copyright regimes in later centuries.)

So, when one specific piece of fan art is commissioned and paid for by one person, and will not be copied, then in my view it isn't a copyright violation; you're not paying for a bootleg copy of something, you're paying for the labor of an artist to create something for you and you only, in a single copy.

Therefore, the important question isn't whether something depicts a copyrighted image, but whether or not it harms the market for the original. That single, one-time image wouldn't. But a copy of the copyrighted novel, released online, would, because—in theory if not always in practice—no one pays for something when they can get the same exact thing for free.

Fan Works and Fair Use

"Fair use" is a U.S. doctrine in copyright law that allows a person to use a limited amount of a copyrighted original work without the permission of the copyright holder and then claim fair use as a defense, but this is under specific circumstances. What is considered are:

1. The purpose and character of the material used
2. The nature of the original work itself
3. The amount of the original work used
4. The effect upon the market of the original work

So, for instance, short quotations from a larger work are allowed for analysis and criticism of the work, even without permission.

So, if a fan fiction (easily reproducible) only uses the characters and settings of an original work and creates its own story, but doesn't charge money for access, then there's an argument that the work could fall under fair use, unless a publisher could show that their copyrighted work was being harmed by the existence of the fan fiction. (Say, if no one were buying the original be-cause of the free fan fictions.)

This is why the biggest impediment to claiming Jake Martin's *Halloween 5* is fair use is the fact that originally one had to pay for access. Martin was prof-iting off of copyrighted material that he didn't have permission to use.

Releasing the book for free is a much better avenue, and it bolsters Martin's argument that he really only was doing this to honor the original work.

Patronage Exception

There may also be an exception when it comes to fan works: patronage. If, say, you support yourself with income from a site where people pay a certain amount every month to support you, then you could create works of fan art or fan fiction for that audience, but that audience isn't paying for it; rather, they're paying to support you, and your creations are byproducts of you living your life.

It may sound strange for me to phrase it that way, but for this reason, pat-ronage might truly be a way to support creators in the fan world. After all, before copyright, patronage of writers by the wealthy was how they were able to focus on writing in the first place, since it didn't matter if their work was widespread or not, or if people distributed their work without permission.

Again, the specific legal parameters of this fall outside of my expertise; I'm just going off of what I understand.

The Disingenuousness of IPOS's Argument

Not Understanding Fair Use

At no point in his video does IPOS bring up fair use. He does, however, argue that if Martin could be brought down because of his actions, then IPOS could be brought down by using copyrighted material in this very video. However, that ignores the doctrine of fair use in favor of fear-mongering to get his point across about corporate greed and the need for resistance against the current social order.

No, IPOS: your use of others' work in your video (1) is used for commentary and (2) does not harm the original market for any of the works. You may not like how copyright operates or its disproportionate benefit to wealthy people and corporations, but you don't get to mislead viewers to get them to support you. Your obligation is to the truth, as it is for all of us. *That* is ethics, not the law.

Now, since its beginning YouTube has been subject to bad-faith copyright claims and poor equality of treatment towards its creators vs. claimants of the violation. YouTube weighs the claims seriously because if they don't, they're violating Section 230 of the Telecommunications Act of 1996. (This is why the onus would have been on Amazon to take down Martin's *Halloween 5*, not on Sean Duregger to inform them of its existence on the site.)

Using a Bad Example

IPOS uses the James Bond movie *Never Say Never Again* as a point of comparison with the *Halloween 5* novelization, saying the former was made without the permission of Eon Productions, the rights-holders for James Bond movies. However, while true that it was made without Eon's permission, *NSNA* was not a violation of copyright because—due to complicated legal matters—the filming rights to the novel it was based on, *Thunderball*, ended up with the company that made *Never Say Never Again*.

This glaring omission means one of two things: either IPOS did not do sufficient research for this example or he is willfully misleading his audience on this point.

His Non-Sequiturs

IPOS, like many of the commenters, claims that copyright exists solely to benefit the wealthy and elite. While that seems to be true in practice, as I've already mentioned, copyright was created to protect creators and ensure that they created new work in the first place.

140

Do I believe the copyright system favors corporate interests over the little guy? Yes. Just look at how long copyright terms are now, thanks to lobbying efforts by media companies. That being said, copyright protects no matter the size of the creator, big or small. I may not be able to sell my hypothetical *Star Wars* novels, but Disney/Lucasfilm is legally prohibited from stealing my sci-fi novel and using it as the basis of a *Star Wars* story—as long as I was able to prove they infringed on my copyright and I enforced that in court.

That brings me to another point: selective enforcement of copyright is not tenable. It doesn't matter if you steal from Disney or from John Doe; you're committing the same crime in both cases. Ethically, one may be worse, but legally, there is no distinction. If we allow pirating of Disney content, we must allow all pirating. (A law allowing pirating only of people who earn under $1 million a year would definitely be a problem, for example; in a way, though going the opposite direction, this is what many commenters argued when saying the *Halloween 5* novelization was okay.) Also, assuming you could, at what point would you draw the line of where copying is okay versus not okay? After all, the reason some people get away with copyright infringement is precisely because they're too small for very wealthy corporations to notice, or, if they do notice, to bother taking them to court; they don't get away with it because people see it as ethically correct.

Corporations are bad, therefore we should be allowed to take from them by violating copyright law is a non-sequitur. I don't disagree with the ethical failings of corporations, but I find it nonsensical that this justifies copyright infringement.

As an example: I recommended Emily Wilson's translation of the *Odyssey* to a friend. Instead of paying money for it, though, this person decided to download a copy for free online. Emily Wilson may be better off than many people, but she isn't a corporate billionaire who treats creative works like products. Still, she was deprived of money that was rightfully hers because someone decided they didn't want to support her work but still wanted to benefit from it. They wanted to get it for free.

Copyright infringement can affect more than just the big corporations, and those who pretend like it can't are being willfully ignorant.

Maybe, as he says in his video, IPOS is okay with people doing whatever they want with his creative works, including selling them for profit. Good for him, and that's his choice. But not all of us are in favor of this system, and as it stands, that policy would only benefit grifters at the expense of creators. We need to change the system, not just how we individually act. That is a sentiment I think IPOS would agree with.

How AI Factors into His Arguments

At the end of the video (made around the start of the 2023 Writers Guild of America strike), IPOS talks about how corporate owners view culture as nothing but a commodity to be exchanged, and thus are more than happy to automate cultural production as much as they can, to maximize profit.

I agree with him.

But in a strange way, copyright could be the antidote to this. Just as copyright was created to protect writers and artists against greedy, unscrupulous publishers, we could use copyright to deal with the new wave of artificial-intelligence chat- and art-bots which draw on copyrighted work to train. After all, if they only drew on out-of-copyright work, not only would they be producing texts that sound like they were made in the Roaring Twenties, but they'd also run out of training data very quickly, because most creative work that has ever been made, and the vast majority of online content in general, falls under copyright.

If these bots would render creatives irrelevant or drive them out of their fields, we would lose so much human-generated art, just as the printing press could also have rendered the act of creating new works pointless (because they'd just be stolen and copied), had things gone differently.

I'm not saying this is our only strategy to deal with AI's effect on creative jobs, but we shouldn't toss out copyright as a potentially very valuable weapon in the arsenal.

My Relationship to Freely-Released Work

Lest you think I'm some copyright evangelist who believes, like Sonny Bono did, that all work should be copyrighted forever, I want to tell you about a couple of my hobbies.

One of my hobbies involves taking pictures for Wikimedia Commons. Many of my photos have ended up on Wikipedia pages, with one of my favorites being the one for *A Concert for Charlottesville*, which became the only freely-available image of that event, as far as I know. (Actually, I took that specific picture just for myself at the time, but when I started taking a lot of pictures for Wikimedia, I realized that I had one that could be used to illustrate the event. I chose it for my example here because it's one of my favorite pictures I've ever taken.) I release into the public domain all of the images I donate to Wikimedia Commons.

The other is one that I've discussed in a previous essay: translating public-domain comics from Spanish into English. Once I've done so, I release my work into the public domain, as well, so anyone can enjoy it for free.

Why do I do these? Well, I enjoy them both as hobbies, for one. For another thing, though, while I'd be required to release my translations into the public domain for them to be posted on the website, I'm not required to make my photos public domain for them to be on Wikimedia Commons. I could choose to require other uses to attribute the work to me if they use my work, or to credit me and share their work under the same terms as mine, as Commons photographer Gage Skidmore does. (Those licenses, by the way, are part of Creative Commons, an organization dedicated to providing alternatives to copyright for artists who want to share their work more freely than standard copyright would allow. While Wikimedia Commons uses some Creative Commons licenses, the two organizations are otherwise unrelated to each other.)

I release my photos to the public domain because I want people to have them as a resource to do whatever they want with them, even if many of the photos would have very limited uses. It's my way of giving back to the world, as well as helping Wikipedia and its sister sites live up to their full potential, because I believe access to knowledge should be universal.

But that belief is also why I've pushed back so much on IPOS's video. I believe knowledge should be available to all, but I also believe that lying in service of an ideological end goal, no matter how noble that goal is or may seem, is never acceptable.

You may also think, based on my principle, that I would be more against copyright, but I'm not. Capitalism does create inequality (not just of knowledge), and as practiced in the Western world — especially in the U.S. — is antithetical to human well-being. As a society, we ought to strive to reduce and eliminate these problems however we can. Maybe that entails a universal basic income, maybe funding more community-oriented works, or maybe something else. But that reform would entail a lot more than simply "fixing" copyright, and would possibly require restructuring society itself around something other than money and non-essential goods and services. Until such time, I support copyright reform, but not abolition.

I will always, however, support the truth above all else.

The Necessity of Mythology

November 26, 2024

The *South Park* episode "Red Hot Catholic Love" concludes with the priest Father Maxi arguing that "when [people] have no mythology to live their lives by, they just start spewing a bunch of crap out of their mouths." (It's worth noting that another plot point in the episode leads to many characters literally crapping out of their mouths, which allows for a literal underscoring of the episode's message.) The quote reflects a broader view of *South Park* creators Trey Parker and Matt Stone that, even if religion is not literally true, it is a necessary and important part of human life because it brings meaning and order to what seems meaningless and disordered.

In the broader context of (1) a recent presidential election that seems to threaten the very existence of religious freedom and a secular society as well as (2) a longer personal journey of mine regarding faith/spirituality and rationalism, this quote resonated with thoughts I've had myself recently, even if the episode is from 2002. Some of those thoughts are as follows:

> *No matter what kind of society we have, a mythology is always necessary for that society to thrive.*

By "mythology," I don't mean something that is fictional, nor by saying that faith doubles as mythology am I implying that faith is inherently false. However, even if there is truth to it, mythology is not about truth; it is about stories of creation, purpose, history, and destiny.

Because we humans are creatures who despise ambiguity and crave answers, a mythology must also arise to provide answers, especially (but not only) in a society without scientific answers to those questions. For most of human history, human-invented mythology was all we had to explain the world and its natural phenomena.

Even though we have no written record of them, we know a group of people whom we now call Proto-Indo-Europeans existed. How do we know? Well, for one thing, the language they spoke is the ancestor to English, Spanish, French, Portuguese, Greek, Russian, German, Albanian, Armenian, and Hindi, among many other current and extinct languages now classified as part of the Indo-European family. But you know what they also left behind in their linguistic descendants? Mythology.

Just as scholars have reconstructed the Proto-Indo-European language by comparing its many descendant languages, they have reconstructed elements of the Proto-Indo-European mythology. Most notably, we have *$Dy\acute{e}us\ ph_2t\acute{e}r$, literally "Day-Sky Father" (the reason why the words "day" and "deity" are so similar in Indo-European languages), the progenitor of Jupiter (Roman), Zeus (Greek), Dyaus (Vedic), and Týr (Norse), among others. Even though these gods don't share all the same attributes, they come from the same source.

In this and other ways, mythology and language are intimately tied together.

Linguist and novelist J.R.R. Tolkien made a similar claim in his lecture "A Secret Vice," wherein he discusses his lifelong love of language creation, the titular "secret vice." For Tolkien, the art of language creation was an end in and of itself; unlike his inheritors such as Klingon, Na'vi, Valyrian, and Dothraki, it was not merely the means toward creating a realistic fictional world. This is precisely in keeping with the fact that Tolkien's day job and life's

146

focus was not in writing stories but in analyzing language, especially Old English: he was a linguist first and foremost.

Tolkien's understanding of language and its relationship to mythology is paramount to his literary work: he claimed that in creating a fictional language, one must also construct a form of mythology to accompany its development. At the same time, he found that "language construction [would] breed a mythology." In a very real way, the world of Middle-earth is a product of Tolkien's linguistic inventiveness rather than his narrative skill, though he possessed the latter, as well.

Just like how the Proto-Indo-European mythology and language giving birth to daughter myths and languages reflects human development over time, Tolkien's mytho-linguistic constructions give his world a sense of reality, of history, that surpasses most, if not all, other fictional worlds in terms of realism—and it's literally a fantasy world!

But what does this have to do with the claimed "necessity of mythology"? Well, it demonstrates the fact that mythology is a byproduct of language and of human cognition. If mythology is an inherently human need (like *South Park* and Tolkien's work claim and demonstrate, respectively), then we ought not to discard mythology entirely, like atheism may ask us to, but instead build our new mythology through new tools and discoveries as we progress as a species.

Just as language can reveal and develop a mythology, so too can the world outside of our immediate linguistic constructions influence the stories we tell about ourselves. In the past, those outside events have been weather, disease, and inter-tribal (as well as intra-tribal) conflict—"tribe" here referring to the political group to which one belonged, from actual tribes to cities to nations.

However, even scientific inquiry develops a mythology because it leads to the discovery of narrativize-able facts. The Big Bang may be true, but it is also our universe's origin story. (The Proto-Indo-European origin story for the universe may have involved the sacrifice of both a human and a cow.) Evolution and natural selection become not only the explanations for how species diverged from a common ancestor (just like Proto-Indo-European diverged into the Indo-European languages), but stories of how we came to develop into ourselves. Instead of being molded from clay, we are molded from our genetic ancestors.

We can understand these true events as part of an overall mythology, and in turn understand — through the same methods of inquiry — that mythology comes from a deep-rooted human need. Science is now meeting this need more and more by providing the how and why.

Problems arise, though, when these truths conflict with the stories we developed before these discoveries were possible. Some, like scientist Stephen Jay Gould and his "non-overlapping magisteria" doctrine, claim that science and religion are not incompatible. But for those who cannot reconcile the two, it becomes a question of which story to internalize and which to reject. For many people, the story with all the answers and which never changes (religion) is more comforting than one that is never complete (because it is constantly developing) and which can, at times, get things wrong. (To be fair to science, it has built-in systems for removing its incorrect conclusions, namely the scientific method.)

Those who value scientific, objective truth may be quick to dismiss traditional religion as superstitious nonsense, but there is value in religious belief: spiritual comfort. I've talked about this in a previous essay, but that is a huge reason why people remain in a faith even if they see evidence that contradicts a tenet of that belief system. They need this comfort. They need this *mythology*.

Proceeding from here, I ask: can we be both rational and mythological? Can we meet the spiritual needs of people where they are while still adhering to the truth?

I believe so. But doing so requires minds that are both open and skeptical, always questioning but never resting, while taking comfort in the knowledge that we have. Perhaps for some that means embracing the "god of the gaps," while for others it means rejecting any spirituality outright and embracing pure atheism.

But our duty as humans is to take care of ourselves, each other, and the greater world. No religious faith commands us to be bad stewards of the world—even if some poor interpretations of doctrine lead to that as a result. We can only fulfill this duty by adhering to the truth and the pursuit of it. In that pursuit, however, we ought not to lose sight of those things which make us human and which matter to many, if not all, of us. If we discard the idea of mythology and the comfort it provides, we risk losing key soldiers in our war for the truth.

After all, if we eliminate our humanity, for what are we fighting in the first place?

How Metafiction Can Be an Effective Storytelling Device

December 7, 2024

To be honest, I've been sitting on this essay idea for more than a year, having conceived it in my early days on Medium but relegating it to the bottom of my drafts. I'd get to it one day, I assured myself.

Then, driving home from work recently, I was listening to the podcast *All About Agatha,* which is dedicated to discussing the works and world of British crime novelist Agatha Christie. On this particular episode, "Interview with Jamie Bernthal, Author of *Queering Agatha Christie*" (April 13, 2019), show host Kemper Donovan made a particular comment about metafictional references in Christie's work:

> *So one of the things I really personally dislike are the meta-moments in Christie when characters say, this is just like a detective novel[.] ... And for me, what they feel like ... is a lack of confidence in the robustness of the world that she's creating, i.e. I know this sounds sort of fake, so I'm just going to hang a lantern on it, so to speak.*

I interpret his statement as referring to the kind of winking, fourth-wall-nudging antics that are groan-inducing, as opposed to the use of a story-within-a-story or similar devices. However, his quote made me think about this article, and about how much I appreciate metafiction within the stories I experience and the ones I create myself. As it happens, I find metafictional techniques to actually enhance the immersion that I have in a story.

Let's use Christie as our starting example. She inserted several characters into her stories who were themselves authors of some sort, in a kind of comedic self-insert, but none are as well-known or iconic as Hercule Poirot's friend Ariadne Oliver, recently played by Tina Fey in the film *A Haunting in Venice* (2023). Oliver is famous in Poirot's world for her Swedish detective character Sven Hjerson, a thinly-veiled reference to Christie being most famous for her Belgian detective Poirot, whom she came to loathe at times. Christie's ability to make fun of herself through Ariadne Oliver is admirable, and while some readers may roll their eyes at how obvious of a self-insert and self-parody Oliver is, she adds flavor to her stories.

But I don't believe that the reason Christie used fictional-author self-inserts or lamp-shaded the genre elements she employed was that she "lacked confidence" in her fictional world, though perhaps she believed these acknowledgements would connect with readers. I believe she did it precisely because she wanted to enhance the sense of reality for her stories.

This is where I bring in my own perspective as a writer. In my novel *Impressions of a Pupil*, I placed a cast list for a play and several short poems into the story, purportedly written by the characters in the story—mostly the first-person narrator. Why did I feel this would enhance the story? Well, the main character/narrator is a budding playwright and hobby poet, so it made sense that he would have written actual work within that fictional world, right? If I could provide examples of his work in the same form and at the same distance from the reader as the actual story being told, then I could have the reader subconsciously see themselves as on the same level as the narrator, because they can look at the stories that the narrator has created the same way they can look at the writings of people in real life, or the same way the narrator himself would look on those stories.

Consider the story world to be underwater, while our real world is above water. Having the reader simply read about a character's experiences, and having them simply hear that there is a story within this story, is like the reader peering into the water from dry land. Yes, they'll understand what you're telling them, but they'll view it through the lens of fiction, distorted. On the other hand, having them be able to read the in-universe creations themselves is like having them place their head underwater; in this scenario, the distortion disappears and the reader sees things in the same way that the in-universe characters do.

The metafiction is immersion.

As I write this, I'm currently working on a novel told entirely through in-universe artifacts and with no narrator, which is known as an *epistolary novel*. The term comes from the Greek *epistole*, meaning "letter" (as in a written message), because originally novels like this were told only using letters. Epistolary novels functioned as a way of allowing readers to feel like they were viewing the private thoughts of, and conversations between, actual people. A narratorial voice would have broken the illusion and added narrative distance between the audience and the story. Epistolary novels—whether they use letters/emails, diary entries, newspaper articles, some other type, or a combination of these—allow for the same type of immersion that I referenced earlier because they give the sense of unmediated access to the fictional world, of the sense that the events depicted might actually have happened somewhere in the real world.

But Christie didn't do that, right? She just had a self-insert who could make real-world references that the audience would get and even laugh at. That's completely different from using fictional documents to add a sense of realism to stories.

You're right. There is a distinction between making those references and having texts-within-texts. But the purpose of both is the same. Seeing a crime author within a detective story lets us readers subconsciously feel more like we're witnessing real events because the novel acknowledges that detective fiction exists, just like that genre exists in our world. We are then mentally pulled into the water without actively realizing it. Of course, this is more effective when we have in-universe fiction to experience, but it isn't completely ineffective if we don't.

———

As a counter-example, consider the world of *The Walking Dead*. The comic and the TV show never use the word "zombie," due to the fact that zombie fiction doesn't exist in their universe. Is that immersion-breaking? Not unless the show stopped itself somehow to speak to the audience directly and say "we don't know what zombies are."

But imagine the characters on the show used the term "zombie." Most viewers probably wouldn't care. But some would. Inevitably, the questions would arise: Where did the word "zombie" come from? Do they have zombie fiction in their world? If so, do their "real" zombies look like the zombies in their in-universe fictional media? If they do resemble each other, is it just a strange coincidence? But if they don't resemble each other, why would zombies be called zombies?

By not wading into these waters and instead refraining from using the word "zombie," *The Walking Dead* is able to, perhaps paradoxically, add realism, because characters in a world without the concept of a zombie wouldn't call these creatures by that name. They'd come up with terms that fit with the zombie behavior, not magically coin a word that doesn't exist in their universe but exists in the real world for these same beings.

This also helps us immerse ourselves as readers or viewers, because we come to recognize that zombies are just a part of the everyday reality of this fictional world. Because zombies never existed in *The Walking Dead*'s in-universe fiction, it feels more possible for this to happen to them than it does to happen to us, because we know zombies are fictional.

Again, I recognize that most viewers don't actively think about this distinction, but its existence supports my point. Some stories use metafiction to enhance their narrative; Agatha Christie acknowledging the existence of crime fiction in her universe helps us feel like her characters could exist alongside us, while *The Walking Dead*'s lack of in-world acknowledgement of the zombie genre helps their situation feel more realistic because it makes them *more* removed from our world.

———

Epistolary novels still exist today, and can perform a number of functions unrelated to immersion. Maybe a novel in text messages aims to capture the unique elements of that form of communication. Maybe an illustrated diary wants to use that form to bring out the expressiveness of the artist-diarist narrator.

But epistolary novels can also be detective novels. I don't mean this in the Agatha Christie sense of "detective novel," wherein a murder investigation could be depicted through, say, newspaper clippings, court transcripts, and phone-call logs. Instead, I mean that in a pure epistolary novel, the reader is asked to play detective themselves. Without a narrator to guide them, they must come to their own conclusions, piece together in their own minds the deeper connections between the documents so that they can have a better sense of the grand picture being depicted.

This is why I'm writing that epistolary novel: so that I can immerse my readers and have them read a tapestry of connected but discrete documents.

Metafiction won't work for every story, but utilizing in-universe works and self-referentiality can create a kind of immersion that cannot be achieved through other methods of storytelling. It can be done poorly, like when it's simply a wink-and-nod to the audience, but at its best, it can draw us into fictional worlds and put us readers in the driver's seat by giving us the clues and asking us to draw our own conclusions.

On Teaching Cursive Handwriting

December 8, 2024

As an English teacher, I may be expected to take the old-fashioned view that cursive is still something we should teach in schools. As a fan of letter-writing, you may think I believe strongly that we should have kids write by hand more often, and thus cursive is necessary for that reason. While I believe it's critical to teach handwriting in schools, I actually have a sacrilegious take: it isn't necessary to teach kids cursive.

I was first taught cursive handwriting in third grade, and as soon as the lesson began, I felt two things: confused and upset. I'd spent the past two years learning how to write in school, and had learned from my father how to write my name around when I started kindergarten. Why was it suddenly necessary for me to learn a completely different way of writing? Mine worked just fine!

It didn't help that some of these letter-forms looked so different from the print forms I had painstakingly learned despite my challenges with reading. As far as I can tell, I was instructed in the D'Nealian script, though it's quite possible my teachers learned the Palmer method when they were in school, just like my dad did.

Some letter-forms are similar to their print counterparts, though it always bothered me that uppercase A looked the exact same as lowercase, just sized differently. Other letters, especially *G, I, Q, S,* and *Z,* looked like they were from another writing system entirely. This made it so much harder to pick up, and I really resented having to learn this. Print writing worked just fine. Why did we have to change it?

The only time I used cursive at all when I was that age was in my signature, and I learned that not from school but from my dad. I watched him sign my school agenda to verify that he'd seen it, and I asked him one day what it was he was doing. Once he explained to me that it was a signature, and that a signature was a unique way to write your name that attested to your identity, I asked him to teach me how to come up with my own. So, we did. Although certain elements of my *T* have changed over the years, the basic design has remained constant. I remember how proud I was to have my own signature, and even in college, I was excited whenever I had to sign something, because it was an act of self-expression tied to my identity.

However, I abandoned cursive as soon as I was able to, returning to print writing and shuddering whenever the word "cursive" was spoken in my presence. It didn't help, I should add, that we were well on our way to adopting computers as a common tool in education, rendering typing something I'd also been learning since kindergarten. Cursive just seemed useless.

Admittedly, my handwriting did change a little during middle school and into early high school, growing quite a bit in terms of legibility. But it was my AP U.S. History (APUSH) class in junior year of high school that transformed my handwriting.

In order to prep us for college, my APUSH teacher didn't have the notes in his PowerPoints like previous teachers did; instead, he would use the PowerPoint slide as an illustration of the subject, and he would talk about it. We were expected to take notes on what we *heard*, and we didn't yet know how to discern important from unimportant information. The result was that I ended up writing fast to ensure that I got down all of what he said that could possibly be on the test, because he said *a lot*.

This crucible led my handwriting, especially the lowercase letters, to evolve very quickly. My *y*, normally by itself and fairly straightforward, morphed into a cursive variant with a loopy tail that always connected to the next letter, probably inspired by the *y* in my signature. My *g* also gained this tail, as opposed to before when its tail would just curve. My *f* gained a loop near the top, even if it began the word. My *r* and *s* never fully morphed into their "official" cursive forms, but the flattening of the former and the shortening of the latter's top helped me realize why the *r* had a flat-top and the *s* looked so weird, respectively.

My uppercase letters, on the other hand, almost entirely retained their print forms, leaving my handwriting as a print-cursive hybrid.

Today, I still write in the post-APUSH style, and even enjoy it. I see in my present handwriting an individuality that even the most quirky of fonts can't replicate, because it is unique to me. This is why I am passionate about writing by hand.

But my students have often said, when seeing my handwriting, things like: "I didn't know you wrote in cursive" and "What does this say? I can't read cursive." But until I began teaching, I never saw my handwriting as cursive at all. In fact, I struggled to use cursive on the SAT when I had to copy out a statement that affirmed I wouldn't cheat. In fact, I had to return to that page to finish it, because it took me so long to remember and then write each word in "pure" cursive, because I was convinced my handwriting wouldn't qualify. I now realize, thanks to my students, that I do write cursive, in a way; it's just not "pure" cursive.

I've come to believe that if cursive is a necessary part of a person's life, it will develop naturally from their print-writing, just like mine did in APUSH. However, print writing is sufficient for today's world, as long as it is legible and won't take too long to write under most time-sensitive circumstances. That, plus a signature, should suffice.

This is especially true due to the advent of computers. Opponents of dropping cursive will point out that students retain more information when they write by hand than when they type, but if that's true (and I believe it is), it isn't *cursive* that matters so much as having a handwriting process of some sort.

Outside of school, it is rare that students need to write a lot of info quickly in situations where computers aren't allowed, so legible handwriting is the important part.

Even computer education, though, underscores this point. When I was first learning how to type, conventional wisdom said to not look at the keyboard and instead learn proper finger placement and keep your eyes on the screen. For me, though, this never settled in, whether I was learning from the school's software or the copy of *Mavis Beacon Teaches Typing* that my mom bought for me. Yet, I still type quickly, according to people who have seen me do it. How did I learn how to type fast? Practice! I just didn't use the normal means.

When I first began typing on a computer, I always looked at the keyboard, only occasionally looking up to check my work. While I did this initially because I felt it was easier and more natural, what I didn't know was that I was rewiring neural pathways and creating a mental databank of words paired with the typing placement I needed to produce them. For example, I could tell you where any given alphabetic letter is on the keyboard, but it would be quicker if you asked me to type a word and I just showed you the sequence with my hands, as if I were actually typing.

Students should still be taught typing, but just like with handwriting, I believe that once students have a basic foundation, they can learn for themselves if they have the right tools and situations to do so.

For instance, no school ever instructed my generation how to type on a smartphone, but if you've ever watched a Gen Z person text, it's like warp speed compared to earlier generations. They're adept at this because they've had ample practice, started by looking at the keyboard frequently, and have had motivation to learn because of what they can get from typing on their phones: entertainment, connecting with friends, etc.

Really, the important elements are (1) the foundation that we give to learners and (2) the motivational structures they have to practice on their own. For me, it was being able to type up my own stories, write fast enough to take notes in APUSH, or text with my friends. Whatever it is for others, we need to focus on those two elements if we want them to retain handwriting or typing skills. Focusing instead on their perfect adherence to prescribed norms of handwriting or typing is ineffective and leads to them tuning out.

The Assumption of Abundance

December 14, 2024

Aside from ignorance/denial about the issue itself, do you know what is one of the biggest impediments to people banding together to pressure their governments to fix environmental issues, especially climate change? The fact that many people, especially Americans, live every day with an ***assumption of abundance***, a sense that (at least certain) resources are infinite.

This is an instinct that I think we all are born with, to some degree. We assume our parents can get us whatever we need, and thus that our needs will be met. However, most of us encounter a moment where we first learn that this isn't true. For some, it's when we see our parents struggle to put food on the table. Maybe it's when we learn the purpose of money. Maybe it's when we ask for something and our parents say no. Or maybe we learn this lesson very young in a place that isn't a Western nation. Whatever the situation, however paltry or significant, we run up against an obstacle to our assumption.

Yet many of us live our lives assuming that nature has no such obstacles, no such limits to what it can provide. Many don't even care enough to dispose of trash properly, and never consider what effect even a small act of littering can have, let alone how a universalizing of that mindset would negatively harm everyone.

This is destructive.

I harbor no illusions that individual action is the primary solution to climate change; fixing that problem requires urgent systemic solutions which de-transition us from fossil fuels—that not only requires government intervention, but also an ability to recognize how most of the responsibility lies squarely on the shoulders of no more than 100 big corporations. Actions should be directed at changing governments and corporate practices, not just individual habits—though those need to be altered, too.

Earth is not infinitely abundant. She has her limits. For some of you reading, that may seem obvious, but for those who have never thought about it in these terms before, maybe this will help to change your frame of reference, and thus your mind.

We're also actively trained to keep this assumption in our minds by advertisements, and by the media that those ads support. We are a society built on consumption, and until we are forced to confront that limit, we will continue to live in ignorance—unless we change our mindset. The question I wish to answer here is this: **how do we escape the mentality of this abundance assumption?**

A Personal Example

One of the ways in which I was recently confronted with my own abundant thinking was with paper. As a teacher, I tend to print quite a bit for my students, despite the fact that they have school-issued laptops. Other teachers have documents to print, as well. In a given day, at one school, we go through thousands of pages and an unimaginable amount of ink. Magically, there is always more paper, and all we have to do if ink runs out is call someone to replace it.

The disconnect we teachers have with the source of these resources, I believe, makes us value the resources less. What does it matter if I print out a few extra packets? We have plenty of paper and ink, and it's always better to be safe than sorry. You never know if a kid will lose a packet, for example. (And,

in fact, the magical appearance of new materials when students lose the originals is probably giving them this sense of infinite abundance, too.)

But this isn't the case. Not only does every page have a financial cost associated with it, but it also has a physical cost. That paper had to be sourced from
somewhere, as did the ink. Even if both were somehow recycled from a previous source, the printer required resources to create and always needs energy
to run, which in my area translates to fossil fuel usage.

There is always a cost, even if we don't see it. The question isn't about there
not being a cost, but on minimizing the cost. We must create in ourselves a
mentality of saving, of restraint, of not assuming abundance. And I'm not talking just about us teachers at my school.

At its most extreme, this mentality would lead to the end of our world as
we know it. Perhaps, then, we have to truly consider the possibility of world
endings in order to understand the problem and break ourselves out of this
destructive mentality.

The Incomprehensibility of World Endings

We cannot conceptualize the end of our world very well, even those of us who
fret doomsday scenarios. When we do contemplate the end of the world, it is
usually in personal terms of how we, our loved ones, other humans, or non-
human-but-living things will be affected. It is natural to consider the problem
in this way, framing it around suffering and death, because those are more
comprehensible to us.

But if we only think in terms of suffering and death, then every day is
someone's apocalypse. Death is a daily occurrence on this planet, as is mental
and physical suffering. While humanity may be a big cause of both today, these
have been around long before us. Ninety-nine percent of the species who have
ever lived are now extinct. The dinosaurs had dominion over the Earth for millions of years, paling our paltry 100–200,000 years of human existence by com-

parison. Still, they died individually, and their time as a species came collectively.

When it did, the universe was indifferent to their loss, and life moved on.

Let us assume we can prolong death forever, and end all human suffering as we know it. In this imagined world, every person is content and healthy, while our relationship to nature is balanced. We have no more wars, and the threat of annihilating ourselves is gone. Let us assume as well that our species will not evolve to a place where our descendants would be unrecognizable as humans, that they would have become a completely new species. Even if we could accomplish all of this, one day the Sun will engulf the Earth, and even if we managed to move beyond Earth, one day the last stars will die, the universe will enter a black hole era, and all we've ever accomplished will be gone and forgotten.

Depressing? I wouldn't blame you if you found it to be. But it's a reminder to me that this world is temporary, that nothing lasts forever.

This isn't to say we should hasten our demise or not try to make the best of what we have. In fact, giving into depressive nihilism would be a great loss to what we could create or improve *now*. The reason I point out the fact that an end will come no matter what we can do is so that we can realize that, in spite of this inevitability, we can still do our best to improve what we can.

Our issue is denial. We deny or ignore the fact of our death, and we deny or ignore the fact that one day we will collectively cease to exist. We pretend, or we delude ourselves into thinking, that everything will go on like it has forever. No matter what, it won't.

But we should not be the agents of our own destruction. That's the difference. Let us accept our temporariness and find meaning in spite of that. Let us work to help our world however we can, to try to do our best with what we have. Let us not hate our neighbors, but build community with them.

If we can cast off the delusion of the eternal abundance of time, perhaps we can also cast off the delusion of infinite resources. Perhaps then we could have a new paradigm of human life in the 21st century.

Perhaps.

Using an AI Therapist

February 4, 2025

It was a mentally bleak morning, and I didn't know what to do. I hadn't seen a therapist in over a year because most therapists only offer sessions on weekdays from 8:00 AM to 5:00 PM, which (aside from the final hour) overlaps with my work schedule. On top of this, I needed to support students for almost the entire day (that's what a teacher does, after all), so I didn't have the luxury of sitting with my feelings and processing them.

In desperation, in the spare moment I had I opened up ChatGPT and wrote the following:

> *I'm feeling very depressed about the state of the world. I'm only talking to you because I can't speak to anyone else at the moment, but normally I wouldn't talk to a chatbot about this. But I need your "thoughts." How do I deal with this sadness?*

I felt pathetic as I wrote it. I was genuinely turning into the main character from the movie *Her*, talking to an incredibly sophisticated computer about problems as complex as depression and coping with it; heck, I even told it that I wouldn't normally talk to a chatbot like this. (Perhaps part of this is due to my years of keeping a diary, where I would sometimes use that kind of language as if I were writing to a real person, even though I never wrote it in "Dear Diary" format or anything.) But I was desperate; I needed to feel a connection, and this was the only way, in that moment, that I could.

Its response:

> *Hey, I'm really sorry you're feeling this way. It makes total sense to feel sad or overwhelmed when the world seems chaotic or full of bad news. You're not alone in feeling this, and your emotions are completely valid.*
>
> *One thing that might help is focusing on what **you can control**. The world may be a mess in some ways, but small, meaningful actions can make a difference—whether it's being kind to someone, supporting a cause you care about, or even just taking care of yourself today.*
>
> *When sadness feels heavy, grounding yourself in something hopeful can really help. Maybe that's spending time with a story that reminds you people are capable of good, listening to music that feels uplifting, or even thinking about what **you want to contribute** to make things better in the long run.*
>
> *Are there specific things about the world weighing on you right now? I'm here to listen.*

While part of this advice is either cliché, obvious, or both, I can't lie: I felt a small bit of relief at receiving this message. It was what I needed, and it was something any good therapist would have provided me... if I had access to one.

And that's exactly what made me want to write this article in the first place. So many people who are in need of quality mental healthcare do not receive it in the United States, because of our broken healthcare industry that keeps therapy expensive, because (like me) they're too busy with work or life, or for other reasons. Seen purely through this lens, ChatGPT could be a godsend for people in desperate need of care but who could otherwise not access it.

But my emotions are very mixed on this. You've already seen how appreciative I am of this technology, but there are issues that I worry about, some existentially.

The first is economical: if we replaced all of our therapists with chatbots, those highly-trained individuals would be another casualty of AI automation.

The second is technical/professional: ChatGPT is not trained as a therapist, nor can it feel emotions the same way a human can. It is great at collecting and delivering information (which makes it a decent research partner), but regurgitation is not what a good therapist does. A good therapist receives years of training, sees their patients face-to-face, brings a human touch. ChatGPT cannot do this. Perhaps one day it will genuinely be the equivalent to a human in terms of emotional intelligence, but it isn't there yet.

The third is humanistic: we are already disconnecting from other human beings as we dive further and further into digital worlds. Social media (as has been demonstrated many times) is not the same as in-person contact, and that's not even considering the harmful effects it has on the dissemination of knowledge. But even I, someone who spends much of his Internet time on Wikipedia and who has almost no social media, have gotten lonelier as the years have gone on. Part of it may be that digital devices occupy the times of my friends, as well, but if that were the case, I would still have the same desire to spend time with others, and they simply don't reciprocate. But I don't have that desire as much. My mind has now begun to prefer singular activities, to prefer media consumption, over human contact. (It also don't help that we work harder and longer, thus further compromising our social lives.) With the loneliness epidemic and our loss of connection to our real lives and the people around us, is it really such a good idea to use a chatbot to provide emotional support, whether it's substituting for a therapist or a friend?

I like that ChatGPT suggested that spending time helping others in the real world was one possible solution to my woes. Again, it may be cliché, but it's also true, to a degree. Helping others and supporting causes you care about are both important, no matter who's president or how much it seems like the world is going to hell. However, I find it telling, as well, what it doesn't say. There isn't advice about calling a friend or spending time with family. Maybe that's just the iteration ChatGPT happened to give me, and if I asked it for more advice, it would include those suggestions. But maybe it also reflects the individualistic mindset that has become so ingrained into our American way of thinking, and which has led in several ways to many, if not all, of our current collective woes.

ChatGPT showed me that it could help me, or even save me, if I were in a low place. It's also made me wonder if we're bargaining away our humanity at the same time.

On (My) Voluntary Childlessness

March 14, 2025

By the wisdom of Christianity, the meek shall inherit the Earth. Whether they're meek or not, however, the only ones we can guarantee will inherit the planet will be children.

In Virginia Woolf's *To the Lighthouse*, the Ramsay patriarchs have had eight children, which in a book concerned with the passage of time is more than just an indictment on the Ramsays' birth-control choices: it's also a comment on immortality. For Mrs. Ramsay, it is her children who represent her best hope of living on after she has died. By the end of the book, not only has Mrs. Ramsay died, but 25% of her children have died as well; her daughter died due to complications of the same attempt at immortality that her mother made eight times, while one of Mrs. Ramsay's sons died due to one of history's deadliest conflicts: the First World War.

To use another cliché: children are the future, and thus, in a reverse sense, the future is defined by children, the descendants of the present. Using this same logic, those without children have no future and also don't deserve the same stake in the running of a country. J.D. Vance, now the Number 2 of the United States, made this same argument in 2021,[12] saying: "Let's give votes to all children in this country, but let's give control over those votes to the parents of those children ... If you don't have as much of an investment in the future of this country, maybe you shouldn't get nearly the same voice." (The thought behind this is also to encourage people to have more children, in response to a declining birth rate in the developed world, including the United States.)

In fairness to Vance, I do think that the voice and needs of the youth should be the most important to a society because they will live with the consequences of the present for the longest amount of time. However, the actions Republicans have taken to reverse progress on tackling climate change, criminalize legitimate protest by those critical of Israel, treat LGBT+ youth like disposable political props, and let old billionaires dictate their policies, have all shown that this professed commitment to protecting the youth is a hollow fiction as opposed to a hallowed reality.

Reasons for (My) Childlessness

There are many reasons why, throughout history, people have chosen (or not chosen, per se) to have a certain number of children, not just for the short-sighted, selfish reasons of the Ramsays and J.D. Vance. When it comes to *not* having children, some people are unable to conceive but want children, others can't afford children so they either have to give up a child for adoption or (if the option exists) not carry the child to term, and some people do not want children to begin with, regardless of their ability to conceive or adopt.

I fall into the final category of childlessness; while I am only 27 years old, I have decided that I don't want to have children, and I want to explain my reasoning here not because I want to encourage others to do the same, but I want you to consider this topic from a perspective you may or may not have ever considered.

Selfishness vs. Selflessness

Whenever I've thought about having children, even going back to when I was in elementary school, I thought about how cool it would be to have someone who looked, acted, sounded, etc. like me in my life. Basically, I wanted a living accessory, even though I never would have thought about it like this when I was a kid. Part of this could be because I am only child, and so I never had a younger sibling to connect with; instead, I had the privilege of a stay-at-home father with whom I was incredibly close, and perhaps that also made me think about wanting to be that kind of person for someone else someday. (I also usually pictured myself having a son far more often than I pictured myself having a daughter, but I think that underscores my point above.)

More recently, when thinking about why I might think children are a good idea, another selfish reason came to me: who will take care of me when I'm older? (This is probably more often on my mind because my parents are both in their sixties now, and so this will start becoming more of a reality for me in the next decade or decade-and-a-half.)

But these are shitty reasons for having children, both rooted in a vain focus on the self. No human being should exist for the exclusive sake of another; all humans are entitled to dignity in and of themselves.

On top of this, a counterargument to bringing a biological child into the world is the fact that so many children are already in the world — and so many will come into the world — who need responsible parents. If I were a responsible parent (though I doubt that I would be a good parent, which is a sub-reason why I don't plan on having children), then I feel it would be an obligation to adopt one or more children instead of bringing another life into the world that I could otherwise avoid creating.

Sparing Suffering

I am a doomer, although I manage to live my life relatively healthfully in spite of that fact. Well, no, at times I am crippled by my anxiety and depression, but things could be a lot worse in terms of its effect on my life. I say that to warn you of what's coming; if discussions about doomer scenarios aren't your thing, feel free to skip to the next section.

I don't know if our society will break down in my lifetime. In some ways, if it were guaranteed to collapse, then I feel like I would be relieved, because then I would have certainty. And death doesn't scare me much; instead, it's pain and suffering that terrifies me.

I see suffering in so many ways in so much of my world and *the world*, and I do not find it morally justifiable to bring a person into the world, because I imagine them suffering like I do, and perhaps they would suffer in ways I can't imagine yet.

On top of this, if we humans are the cause of most of the world's suffering, then by having a child I would be adding another polluter, another potential corrupt politician, another potential greedy individual, into the world. Another tick in the "con" column.

I do not have the option of choosing whether I was born or not; none of us do. And (thankfully), I've come to realize that no matter how depressed I get, it is better to stick around and try my best to make the world as good of a place as I possibly can. But I do not like the idea of deciding on someone else's behalf to expose them to suffering, or to cause suffering indirectly because of any negative effects their existence would have.

That actually leads into the final main reason:

Community Is Everything

Lower childbirth rates would be a benefit to nature, because it would mean fewer polluters and fewer consumers of resources. However, I am not a nature worshipper. I recognize that we humans rely on nature to survive, but I appreciate nature first and foremost because of the benefits I receive from it; I admit, I see it as a means to an end (my health) before I see it as an end in and of itself. Like I said, suffering is what scares me, and when nature suffers, humans suffer. But if all humans disappeared simultaneously, so would all pain and suffering. Nature would survive and/or evolve. It's done that for billions of years, and if your instinct is to point out that maybe this time it's different, you know what my answer is? Maybe. But one day the entire universe will die. That's guaranteed. It's the suffering that's the big concern. (And when plants and especially animals are suffering, I *am* heartbroken by that.)

However, I find another, major benefit to humanity if we engage in a controlled population shrinkage over the course of a few generations of lowered birth rates: a greater allowance for the development of extended communities. We humans evolved as social creatures and lived as tribes for most of our history; it is only with large, populated cities that we could finally not know everyone who lived in our community. It's no accident that the nuclear family has become a cornerstone of nations with large populations: when most of your neighbors are strangers, the ones you rely on first and most are those who raised you, those you were raised with, and those you raised.

We need a different definition of community, one where strangers rise to the occasion of helping others, where decisions aren't made by actors hundreds of miles away but in our local areas (as much as possible; some things require large-scale action at a higher level). We need to stop focusing on creating a future that best suits our immediate family needs at the expense of others, and we need to start working toward building a better future together, with a person-first mentality. It won't be easy, but it would be a fairer, more just world.

Again, I'm not advocating voluntary extinction; I actually think that humanity has quite a bit of good in it. But we don't need eight billion people, and it's either reduce our numbers peacefully and build more resilient communities with those who are here, or continue to be selfish and test the systems we rely on. The latter could even lead to population control measures which would be—to put it lightly—more immediate, direct, and violent.

Focusing On What We Can Do

Another character in *To the Lighthouse* makes a different attempt at immortality: Lily Briscoe makes art, specifically paintings. Like her, humans throughout history have made art as a way to communicate across space and time, because they wanted to be remembered, they wanted to connect with other humans, or they wanted to express themselves. I find myself following the Briscoe example in focusing on my creative pursuits, but I find myself also doing the community-focused route by teaching at a high school.

I don't believe in false hope, that born of blind optimism, and I don't act that way, either. At times, I am able to move forward not because of optimism or because of emotional reasoning (i.e. anger or sadness), but because of logic: *nothing changes if we don't do anything*. The choice is thus made for me: *I must keep going*. I will do what I can to make the world better. That isn't optimism, it's realism, and for me at least, that's more comforting than any kind of blind faith or hope. *I have found a strength within*. This comes not from trying to outrun inevitabilities but in living with them, in working with and around them, and in accepting the things I can and cannot change. For me, this acceptance includes realizing that my reasons for having children are outweighed by my reasons not to have children. And I've learned to be okay with that. I've learned that instead, I can focus on what I bring to the world.

Ultimately, whether you conceive children or decide to stay childless like me, consider your actions as much as you can, and learn to accept the truly inevitable while improving what you can. That's all most of us have control over, and I truly believe the world would be a completely different place if we changed how we thought about death and about what happens before it.

Has There Ever Been a Photo-Comics Masterpiece?

March 31, 2025

If you're a fan of comics, you can almost certainly name works of that medium which are worthy of the title "masterpiece." Maybe you're thinking of *Maus*, *Watchmen*, *Saga*, or a number of others I haven't named. But unless you're a super fan, I bet you can't even name a single comic book made up of photos, which are called "fumetti" or "photo-comics."

Why is that?

No, seriously: why is that the case? We've had photography for about a century and a half now, and have been able to reliably print it for a majority of that time; today, we have photos at our fingertips, thanks to the Internet and smartphones. In fact, if you're an Apple user, you can take a photo and insert a word balloon onto it using the built-in Photos app. (This might be possible on other phones' built-in apps, but I'm not sure; it's definitely possible with third-party apps.) Yet we have no great works of the medium that are widely known.

I think the obscurity comes down to the relative lack of examples, which is in turn due to the limitations of the photo-comic as a medium. In order to illustrate these limitations, I'm going to use an example of a photo-comic that I think works well:

The Brick Bible

A 12-year labor by creator Elbe Spurling, *The Brick Bible* is an adaptation of the Bible using photographs of posed Legos (or Lego, if you prefer). The need for dialogue leads to the use of word balloons and caption boxes, while sequential images combine to tell a given story from the Christian holy text. Therefore, *The Brick Bible* is comics made up of photos, therefore photo-comics.

Spurling's meticulous work in using Lego figures and sets to tell stories in comics form is honestly both mesmerizing and awe-inspiring. It represents some of the best that can be done with the form, and I believe any aspiring photo-comics creator should take note of it as potential inspiration for their own project.

But here's the thing: Lego figures are *posable*, and therefore controllable in the same way a drawing is controllable. In a sense, Spurling is just making 3D comic-art. That doesn't detract from her incredible accomplishment one bit, but it definitely isn't the same as having models pose for photographs in historical costume to actually depict the Biblical figures.

And this is what brings us to the fundamental limit of photo-comics: posability.

Posability

One key draw of the comics medium is that it can allow a single voice to tell a visual narrative. You don't need the million-dollar budgets of movies and tons of CGI to tell a story set in a fantasy world; all you need is a pen and paper, or digital drawing tools. When drawing, you can pose figures however you'd like, even to the point of distorting bodies to get a dynamic pose, a la Jack Kirby.

Let us consider the movies vs. comics comparison even more. Specifically, let's think about a no-budget film, one made by, say, high schoolers or college students. Even in this instance, you have to secure actors, filming locations, synchronized schedules, editing software, competent direction behind the camera, etc. Getting all the resources together to make a photo-comic with real people would require a similar level of involvement as making that small film. Why not just make a film in that case? What is so unique about photography in comics form that justifies the work involved?

Even one person making a photo-comic by themselves would have difficulty thanks to the posability problem; if that one person is the subject, they have to be both photographer and actor simultaneously, which is *incredibly* difficult. Sure, you can set a camera on a tripod and time-delay the picture, but you couldn't both pose for the camera and see your possible picture simultaneously, unless either (1) you were close the camera, like with a selfie, or (2) you had another piece of equipment that would let you view the setup remotely, but you'd have to be able to hide this setup before taking your actual photograph. So, not impossible, but difficult.

To use myself as an example, I once added a speech balloon to a photo of my cat: I couldn't guarantee that she would be in the right poses for multiple images, so the best I could maybe do would be to work around what I'm able to photograph of her. However, the pictures would then be dictating the content, rather than the other way around.

Stills and Screenshots

Aside from posable figures, another work-around for photo-comics is to use screenshots.

In fact, before home video, certain films and even TV episodes would be made available to re-experience at home by taking stills from the movie and overlaying narration and word balloons on top of them. This is like a novelization, but in picture form. This was easier to accomplish than creating a photo-comic from scratch because the actors were already posed in the film. This method also did not encounter the problem of "why bother if it's the same effort as a film?" mentioned at the end of the previous section; the film had already been made, and thus the photo-comic was an adaptation/supplement, not a standalone work.

"Breaking Ted"

I actually once considered doing something like this for a final project in college. I was taking a course on the show *Breaking Bad*, and for the final assignment, I wanted to do something creative. My initial idea was to make an edit of the show which only featured scenes with Ted Beneke, a side character who acts as a foil to main character Walter White. Why did I want to do this? Well, because I realized that if you told Ted's story, you'd actually get something very similar to Walter's in terms of desperation leading to criminal choices. I was going to call it "Breaking Ted." (Extra points if you get the pun in terms of what happens to Ted.)

However, I couldn't figure out how to pull that off. My second idea, then, was to make this adaptation using screenshots, captions, and dialogue balloons. The amount of work in the undertaking made it unviable for me at the time, but it's always stuck at the back of my head.

Had I gone through with the project, it would have been a good example of screenshots used to create a photo-comic.

Concerned

For an example of an actual photo-comic that employs screenshots, shows good use of posability, and was actually pulled off, I direct you to Christopher C. Livingston's *Concerned*, a fan comic set in the universe of the *Half-Life* games. The comic was produced by taking screenshots of characters posed in deliberate ways by Livingston, and was created to parody/comment upon the games, as well as provide a humorous explanation for events actually witnessed in *Half-Life 2*.

Despite being made as a fan effort, *Concerned* is a genuinely good example of what the medium of photo-comics can accomplish. Yes, I would say that it is an instance of photo-comics, even if all the pictures were made using a game engine. It may not be photo-comics in the purest sense, but it is adjacent to that, still worthy of a more generalized category.

One Contender

Dutch artist Ype Driessen is perhaps the world's only — or, at the very least, its most popular — photo-cartoonist. He has developed a name for himself by producing photo-strips (usually about four panels per entry) that comment on life, often humorously, sometimes seriously, and on occasion, somehow both simultaneously.

In 2020, Driessen released a photo-graphic-novel in his original Dutch, which was republished into English in 2023 under the title *The Last Gay Man on Earth*. The story follows a fictional Ype over the course of a week as he agonizes over whether or not to join his boyfriend on a trip to the United States. His hesitation is due to a fear of flying, but the book explores some of Ype's other fears when it comes to different parts of his life, like his creative works and him getting older.

The Last Gay Man on Earth, Driessen's first photo novel, takes place over the course of a week, with all but two chapters marking a day and each ending with a dream that explores Ype's inner psyche. The book is also self-reflexive about creating a photo-comics masterpiece, and makes that an explicit focus of the in-universe character: on page 25, while speaking with his boyfriend Nico, Ype even imagines the possibility that his planned photo-novel could "be a masterpiece and a best-seller, translated into a hundred languages ..." Thus, *The Last Gay Man on Earth* puts the question of creating a photo-comic masterpiece at the core of its narrative. While we see Ype working on his photo-comic strips in one scene, we never see him work on the book; however, the book does get mentioned often, like a specter haunting him. Will he get it done, and will it be good?

179

To digress for a moment, the scene that shows Driessen's process does reveal two important facets about how he creates his work. First, it's made clear that he does use a remote-control device after he's set up any scenes that he's in, which confirms that this is a viable and in-use method for overcoming the actor-photographer conundrum that I mentioned earlier. The second is that he's shown scripting his comics through a thumbnail process, including the dialogue he'll eventually include, so that he can know exactly how he wants the scene to look. For pictures in which he appears, this allows him to set up the shot while behind the camera and then simply walk to his spot in the frame and then take the picture while in frame. Driessen has found clear ways to solve the posability problem.

Overall, *The Last Gay Man on Earth* is a fascinating read that stands up on its own as a story but could very well be the first masterpiece of the photo-comics novel form, equivalent to the groundbreaking graphic novels that helped gain mainstream respect for the comics medium.

The only issue I had was with the start of the Friday chapter, a therapy-session scene which goes from pages 115 to 120. Although the scene sets up a somewhat effective gag at its end, and despite the fact that it gives us a glimpse into the Ype character's childhood and psychological life, it has a major flaw: the therapy session is mostly telling, with very little showing. For those five and a half pages, all we see is Ype's face as he talks and talks (with his therapist responding), and while his expressions change, the scene has no visual diversity beyond that, which holds it back. I admit that this setup served the story, but comics is a visual medium that uses multiple images to progress a narrative. If the images are functionally static and the text is doing the heavy lifting, it's not a comic so much as it is a prose work with pictures behind the text. It's clear that Driessen has talent for creating photo-comics. Based on that, he could've used the therapy session as narration while the images illustrated what he was recounting, in a flashback format.

While this flaw was nowhere near fatal to the book as a whole, it was a weak spot that needed to be pointed out, because this is about form and medium.

There is so much more that could be talked about when it comes to *The Last Gay Man on Earth* in terms of form and composition, but that's not the focus here. This is: from what I've read, I'm confident in saying that the book is evidence that there has been at least one great work of the photo-comics form.

Do We Need Negative Film Reviews Anymore?

May 3, 2025

I used to view two YouTube movie reviewers religiously: Jeremy Jahns and Chris Stuckmann. (I'm sure I'm not the only one who did.) I first discovered Jahns in early 2015, as I remember his review of *The SpongeBob Movie: Sponge Out of Water* being the first review that I watched by him. I know I discovered Stuckmann second, and it would have been within that year, but it was definitely months later.

While I was a huge fan of both, and always hoped they would do a crossover review during that period (though they did appear on the Screen Junkies YouTube channel together once in late 2016, though it was for the show's "Movie Fights" segment), it quickly became clear that the two of them had very different review styles, reflective of their different backgrounds and interests. Jeremy was once a projectionist at a movie theater, and I've always viewed him as a "film bro": he's the kind of guy who watches movies from the fan or audience's perspective and reviews movies this way, with his unique ratings system. On the other hand, Chris has been interested in film from the creator's perspective, having made home movies—including an *Indiana Jones* fan film—since he was a teenager, and so his reviews have come from that perspective, although he also had a fanboy element to his reviews, as well.

Like him or not (and there are controversies that have popped up over the years that you can find but which aren't relevant here), Jeremy hasn't significantly changed his style of reviewing for over 15 years: he still has the red background, he wears that signature leather jacket, and he's energetic. Most importantly for this essay, he continues to put out his "worst movies of the year" list. Chris no longer does that, nor has he made an entry in his "Hilariocity" series—where he reviews bad movies that are hilariously atrocious, hence the name—since 2022, nor does he really put out negative film reviews anymore.

Fans of his traditional channel have never forgiven him for this. They see him as a Hollywood sellout who either doesn't want anyone to criticize his debut movie, *Shelby Oaks* or doesn't want to upset colleagues. On the latter point, I believe they're correct, but I also understand his point of view: Chris has always wanted to be a filmmaker, and his channel has been a vehicle for that passion since 2011. His change in style isn't cowering to something new; in actuality, it is a reflection of the channel's original purpose.

But the Internet, and YouTube in particular, *craves* negativity. There's a reason why some of Chris's most-viewed reviews are for bad films. It's also why, when Chris released a rewrite of a *Batman v Superman* scene on Twitter in 2016, he was hit with a flood of what can only be called cyberbullying, and even years later was still getting comments along the lines of "Tell that to Zod's snapped neck," a reference to the rewrite. (No, I don't think his rewrite was great or anything, but the idea of harassing someone for writing a bad scene *that they posted for free on the Internet* is a sad reflection on the harassers. It has nothing to do with the writer at that point.)

Because of this love of negativity, commenters have seized their chance to remind others at every turn of how much of a sellout Chris is, including by posting comments on Jeremy's worst-of-the-year videos talking about how Chris Stuckmann would never do something like this anymore. (Bordering a bit on obsessed, aren't we?)

You know the best way to show Chris that you dislike his channel's change? *Don't watch.* It's that simple. Support Jeremy or the tons of other reviewers on YouTube or elsewhere who are still willing to negatively review a film.

However, what has stuck with me (no pun on Chris's name intended) from these comments, and made me seriously think about this topic, is one specific idea: Chris is no longer a true film reviewer because he only reviews films that he likes and is unwilling to put a negative review on his channel.

You know what? I cannot 100% dismiss this idea. But when I think about it, I wonder the titular question: do we need negative film reviews anymore?

Traditionally, film critics were there not to assess a movie's aesthetic quality as much as they were there to help audiences decide whether or not to spend their time and money on going to the theater to see the movie in the first place. This function found its apotheosis in Roger Ebert and Richard Roeper's famous "Two Thumbs Up" phrase; the thumbs-up-or-down embodies the binary question at the heart of this type of film criticism: to see or not to see.

But that was in the pre-Internet era, where the only visual competitor to movies was the television. Now, with the deluge of content that we have thanks to the Internet and smartphones, it seems like the point of a film review could shift: instead of telling you whether or not to see a movie, maybe the review exists just to make people aware of the movie at all. In 2019, almost everyone on Earth was aware of *Avengers: Endgame*, but how many American viewers had even heard of Céline Sciamma's *Portrait of a Lady on Fire*? How many are still unaware of the film?

In our age of content oversaturation and blockbusters dominating the movie theaters, bad non-blockbuster movies might not even need to be negatively reviewed; they might just be forgotten or unknown. At the same time, if, say, you really like Chris Stuckmann's reviews and you notice that he hasn't reviewed a movie that everyone else is discussing, couldn't that speak quite loudly to his thoughts on the film, as well?

———

I actually think negative reviews still have an important place in film criticism. But it feels almost like the desire for negative reviews nowadays, especially as reflected in the backlash to Chris's decision to not make them, is more about the Internet's love of toxic negativity rather than a concern for the loss of an important critical element. (Again, Chris is *not* the only film reviewer out there, so it isn't like we've lost *all* negative film reviews due to his decision.)

At the end of the day, I think it's Chris's decision as to where his channel will go, and I respect him for reducing the negativity his channel puts out, regardless of the reason he decided to do it. But his decision, and the overreaction it encountered, made me question negative film reviews and how they interact with broader Internet trends regarding negative, sensationalistic content and algorithmic incentivization of that type of content.

There is no simple answer to this question, I've come to realize. I hope that we continue to consider this question, but do so with nuance.

12 Great Books to Read Right Now

May 20, 2025

In the spirit of the times, I wanted to share a personal reading list; the following is a set of books that I would recommend to anyone thinking about some particularly salient topics in today's world. The selections have been placed into certain categories that represent a contemporary anxiety or topic of discussion. Keep in mind that this list is not exhaustive, of course.

Authoritarianism and Autocracy

Antigone by Sophocles (play)

To whom should you be loyal: your family, your state, or yourself? That's the question at the heart of Sophocles' *Antigone*, wherein the title character must choose between burying her brother, Polynices, or obeying the decree of her uncle (who is also the city's ruler) that Polynices' body must be left to rot outside the city because he was a traitor.

Seamus Heaney's 2004 version, *The Burial at Thebes*, is also worth a perusal for fans of the play; Heaney makes clear his work is a commentary on the Bush administration's foreign policy, which has resonance with the Trump regime's own actions at home and abroad.

Julius Caesar by William Shakespeare (play)

Shakespeare's *Julius Caesar* is about more than just an assassination, which only occurs in the third of the play's five acts. Its main focus is on the fall of a republic into a dictatorial empire, where the commoners come to love a strongman leader and, after his death, are persuaded to support his successors, who use Caesar's popularity to seize power for themselves. However, most of the conspirators who kill Caesar, it becomes clear, did so because they were jealous of his power. Only Brutus, it seems, was genuinely determined to do so in order to save his republic, just like his ancestor helped overthrow the Roman Kingdom and establish the Republic.

There's a reason the Public Theater's 2017 production, with Caesar dressed to look like Donald Trump, incurred so much ire. The right-wing took it at face value and saw it (seemingly) depicting the assassination of the sitting head of state (whom they also, incidentally, loved). But the play is not at all an endorsement of Caesar's assassination; in fact, its depiction of that event leading to Rome's downfall is exactly what makes it, if anything, anti-assassination. Thus, it was really a confrontation of left-wing hatred toward Trump, which makes more sense considering New York City is very Democratic.

The play's treatment of this delicate, complex subject matter was radical even in its time, when concerns about Queen Elizabeth I's age and successor were on the public's minds, and as we are currently in another volatile era politically, it retains that relevance.

Intellectual Freedom

Inherit the Wind by Jerome Lawrence & Robert E. Lee (play)

Written as an allegory on McCarthyism, *Inherit the Wind* is a play that fictionalizes the Scopes Monkey Trial, where a Tennessee teacher was put on trial for daring to teach his students about Darwin's theory of evolution by natural selection.

During the 2023–24 school year, I had my 9th-grade English students read/perform this work as a class. At the time, I was tying it specifically to the issue of book banning, because the play as a whole isn't about evolution as much as it is about the right to think for oneself, to be allowed to live without governmental or societal restriction of thought.

It's worth noting, as well, that the co-playwright Lee was not, of course, the same Robert E. Lee who fought for the Confederate States of America. Perhaps, though, it is a fitting historical irony, since another debate of the 2010s and 2020s centers around the memorialization of Confederate figures.

The Library by Andrew Pettegree & Arthur der Weduwen (nonfiction)

Stretching from the first repositories of knowledge to the digital superhighway of information known as the Internet, *The Library* is a history of that institution throughout recorded human history. Not only for bibliophiles, the book will change how you see the role that access to information has played and will continue to play in human life for as long as we defend libraries. But that's the challenge: we must defend them.

As I write this, libraries and the freedom to read — which is tied to the broader freedom to access information of any sort — are under siege by forces who seek to restrict access to knowledge, who want all narratives to be ones that comply with their view of the world. (Just look at the recent firing of the Librarian of Congress to see the highest-profile example yet.) *The Library* may not have been written precisely for this moment, but it is most certainly relevant to it.

Technological Advancement

Frankenstein by Mary Shelley (novel)

One of the foundational works of science fiction, *Frankenstein* is preoccupied with scientific possibility run amok by godlike ambitions. It may be the source of a classic monster, but its true conflict centers not on the monster and the monstrous, but on the ability to create life, and the dangers such artificial life could pose to humanity.

In an age of advanced artificial intelligence, Shelley's novel takes on a new relevance.

R.U.R. by Karel Čapek (play)

The source of the English word "robot," *R.U.R.* (which stands for "Rossum's Universal Robots") was written in 1920 but set around the then-future-year of 2000, the equivalent projection of guessing events in 2095.

As I said in a previous essay of mine comparing the two works, *R.U.R.* is a great companion to *Frankenstein*: both deal with artificial life and the threats that it could pose to humanity. However, whereas *Frankenstein* focuses on one monster, Čapek's play depicts the results of mass-production of semi-sentient beings. You can imagine the end result.

While predictable by modern standards, Čapek's work is a landmark in science fiction just as Shelley's novel is, and likewise is something that completely resonates with the times.

The Corporate Influence on Politics

The Appeal by John Grisham (novel)

I was originally going to dedicate an entire essay to just this book, titled "The Greatest American Novel of the 21st Century." When I realized that (1) this would seem like an overstatement in comparison to the Pulitzer winners, Booker winners, etc. and (2) I didn't have enough content to really justify an entire essay, I decided that it could fit on this list.

The Appeal follows the aftermath of a trial where a chemical company is found guilty of polluting a local Mississippi town and causing cancer among its residents. While the little-guy Mississippians celebrate their victory, New York mogul Carl Trudeau, who owns the company, schemes to elect a friendly judge to the Mississippi Supreme Court, so that it will hand down a ruling in his company's favor. (However, the candidate who is recruited to run is not aware of these machinations.)

What follows is a sprawling story of political power, corruption, the influence of money on elections, and the disaster that arises when the justice system is politicized and weaponized. *The Appeal* predates the 2010 Supreme Court decision of *Citizens United v. Federal Election Commission* by two years, yet it seems to so perfectly depict the issue that I was on first read convinced it was written in response to that decision. (I read the book in 2012, though I'd listened to a small snippet of the audiobook with my mom in 2010 or 2011.)

I don't know if Carl Trudeau is directly based on Donald Trump, but it would not surprise me in the slightest to learn that Grisham had at least used Trump as one model for his money-hungry New York billionaire with a much-younger wife and at-the-time very young child.

It isn't an uplifting book, but *The Appeal* thrills and enthralls in the modern political context, and I'm frankly shocked that it's never been adapted into a TV show, especially in our current era of prestige TV.

The Puritan(ical) Spirit in America

The three works listed in this category would best be read in conversation with one another, and are listed here by order of publication.

Superstition by James Nelson Barker (play)

Published in the 1820s, *Superstition* follows the story of Charles, a young man in Puritan New England who, along with his mother, is persecuted by the tyrannical Reverend Ravensworth on the charge of practicing magic. The play, written in verse, prefigures the preoccupation with Puritan repression as seen in *The Scarlet Letter* and *The Crucible*, and because of our current moment seems almost baked into our country's DNA. Although outdated in several ways, *Superstition* still holds up overall, to an unfortunate degree.

The Scarlet Letter by Nathaniel Hawthorne (novel)

When Hester Prynne gives birth to a baby girl well after her husband is presumed to have died, it is clear to the citizens of her Puritan town that she has committed adultery. Thus, she is forced to wear a scarlet "A" embroidered on her dress, and is forced to be a semi-outcast, living outside of town.

One of the first American bestselling books, Hawthorne's masterwork touches on themes of sin, intolerance, and sexual hypocrisy, all of which remain relevant today.

The Crucible by Arthur Miller (play)

The finale of this aforementioned trilogy, Arthur Miller had the same target in *The Crucible* as Lawrence & Lee had with *Inherit the Wind*: McCarthyism and its threat to the freedom of independent thought. While researching Salem, Massachusetts, Miller found parallels between the witch-hunts and the anti-communist fervor of the Second Red Scare, which he dramatized in what is now his most-performed play.

In an age where the U.S. government seeks to root out practitioners of "diversity, equity, and inclusion," defund services that don't align with Donald Trump's narrow agenda, and label anyone who disagrees with the official government position as enemies of the nation, this work stands as a powerful testament to both the damage this mindset can cause and to the powerful example set by those who defend their principles at all cost.

Communication & Connection

How the Post Office Created America by Winifred Gallagher (nonfiction)

Before we had texting, email, phone calls, or even the telegraph, we had the postal service as our only means of transporting information across large distances. Winifred Gallagher's *How the Post Office Created America* charts how this vital service connected a young but ever-expanding nation, as well as how those aforementioned newer technologies interacted with the traditional post.

Published in 2016, the book's only lack is information on the much-needed Postal Service Reform Act of 2022, which was passed to address issues with the Postal Accountability and Enhancement Act of 2006, which came to threaten the existence of a functional postal service.

To Obama by Jeanne Marie Laskas (nonfiction)

One of the most unique books I have ever read, *To Obama* is a collection of letters sent to President Barack Obama during his eight years in office, as well as some of the responses he wrote back. Some letters to him express hope, others fear, and even others hatred. What really sells the book, however, are the profiles Laskas features of some of the letter writers before she shows the reader that person's actual letter. This connects the reader to these average Americans who wrote to President Obama, and it reminds readers that behind each of those letters is a human story, even the ones that are printed without that context.

I do not exaggerate when I say that this book was life-affirming and — although featuring work from eight years ago at the most recent — reminded me of the humanity I share with "my *fellow* Americans," to use that common refrain and add my own emphasis. It's that fellowship that we've lost in the past 15 years, and although I don't know if we will ever get it back, this tangible evidence of its existence is enough to inspire hope and, hopefully, action toward its restoration.

My Stupid Obsession with the College Board AP Literature Exam

June 3, 2025

When I started applying for high-school English-teacher jobs in the spring of 2023, I decided to prepare for teaching by doing something very specific: buying a book of 500 questions that could appear on the College Board's Advanced Placement English Literature exam. I wasn't expecting to teach this course, but I felt like this would be a good way to get back into the English curriculum for someone who had studied an adjacent topic — media studies — in college. After all, what is English class but preparation for this exam in one's senior year of high school? What would it involve other than studying and writing about the classic works of literature? (Though this wouldn't have been a completely sarcastic thought at the time, it is in hindsight.)

Well, as it turned out, the English classes I taught for the next two school years were focused on building skills rather than learning texts. I was told that specifically: "We teach skills, not texts." And you know what? Part of me agreed. Memorizing lines and themes from *Romeo and Juliet* isn't worthless, but in an age where multimedia literacy is a must, I agree that English class should accommodate newer media forms so that students are better prepared for the Information Age once they leave high school. After all, that's what my major in college was focused on, and if anything, that major made me *more* prepared to teach in this new format.

Still (perhaps because *I* was taught this way), I felt it was important that we read at least one text together, so I managed to squeeze in the play *Inherit the Wind* for some of my English classes during my first year of teaching. Plays are shorter than novels and thus are easier to fit into the curriculum; plus, they are inherently well-suited to popcorn reading—where students switch off reading certain parts aloud—because they have specific roles to be assigned for performance. It also helped that many of these students were theater kids, as they were overjoyed to be able to do some theater during English class.

But, yes, the AP Literature exam. I think the reason I was obsessed with it, and the reason why text analysis was still a lingering thing for me when I started teaching, was because of how highly regarded the texts were when I was an AP Lit student in 12th grade. That year, we read (among other works) *Macbeth* and *A Doll's House*, which I mention because I still vividly remember my teacher's rendition of (1) the Scottish thane and (2) the famous door-slam at the end of *Doll's House*. My teacher, Mr. Bolt, made it clear how highly regarded these works were, and I was in awe of them—and of his style of teaching, as well.

Mr. Bolt also helped introduce me to deeper reading of literature thanks to recommending Thomas Foster's book *How to Read Literature Like a Professor*, which truly was a monumental book for me: for the first time in my life, I understood how teachers could draw these deeper connections in fiction, how they could read a character as a stand-in for the devil, for example.

I'd been writing fiction for about eight years already at this point, but after taking AP Lit and reading *How to Read Literature Like a Professor*, something changed in me: I wanted to write a work worthy of being used on the exam, or to be studied in the same way that the classics were studied by my teacher or by Foster's book. Great literature was clearly written to be picked apart by experts and then explained to the regular denizens of society. I was a fool for

194

trying to write works simply for fun.

My sense of inferiority may also have been fed by the fact that I wasn't able to get a 5 (the highest score) on either the Lit exam or the AP English Language exam in 11th grade: I got a 4 on both. What writer of any merit could stoop so low?

Between my interest in studying film and a bad experience my first semester of college in a creative-writing course, I moved away from English (outside of mandated college courses), majoring in media studies/analysis, like I mentioned before. But while fate brought me back to teaching English, I'm grateful for the skills I learned from my major, as well as the new perspective it gave me on other forms of media. When you study news broadcasts, comics, video games, movies, TV shows, and other media with the same critical lens that traditionally was applied only to literature, you come to realize that great stories can exist in any medium.

After I started teaching English, I had my epiphany: The best literature is never that which is written for a test or for the analysis of others in an academic context; it is that which is written for the people and which connects deeply with human concerns. The study of the text is a byproduct of its greatness, not the reason for its existence in the first place.

William Shakespeare didn't write his plays to be read and studied for the ages; he wrote them to entertain and connect with the audiences of Elizabethan and Jacobean society. In fact, he possibly expected that most of his plays would never be printed officially; only about half had been published in some form before his death.

Mary Shelley's *Frankenstein* is one of the most influential novels ever written, if not the most, and yet it was a product of a mental exploration, the classic "what-if" set-up that animates many great works of fiction. In her case, the what-if was the following: what if we could create life itself? In playing god, what could come as a result? Well, the result of the novel was essentially the birth of science fiction.

To take a non-traditional example (though it is now becoming canonized): Alan Moore's *Watchmen* comic is a reflection of the 1980s, but it asks enduring questions regarding power and powerlessness in society, regarding technological progress and its effect on the individual, regarding the question of propaganda, etc. It's a comic book (a traditionally denigrated form) about superheroes (a traditionally denigrated genre), but it speaks to and beyond its moment, about something beneath its surface level. That is what makes it commensurate with great works of literature, in a way that few if any other superhero comics ever are.

———

When Jerome Lawrence and Robert Edwin Lee wrote *Inherit the Wind*, they were dramatizing the Scopes Monkey Trial, where a Tennessee teacher was put on trial for violating a state law against teaching evolution. That is what the play is about... on the surface. However, it was written in the context of the McCarthy era, where anti-communist fervor demanded intellectual orthodoxy of every American; those who refused to follow along were shunned and even lost their jobs. *Inherit the Wind* is a direct response to this era, and it is a plea for intellectual freedom, for the ability to think for oneself.

This is precisely why I chose *Inherit the Wind* for my class to read during the 2023–2024 school year. It was (and remains) an era of book banning and silencing of unorthodox voices by those in power, whether because of "critical race theory" (in reality, any book that discusses race in a way the regime deems antithetical to its interests), because of "LGBT indoctrination" by the "rainbow mafia" (i.e., any attempt to depict queer people as human beings and not Hellbound pedophilic predators), or another reason. I did not teach the play because I wanted my students to share my exact feelings on the matter. My goal is not, and never was, to get them to think how I think. My job as a teacher is to equip them with the skills to think for themselves, to be able to assess information and come to their own conclusions based not on their biases but on careful consideration of the facts.

———

To be clear, I don't think the AP Lit exam is irrelevant. It is by nature a standardized test meant to assess students across the country in a uniform way; it *has* to do that in order to fulfill its assessment goal, which is to answer the following question: "Did students gain a college-level understanding of literature?" For this purpose, it works well enough.

However, the standardization is a result of necessity, not because that is the way we must teach literature to all students. It's also an *incredibly* stupid way to go about trying to write a work of literature; to ask "will the AP Lit gods deem this worthy of study?" and use *that* as the basis of writing is going to *at best* result in formulaic (and possibly also archaic) writing. Needless to say: don't do this!

If anyone reading this has felt similarly, I hope this has helped purge you of the same mentality I once had. If you're a writer, it's no way to go about creating good work. If you're a reader, however, it's also not beneficial to see literature only in relation its use as an assessment tool. Literature is meant to be alive, engaging, relevant, and nuanced. Do not let the AP Lit exam, or any similar assessment, take that away.

What Defines Comics?

June 6, 2025

In my first-ever published book, *Narrative in Action*, I spent quite a bit of time on the topic of comics. In fact, I devoted a whole chapter to the medium under the title of "sequential art" — a term coined by comics pioneer Will Eisner and used frequently in academic discussions not only of comics, but of comics-like media. In the book, I defined sequential art as "a sequence of images used to tell a narrative," and I defined comics as a form of sequential art. At the time, however, I distinguished comics as being "mass-reproducible sequential art." This way, digital comics which remained on a person's computer would be included, since they had the potential to be mass-reproduced, but a sequence of paintings wouldn't in and of itself be considered comics.

Part of this was a result of trying to pin down the definitions and essential qualities of different media, which was the whole point of *Narrative in Action*'s second half. I was also trying to accomplish something similar to Scott McCloud's work in his seminal *Understanding Comics*, albeit for all media that I could identify as being unique and not part of a larger category. When I wrote those definitions, I really believed that those definitions were perfect, that I had found a definition for comics that could be used as part of comics-studies and academia more broadly. (I had my head in the clouds a bit, but dreaming of heights helps us keep our aspirations up.)

While I stand by the definition I used for sequential art, I've come to change my view of what comics are, and in doing so have learned just how fluid certain media categories can be.

———

It all really starts before I even developed my definition of comics for *Narrative in Action*, though at the time I wouldn't have realized it: because of a series of fortunate events, I ended up taking a class on comics in my final semester at the University of Virginia with Sean Duncan, something I've mentioned before in these essays. I had wanted to take the course from the beginning, but I felt like I didn't belong in it, because we would be expected to draw, and I can't draw well to save my life.

But because of a mistake I made in a different course that would have resulted in my grade tanking, I switched into the comics class. It turned out to be one of the best decisions I had ever made, because that became one of the most artistically informative classes I ever took. And you know what? I eventually did end up making a four-page comic using drawings… but I'm getting ahead of myself.

The night before my first day in the comics class, I was experiencing a significant depressive episode, and, according to my journal:

> *I took a picture of myself while sitting in [my dorm's] first-floor entryway, because I'd been meaning to create a photo-comic for a while and decided that it would be good practice for thinking about sequential art, since [the comics class] starts tomorrow. I wanted to document my depression. I'd meant for it only to be a study of my face, hence the original title "Faces of Depression," but I ended up talking about memories from a few years ago [...]. It was this rumination on my face, my façade, my experiences (I wanted to make it longer, but I cut it off before it got too large), and depression. I thought it was wonderful and very therapeutic, and I would like Professor Duncan to read it. Its final title is* Facing Depression, *which reflects the original title while also being a bit more complex of a title, like the work to which it refers.*

Employing the photo-comic method, something I imagined I could lean on during the class, made me more comfortable with the idea of making comics in general. However, it was the method that I used to piece the comic together, not the technology, that really matters: I made it using Microsoft PowerPoint, with each slide its own panel.

But was this really a comic? Adhering to Scott McCloud's definition in *Understanding Comics*, comics is "juxtaposed pictorial and other images in deliberate sequence." (That would probably annoy him, since apparently McCloud has had many readers want to discuss that specific definition, and who take it much more seriously than he does.) I could argue that the images were juxtaposed by having them set in sequence, but a stricter and more common definition would require that both images be visible simultaneously for them to be juxtaposed, a definition which would exclude *Facing Depression*.

In an episode of *The Illustration Department Podcast* (February 27, 2024), Scott McCloud points out that digital comics where "panel one just fills the screen, and you click and you get panel two, which fills the screen ... like a slideshow" do not have their images juxtaposed in space, like traditional comics. However, McCloud admits that this is a "loophole" that tests his definition of comics, and if those single-image-per-view experiences aren't comics, then it isn't clear what exactly they would be. So, even McCloud admits that PowerPoint comics might skirt into a gray area; it was that admission that brought me back to the topic of this essay.

In another podcast episode, this one for *Comix Experience Graphic Novel Club: The Interviews*, "Scott McCloud for Understanding Comics" (September 8, 2022), McCloud states: "I think the page might actually be hobbling us a little," because there becomes an emphasis on creating an engaging page composition (like a spread or double-page spread) that catches the reader's eye, but that creates a pausing effect and pulls focus away from the panel-to-panel storytelling. In his mind, the best comics have "a kind of cascading momentum from panel to panel."

Contrast this, then, with an argument made by the YouTuber "The Nerd-writer," who argues that Art Spiegelman, creator of the Holocaust comic *Maus*, views the page as the storytelling unit of comics. In his video "Maus: How To Design A Comic Book Page," the Nerdwriter discusses how in *Maus*, as in many comics, time is made spatial on the page, where past, present, and future exist simultaneously for the reader. For a story so preoccupied with the effect of the past on the present, this viewpoint and design philosophy fits perfectly.

So, how to reconcile these interconnected but somewhat conflicting views on comics? What is the fundamental unit of comics, the page or the panel? Can we have a comic where each image is experienced separately, or must images be juxtaposed together in space for a work to truly fit into the comics medium?

———

"Children's picture books use images in sequence, but the images play a secondary, illustrative role to the words, whereas in comics, words play a secondary, explanatory role to the illustrations." This was my argument in *Narrative in Action* for why illustrated books do not fit the definition of comics. However, like with my attempt to define comics based on mass-reproducibility, I was going off of a vibe and attempting to create a definition which fit with what *felt* right, without considering the possibility that I could be wrong. What if children's books are a form of comics?

In thinking about this, and about the fundamental unit of comics, I created a set of Venn diagrams. The first is how to consider comics in terms of three elements: images, text, and sequence:

- IMAGE & TEXT: Single-panel comic
- IMAGE & SEQUENCE: Wordless comics
- TEXT & SEQUENCE: Image-less books
- IMAGE, TEXT, & SEQUENCE: Traditional comics

The second Venn diagram is how to classify comics based on whether their fundamental unit is the page or the panel:

- PANEL: Comic
- PAGE: Illustrated book
- PANEL & PAGE: Traditional comics

Utilizing these two analytical resources, we can not only classify traditional comics, but also single-panel comics (which McCloud in *Understanding Comics* labels as "comic art," but argues are not comics because they lack sequence), wordless comics (like those of Frans Masereel and Lynd Ward), and even written narratives without pictures at all! We can also fit illustrated books into our understanding, if we allow for the fundamental unit to be the page only (as in, there are no panels).

Best of all, what this classification allows us to do is view comics as part of a pictorial-narrative tradition dating back throughout human history, and not just something that required the printing-press technology, like my old definition did. Comics are much more fundamental to the human story than we previously understood, and this framework, I hope, helps contribute to that new lens.

Update #1

I've since delved more deeply into McCloud's work, and I've learned about his emphasis on "designing for the device." In a 2014 blog post about his then-upcoming book *The Sculptor*, McCloud says "This book is designed for print and as far as I'm concerned, the paper and ink version will always be the 'real' version," whereas a digital version would be an *adaptation*; it would be an approximation of an experience designed specifically for the physical page. He says he would feel the same about a print version of a digital-first comic; in either scenario an artist has had to "castrate their work to suit multiple formats." [13] McCloud has been an evangelist for the unique opportunities provided by digital comics ever since his 2000 book *Reinventing Comics*, and he has experimented quite a bit in that form ever since, blazing a trail for future artists that still has not been well-traversed. But a comic should not be hindered by expectations that it will be adapted into another form; instead, an artist ought to decide which medium—digital or print—they will use to tell their story and then design their comic around that form.

This is an example of "medium essentialism," the idea that each form of art has unique properties that it should seek to emphasize and display, rather than attempting to imitate other media forms. For example, a film should not try to be a play, for it cannot mimic the immediacy that a play has when performed live in front of an audience. Rather, a film should use its unique elements to give the audience an experience only a film could provide. And it can! If in a play the audience is stationary and the stage-world is what moves, in a film the audience is transportable: they can be taken to real locations anywhere in this world or a fictitious one that special effects and computer-generated imagery can create.

Alan Moore, when discussing his and Dave Gibbons' comic-book *Watchmen*, stated: "What I'd like to explore is the areas that comics succeed in where no other media is capable of operating." [14] Then, in discussing his work retrospectively in 2008, he shared similar sentiments: "If we only see comics in relation to movies then the best that they will ever be is films that do not move. I found it, in the mid 80s, preferable to concentrate on those things that only comics could achieve. [...] most of my work from the 80s onwards was designed to be un-filmable." [15] Comics have at times tried to reach for legitimacy by imitating techniques from film; while other media can inspire new ideas, methods, and techniques in a given medium (superhero films often take their visual cues straight from comics, recreating them with computer effects), a medium thrives best when it explores and expands its intrinsic and unadaptable capabilities.

Returning to The Nerdwriter's deconstruction of *Maus*, we can see the principle of medium essentialism in action, but within the sub-medium of print comics: Art Spiegelman uses the page as a unit to juxtapose past, present, and future simultaneously; instead of the page being a byproduct of the demands of print, it becomes the uniquely-suited vehicle for this particular story. And Spiegelman wasn't the only one. "I found myself competing with the movie camera. I had to compete with the camera," said comics legend Jack Kirby. "I tore my characters out of the panels. I made them jump all over the page." [16] Many of Kirby's predecessors simply recreated standard newspaper strips in the comic books, which made sense, since originally the books were reprints of strips. However, Kirby realized that he could utilize the page-as-unit to create something intrinsic to the printed comic book, a method the comic strip never could have accommodated.[17]

One wonders what Kirby, whose experience in animation influenced his comic-book work, would have done with the limitless potential of the web. In *Reinventing Comics* and his web-based work since then, McCloud has championed the idea of the "infinite canvas." A breakaway from comic-book formatting just as radical as Kirby's breakaway from comic-strip formatting, the "infinite canvas" is the realization that, on the Internet, artists are not limited to the page in the way they are in print. Instead of viewing the computer screen as a panel or a page, McCloud insists we see it as a window, one that can display one part of a comic at a time, while allowing the comic as a whole to take on any shape and any size its creator desires. For example, a comic adaptation of Dante's *Inferno* could have a spiraling downward shape, mimicking Dante and Virgil's descent into the deeper levels of Hell.

If we're designing for and wedding our comic to the web, then we ought to take a page out of Jack Kirby's book (pun intended) and break the bounds of what was previously possible. Just as no comic strip could reproduce what Kirby did with the page, no book is capable of reproducing an infinite-canvas comic, if one commits to exploring the full possibilities that it presents.

Some comic strips, however, do seem to be able to hold up when collected in larger volumes, especially narrative ones as opposed to the gag-a-day strips. For example, Alex Raymond and John Prentice's detective-strip *Rip Kirby* (no relation to Jack) would present three panels of day, every day of the week, and would take a few months to tell a complete story. (Occasionally, you'd have two panels or four panels, but their overall horizontal length would be the same as the three-panel setup.) How fans kept track of these stories, I don't completely know, because they hold up well when the daily strips are read back-to-back, providing a compelling reading experience comparable to a well-written graphic novel. There is one clue, however, that might shed some light on how reader attention was kept day-after-day with only three panels of story. Aside from the first and last sets of three in a story, each day's panels follow a pattern: the first panel acts as a soft recap of what's just happened or of something that happened further back in the story, the middle panel propels the story forward, and the third panel acts as a cliffhanger, with stakes from the very small to the very large. Sometimes, this process does mean that, say, Panel 1 on Day 2 will repeat some of the information from Panel 3 of Day 1, but this problem is the exception that proves the rule. Unless you're primed to notice the recap-progress-cliffhanger pattern, or you're taken out of the story by repeated information, you don't notice the original structure and the story feels natural when read in one sitting.

I don't know what McCloud's answer would be to this example. Would he claim that *Rip Kirby* would have been better served as a comic book or even a series of graphic novels? Or would he instead argue that the recap-progress-cliffhanger structure—a product of the original medium, that of the newspaper strip—is actually what makes it so compelling on re-read? Could it be that *Rip Kirby* and strips like it demonstrate exceptions to the "castration" that a work of comics experiences when moved from one "device" to another? Could some stories actually *benefit* from being adapted from one medium to another (if we view comic strips and comic books as different media)? Or is *Rip Kirby* only "pure" if experienced three-panels-a-day, as originally designed? (I should note that, according to an introduction of one of the *Rip Kirby* reprint volumes, some people would cut out each strip and save them to be re-read once they'd collected an entire story.)

Update #2

On his website, www.scottmccloud.com, Scott (we're on a first-name basis, apparently) has a set of webcomics, most of which attempt to explore his concept of the infinite canvas. For example, *My Obsession with Chess* is a memoir about McCloud's relationship with this game, from his childhood introduction to his continuing interest with it as he got older; it's told on the "canvas" of a chessboard, where each panel is another square progressing diagonally down the screen, like a scroller. He has another set of comics, though, from 2000 to 2001 called *I Can't Stop Thinking*, wherein he expands on his work in *Reinventing Comics* in a way he could only do online, providing comics-based tutorials for aspiring web-comics creators.

Much like McCloud with his concepts in *Reinventing Comics*, I also couldn't stop thinking about my attempts to categorize comics; this reached its apotheosis when I asked myself: what if we combined all *five* of the elements of traditional comics (image, text, sequence, panel, page) in different ways to see what would result? Well, it gave us 26 combinations (anywhere from 2–5 elements combined together), with a couple of them unable to be properly conceptualized (**Image, Panel, Page** and **Text, Panel, Page**), leaving us with the final tally of 24. Although I started building with just combinations of two, we can use this framework in a subtractive way, as well, to see how removing one of the five elements changes the essence of the product. I can't share the combinations in the same way I formulated them, since I used PowerPoint to create an illustrated approach. However, I can provide them in a list format to give you an idea of what I conceptualized:

1. IMAGE, TEXT: a picture with a maximum of one word.

    a. Without "sequence," we can have neither multiple images nor multiple words. Both elements can work together, but they must each be singular.

2. IMAGE, SEQUENCE: multiple images but ones which are not differentiated based on panel borders, and where no text is involved.

3. IMAGE, PANEL: a wordless picture in a frame set against a larger background.

    a. Without the larger background, we couldn't tell that the panel existed. However, this background is not a page in this instance; it's just a canvas, a differentiator from the panel.

4. IMAGE, PAGE: a single picture on a printed document, or one which fills up the entire screen and is not differentiated from the background, because we have excluded panels from this instance.

    a. Here is where we take our first dip into "print-only" territory.

5. TEXT, SEQUENCE: multiple words strung together, like I'm doing right now.

6. TEXT, PANEL: Text inside a panel, set inside a frame against a larger background. (Basically a text box.)

7. TEXT, PAGE: a single word on a single page.

8. SEQUENCE, PANEL: a series of panels, without images or words inside of them.

9. SEQUENCE, PAGE: multiple empty pages.

10. PANEL, PAGE: an empty page with an empty panel.

11. IMAGE, TEXT, SEQUENCE: a picture with multiple words, multiple pictures with one word each, or multiple pictures with multiple words each.

12. IMAGE, TEXT, PANEL: a picture with one word set inside a frame against a larger background.

13. IMAGE, TEXT, PAGE: a picture on a page with one word.

14. IMAGE, SEQUENCE, PANEL: a series of wordless pictures inside multiple frames set against a larger background.

    a. By definition, you cannot fit multiple pictures inside a panel, because the panel is what separates the pictures.

15. IMAGE, SEQUENCE, PAGE: a series of wordless pictures on a single document or across multiple documents, one per page.

    a. Could multiple images on a page, without panels to differentiate them, still have a separation that traditional panels provide? (Say, if you could tell that you were looking at a person at two different moments, not clones.) This is an unresolved question.

16. TEXT, SEQUENCE, PANEL: words inside one or multiple panels, which they are set against a larger background.

17. TEXT, SEQUENCE, PAGE: multiple words on a single document, multiple words on multiple documents *(taken to its logical conclusion, this is just a book filled with writing)*, or one word across multiple documents.

18. SEQUENCE, PANEL, PAGE: a series of empty panels on a page, or across multiple pages without any images or text.

    a. Can a multi-page panel exist, or would it simply be read as a page, like with a spread? This is an unresolved question.

19. IMAGE, TEXT, SEQUENCE, PANEL: a combination of words and images in series set inside a frame; theoretically, some panels might only contain words, some just images, others both.

    a. This is our "infinite canvas," because the page has been removed from consideration *but* we have all other elements of comics.

20. IMAGE, TEXT, SEQUENCE, PAGE: A combination of words and images in series across multiple pages.

    a. Illustrated children's books which have only one image per page, but which also contain text, would fall under this category.

21. IMAGE, SEQUENCE, PANEL, PAGE: a series of images inside frames on a page or across multiple pages.

   a. These are your wordless or "silent" comic books.

22. IMAGE, TEXT, PANEL, PAGE: a single image with one word inside a frame set against a larger background of a document.

23. TEXT, SEQUENCE, PANEL, PAGE: a series of word-only panels on a page or across multiple pages without any images.

24. IMAGE, TEXT, SEQUENCE, PANEL, PAGE: this is our traditional form of comics.

You'll note that not all of the 24 categories above would fall under "comics," even with the loosest definition. That's okay. We aren't trying to claim that all of these are comics, just that these are the results of the different combinations of traditional ingredients. (The two that didn't work, **IPP** and **TPP**, don't work because they require a singular image or a singular word to be simultaneously inside and outside of a frame and both occupy and not occupy an entire page. If you can figure out how that might work, my hat goes off to you.)

Now, let's take the subtractive approach. First, do we need a page for something to be a comic? Well, I'd argue *no*, since Scott McCloud et al. have demonstrated the ability for an infinite-canvas webcomic to exist.

Do they need to have panels? I would say *yes*, because if you're not dealing with a page, the panel is the only unit you can use to separate your images from one another (and thus delineate separate moments). But maybe, like with the question on combination #15, you could get away with a panel-less comic somehow, though in that combination you have the page as a fallback unit.

Do they need to have a sequence? I would say *yes*, because even if we were to count a single cartoon image as a "comic" (which McCloud does not), we would still lack context that could only be provided by a sequence of words to fill in our gaps of knowledge.

Do they need to have text? I'd say *no*, because there are plenty of examples of "mime" or "silent" comics that exist, like the work of Masereel and Ward.

Do they need images? Well, I'd argue that's the most integral part of comics, since the assumption is that at least one picture is required to meet a minimum definition of the medium. So, *yes, absolutely.*

So, if we look at what we *must have* to make comics, we need images (almost certainly differentiated by panels, but again, there may be an exception to that) and sequence, which gives us... *sequential art!* (if we take "art" to refer to visual imagery). It seems that, even under this system, we return to the pithy but apt definition used by Will Eisner to delineate comics as a medium.

Politics as Theater and Ritual

June 9, 2025

My home state of Virginia has an election every single year, due to its state elections happening on the off-years between federal ones. This year, 2025, we elect our governor, lieutenant governor, and attorney general, as well as all 100 seats of our lower legislative chamber, the House of Delegates. (In 2023, we elected our state senators as well as our 100 delegates, who serve four-year and two-year terms, respectively.)

Because of the perennial election season we experience, and the fact that Virginia state elections act as potential bellwethers one year after and one year before presidential ones, elections are an inescapable topic for Virginians — unless they tune it out, of course.

But to tune out politics is to not only ignore one's responsibility of doing their best to help contribute positively to the world; it's also willingly ignoring the *cultural* function that politics and elections serve. Now, that might sound strange at first glance; elections don't serve a cultural purpose, they serve a practical one: electing leaders. But perhaps bringing in the comparison to theater will illuminate this element of politics.

———

It's theorized that Ancient Greek theater — from which all Western theater derives — emerged from ritual. Perhaps as part of some kind of rite, the ritualistic performers started to not only recite the myths, like the bards would speak the stories of ancient epics, but pretend to be the mythical figures. This, in turn, would lead to the emergence of theater as a unique tradition in Athens, one that also served a cultural function as the subject matter for plays was either mythical or historical—a distinction that ancient Athenians didn't draw as tightly as we do today. The attendance of all free male citizens at theatrical events was also a *requirement*, showing that these events were more than just diversionary entertainment for the Athenians.

Athens, however, also gave rise to the first instance of democracy in the Western world. Under its system, all male citizens were expected to participate in helping run the city in some form, which made Athens a direct democracy (for some), as opposed to the representative democracies that, at least on paper, many Western countries are today. So, to the Athenians, some form of participation in theater and some form of participation in government were both mandatory.

That certainly does tie politics together with theater, which itself drew on ritual, but it still doesn't connect us to how politics can be seen as both theater and ritual in the modern world.

To demonstrate this, let's begin with elections themselves.

Elections as Rituals

We can think of voting as a kind of ritual, where all voters assemble in designated locations to cast their preference for which candidate should hold a given office. The voices of the people are then collected into one, and a determination (usually a singular determination, a choice of one candidate) is made as to who will represent the people. It may not involve animal sacrifices or anointing of holy bread and wine, but it is ritualistic, nonetheless.

Continuing the ritual, what happens next? Well, usually within two or three months, the chosen candidate is inaugurated into office, usually by being sworn in, at least in the United States. This process of anointing power upon given people is inherently ritualistic, because an ephemeral, almost spiritual idea — power — is placed upon the "chosen ones."

The expectation in a representative democracy is that each elected person "represents" (in both a literary and a political sense) a group of people, whether that be a district or an entire country. In essence, that person or that group of people *are* the people, per the ritual of voting that gives them the "mandate" (air quotes) to act in the public's interest. Again, as if by magic, the people become embodied within them, and they are in turn entrusted to carry out the will of the people, while also acting as guardians of the people's interests — in other words, they are both the electorate embodied as well as a check on the electorate's impulses.

Consent

When elections fairly and accurately represent the people's interests, the outcome of this ritual can be said to represent the "consent of the governed," the hallmark of any democracy.

However, when the process is manipulated, when the ritual is still enacted but the people are led to support something through deception by the already-powerful or those seeking power, then the power-seekers can be said to be "manufacturing consent." In this case, the ritual has been manipulated for gain beyond its purpose.

Consent can also be manufactured through governance, the part that comes after the inauguration.

Governance as Theater, and Thus Ritual

The placement of power into the hands of the few allows for them to be a focusing rod for the political power of the entire people, sharpening disparate interests into specific policies. This includes, but is not limited to, the passage and implementation of laws.

Consider how laws are passed in the United States. Members of Congress

213

are elected by the people, then represent them in either the Senate or the House of Representatives. Both chambers of Congress have specific procedures and rules, however, for conducting their day-to-day business. There's nothing in the universe that says these specific rules must be adopted; no, they're adopted or maintained because of tradition, because they allow for the organization of the chamber itself—regardless of the chamber's efficacy in representing the people's will through these rules.

The most obvious of these rules is the (typical) requirement of a simple majority for approval; that's 50% plus one vote. Why do it this way? After all, the papal conclave, for example, requires $2/3$ support to elect a new pope. As of writing, the Senate requires $3/5$ of its members to pass a non-reconciliation bill through its chamber. So, again, there is nothing out there in the universe that says 50% plus one vote is the proper way to conduct business.

In fact, all it boils down to are votes recorded by voice and on paper, just sounds and ink marks. No, it is not the procedures themselves that hold power, but the people who run them who infuse the procedures with that power. Those people, our representatives, in turn draw their power from us, from our consent and our willingness to accept these rituals as having power.

Then, if the president signs it, takes no action but Congress remains in session, or has a veto overridden, the bill becomes a law. But like the votes in Congress, a law is simply lines on a paper. It is the people's willingness to follow the laws which gives the laws their power, their sacredness.

That being said, not all of us have an equal say in how much power a law has. Courts have ritualistic power to interpret the law, while the executive branch has the ritualistic as well as physical power to enforce the law. It is that physical power which gives the ritualistic power more weight. However, that physical power possessed by the executive can be abused, even (but not always) to the point of going against the consent of the governed. At that point, it is not so easy to stand against the law, to in essence personally nullify it.

However, if enough people refuse to adhere to the sacredness of the ritual's outcome, if enough people decide that the law is unjust and stand against it, then this action (which is traditionally called "civil disobedience") can result in the nullification of the law's effect, even if a law isn't ritualistically repealed.

And that shows that the ritual itself is hollow, doesn't it? Without the support and consent of the people (or, at least, without the consent of a sufficient number of them), the law is meaningless, merely an ephemeral product of an ephemeral process.

Because of this fact, elections should not be seen (at least merely) as about choosing a government, but about the ability to choose to alter government, as well. However, elections are only an outlet for change on the rare days when they're held, and thus should not be seen as the only valve for the people's exercise of their own power.

All politics is theater, in one form or another. It is not the enactment that matters, but the agreement of the spectators.

Update

I think the theatricality inherent in politics is why we love fictional dictators like Emperor Palpatine in the *Star Wars* movies (where he is a campy and charismatic villain) while most of us abhor actual fascism, as depicted in the *Star Wars* TV show *Andor*, wherein the Galactic Empire's fascist rule is seen from the perspective of everyday people. In those circumstances, fascism isn't this fun theatrical performance that draws you in and allows you to enjoy the story, but an oppressive force that harms the people and needs to be defeated.

That theatricality, however, may also be why so many people *are* taken in by real-life fascism, and why they are willing to ritualistically surrender their power to a person or group of people who clearly don't care about the people's well-being. Fascism, then, represents the ultimate usurpation of political ritual.

The Paradox of Technology in the Workplace

June 10, 2025

Efficiency. That's the word used to laud technological progress for decades, if not centuries. The addition of new technology means an easier path to accomplishing certain tasks, and thus, we humans ought to cheer on this progress for the good that it will bring to all of us, especially in terms of reduced work.

Traditionally, the fear with new technology — from the actual Luddites protesting textile machines to the modern-day concerns over artificial intelligence — is that it will replace the human worker, and that ownership of capital will be what matters. Forget the days of "real labor"; in this new world, it's either leisure or destitution.

In other words, both the techno-optimists and the Luddites (using that term in the wider sense) emphasize the replacement of manual work by machinery of some sort. But in my experience, that isn't the only possibility that can come from the adoption of new technology. In fact, I've observed a seemingly paradoxical result in terms of new technology, at least in my work place:

> *Technology that makes us more efficient at a task leads managers to place more tasks upon us.*

This thought occurred to me when I was working on my school-issued laptop

(I was teaching 9th-grade English at the time) and realized that I was getting overwhelmed. Between lesson planning, email responding, data collection, documentation of planning and curricular alignment, data reflection, and other tasks that aren't immediately coming to mind, I was on that laptop *a lot*. I thought to myself: what did people do before the laptop was available, before email was universal?

Well, parents would have to schedule a conference with the teacher if they had a question; at best, they might have been able to speak to them on the phone, during school hours. (Once you left the building, you were no longer "on call" as a teacher, barring an emergency.) Data collection could happen, but it was much slower and thus assessments for that purpose had to be given out more sparingly. Now, we teachers were on call no matter where and when thanks to email and cell phones (parents don't usually have our numbers, but our administrators do), and because data is so easily collected electronically, we can assess our students with every assignment like it's the yearly standardized test. And all the emphasis is placed on the documentable, with a marked decrease in emphasis on what happens socially, between teachers and students, inside the classroom.

Now, if this increased workload benefitted students or teachers, I would champion it. But it doesn't. If anything, it harms both groups, because it puts additional expectations on teachers, which takes more of their focus away from the kids, in order to meet the criteria of certain data points. Yes, data is helpful to gauge student learning in steps, but if it's all about the data, then the instruction becomes focused around preparing students for the tests—for the data collection—and not around preparing them for the world outside of the classroom.

At that point, you might as well just have an AI train and assess students, if all that matters is their ability to memorize information, regurgitate it on an assessment, and then promptly forget it; at least then it'll be easier to score the assignments!

Oh, wait, I probably shouldn't be giving anyone "ideas" about that...

———

My discussion so far has been through the lens of education, since that's where my experience comes from. However, this paradox goes beyond the realm of education, and it comes into play in any workplace where technology can facilitate either surveillance of workers, constant communication between workers and their clients, or both. (Yes, in essence, students and parents are clients in relation to the teacher. If that seems crassly commercial, then I've actually made my point quite successfully.) Lawyers don't give out their personal numbers to clients, and they're allowed to turn off their work at night — at least, they are if they're the partners.

That's really what this is about, and in fact it does go back to the question of ownership of capital. To continue with the lawyer example: law-firm partners dictate the hours and expectations placed on the non-owner associates; some are reasonable, fair, and respectful, while others can be demanding, unreasonable, and/or flat-out ridiculous. But, depending on the availability of work at a better firm, the associate does not have the same power — in the socioeconomic sense — as the partners do.

Apply this thinking to any firm, and it comes to make complete sense why unionization is good for the workers, as well as why it's so vehemently opposed by the owner(s). Unionization, while admittedly not always a perfect system, allows for the reclamation of power by the commoners over their lords — I mean, over their employers; pardon me, sometimes I get the two confused. But yes, as I was saying, by banding together, by combining their small individual power, those on the bottom rung are able to better take action to protect themselves and advance their moral rights over those who have the power to, if they so desire, turn many to poverty by the flourish of a pen or the click of a mouse.

The reasons for certain industries having unions or not having unions varies, and it may be completely different on a state-to-state basis in the United

States, never mind how it works in the rest of the world. For instance, New York State has a robust (if, again, imperfect) teachers union, whereas unionization has only just now started to really come to Virginia public school districts, where I work. (This is thanks to the state legislature removing the ban on collective bargaining in 2020, which has already notably benefitted teachers in the state.[18]) However, according to *Education Week*, 37 states ban strikes by public workers,[19] which includes teachers; although this is not the same as a prohibition on collective bargaining, it does somewhat defang unions in those states by taking away a key action available to make those in power listen and respond to their concerns.

"But Ryan," I hear some naysayers bemoan, "unions seem great and all, and sometimes they are, but they allow members to skirt accountability and get paid more for doing the same work; people can be lazy and not get fired!" (Maybe the argument would be more complex than this, but I'm trying to simplify, not to create a strawman but to synthesize potential complaints.) When it comes to teaching in particular, due to the shortage of and therefore demand for teachers, it's hard to get fired anyway. On top of that, many — if not most — teachers enter the profession because they care about their job and want to make a difference in students' lives and, through that, the community as a whole.

As I've made clear before, in this context I can really only speak to teaching and not to other professions' experiences, but my response to most complaints regarding unions is this: the pros outweigh the cons (pun not intended but welcomed after the fact). Better that workers have mechanisms of power to agitate for and receive livable wages and working conditions rather than punish all workers because of the bad actions of a very small portion of them.

———

You don't have to love your job. For many, if not most, a job is simply the means to get money for groceries, rent, and some luxuries. There's no shame in that, and I hope I didn't even indirectly imply that by what I've written here.

But *every* worker deserves dignity, respect, and a fair wage, no matter their profession.

Actually, the only exception I'd seriously consider would be politicians, but that's more so because we live in a system where their job is usually on the line only one day during their term and thus, politicians form an elected oligarchy (see "Why 'Democracy' Has Always Been a Misnomer"); on every day but Election Day, they are more like bosses of the people than employees of them.

So, if the increasing workplace demands due to technology are what finally drive you over, or if you've been a fan of putting more power (economic and otherwise) back into the hands of the people, *agitate* for it. Change comes not when the people have power, but when they exercise the power they have.

And for the cynically-minded out there, I do have one last thing to say: teachers who aren't overworked are more likely to help their students, and thus their communities, achieve higher. Just as in other fields, treating workers fairly has benefits beyond just the workers.

Memes and Political Cartoons

June 11, 2025

At the high school where I used to work, there was (and may still be) an end-of-quarter assignment that we English teachers gave students: make a public service announcement (PSA) about an issue. Usually, there was a list of pre-approved topics for students to choose from, or students could come up with their own issue to address with their PSA. Also usually, for the pre-approved topics, either the class had done reading on them beforehand or students were expected to read pre-selected articles before they made the PSA on one of those issues; if doing their own issue, they were expected to do their own research.

In order to prepare my students for this assignment, I created a Google Slides presentation walking them through how — using just their school-issued laptop and the software (I believed was) available to them through that laptop and their school Google account — they could create an editorial cartoon (also called a "political cartoon"). Students were then expected to use that process, or other means, to create their own cartoon addressing an issue. No, it wasn't the same thing as a PSA, but an editorial cartoon was a step in that direction: political cartoons' quick, clear messaging allowed for a great example of how a message can be expressed visually, which is the skill students would be expected to demonstrate in making their PSAs.

To make my example, I struck a pose intentionally reminiscent of the Uncle

Sam "I Want You" posters and then I used Canva to remove the background and create a cartoony effect on my pose. In order to sell the whole patriotic theme, I added an American flag as the new background and voila, I had my template.

The real question was: what message would I convey with the image?

I knew I was going to put all these instructions and examples into a Google Slides presentation so that students could follow the process step-by-step, but that also meant that I needed a message for the cartoon to convey. I decided to have it be a simple one that fit completely with the design, and delivered the message using a speech balloon because (1) I have a huge fondness for speech balloons, but (2) trying to fit the message underneath in quotes just wouldn't work, because... well, I already had spaced out the cartoon for the size of a Google Slide, so I couldn't suddenly fit a text box underneath without cutting into the design. Thus, with a red-colored speech balloon and white Trebuchet text, I had my cartoon version say: **PATRIOTISM IS A VIRTUE!** (The all-caps was meant to be reminiscent of classic speech-balloon text, which is tradition-ally in all caps, not to indicate screaming. Perhaps there is something appro-priate, though, about having it be in all caps aside from — or, depending on how you look at it, *because of* — tradition.)

However, I wasn't completely satisfied; after all, most political cartoons do have that messaging separate from the cartoon, even if they incorporate some dialogue. So, I made a second version from the template, still not exactly like, but closer to, how an actual editorial cartoon might operate. Instead of using the speech balloon, I created a white box, put it off to the top-right of the image, and wrote, in black Impact font, a completely different message: **When your entire personality is just "MURICA!"**

I left both versions in the slideshow as examples, but when showing the second version to my students, I admitted that I'd basically just made a meme. (When making it, I was aware that using the Impact fond would make the im-age meme-like; my intent was to make an example for the Internet age.) But as

I thought it over more, I realized that this was kind of an apt way of thinking about editorial cartoons through a modern lens: certain memes could be seen as a type of modern political cartoon, and, conversely, political cartoons could be seen as a precursor to a certain type of meme.

———

According to the *American Heritage® Dictionary of the English Language*, the original meaning of the term *meme* is "A unit of cultural information, such as a cultural practice or idea, that is transmitted verbally or by repeated action from one mind to another." The term was coined by evolutionary biologist Richard Dawkins in his 1976 book *The Selfish Gene* as a unit for cultural-informational transmission in the same way as a gene is a unit of biological-informational transmission. However, the modern and currently more common usage of the term refers to usually humorous images, sounds, video clips, quotes, or even ideas that go viral online and are both spread and remixed by many users.

The kind of meme I had in mind when first making the comparison to political cartoons is the type known as the ***image macro***, which Wikipedia defines as "a piece of digital media featuring a picture, or artwork, with some form of text superimposed." One notable form would have a picture with humorous text above and/or below it in the Impact font. In keeping with the definition above, image macros only become memes when either the underlying image, the text, or both get remixed by other Internet users.

The sense of humor is definitely of the Internet era, but the combination of images and text is arguably as old as the written word. However, the first of what we call "cartoons" were satirical sketches printed in the British humor magazine *Punch* starting in the 1840s.

Lest you think that serious cartoons are a much more recent phenomenon, take a look at the editorial cartooning of Thomas Nast. Nast's pioneering work in the form of editorial cartoons employed visual shorthand and oftentimes underlying text to convey a complex political comment on the times, popularizing the donkey as a symbol for the Democratic Party, creating the elephant symbolism for the Republican Party, and using the Uncle Sam character, as well. Nast's work—while not always sensitive in some of his depictions by today's standards—appealed to all levels of literacy precisely because the work could be understood visually, with the writing playing a secondary, explanatory role. His broad societal reach is what earned him a lasting place in cartoon history.

Political cartoons are also "quick, in-the-moment commentary, whose artists have to educate themselves on complex issues and craft well-informed opinions in a single take," as the Association of American Editorial Cartoonists said in a statement.[20] (The statement was made in response to the announcement that the Pulitzer Prize for Editorial Cartooning was being renamed in 2022 as the Pulitzer Prize for Illustrated Reporting and Commentary. The change was to make room for comics-journalistic pieces, but those really do seem to crowd out the field in the category, whereas ideally editorial cartoons should also be present. I agree with those who think they should have their own category.) It is the editorial cartoon's immediacy—its ability to, at its height, deliver a gut punch and an intellectually riveting and/or hilarious take on an issue—that makes it so powerful.

That's also something it shares in common with memes. Memes just don't have a deadline.

Like cartoons, the primary function of the image-based meme may be for humor, but, especially since the 2016 election, they've come to intersect straight with politics. It has to be acknowledged that memes have become a weapon in the culture war used to spread racism, anti-Semitism, homophobia, sexism, etc. And this is also part of how they draw on the same tradition as the editorial cartoon: their message can be easily accessible to a wide audience. Thus, these memes can serve as an effective tool of recruitment and propaganda. (They can also act as a humor-filled smokescreen that can obscure hateful intentions.) Their users' opinions may not be morally legitimate, but they are spreading political takes to a mass audience the same way editorial cartoons have since

Thomas Nast. (In fact, perhaps Nast's less politically-correct cartoons really are his era's equivalent of this kind of meme.)

For an example of where right-wing memes and political cartoons are virtually indistinguishable, look no further than the work of cartoonist Ben Garrison. For just one example, Garrison's work openly celebrates the January 6th insurrection: a cartoon posted just one day after the event depicts it as a necessary confrontation of the Washington swamp monsters by true, patriotic Americans. (This cartoon also got him banned from both Twitter and Facebook at the time.) In a post accompanying that cartoon,[21] Garrison also asserts that:

- Kelly Loeffler lost the 2020 Senate election in Georgia due to rigged Dominion voting machines.
- Mike Pence, Mitch McConnell, and Mitt Romney are "traitors" (because they, you know, respected the Constitution and—for once in Mitch McConnell's life—told the truth).
- His home-state senator, Steve Daines, will no longer get his vote due to Daines being offended at the insurrection that threatened his life and the lives of his colleagues.
- The insurrection became violent because of left-wing plotting meant to make the right (Trump supporters in particular) look bad, including intentionally making the Capitol vulnerable to attack.
- Trump won the 2020 election in a landslide.

Unsurprisingly, he now treats Trump's return like the Second Coming. (I guess it technically is, in a way. Many Republicans were also certainly coming a second time after watching the 2024 results, just as they did in 2016.)

Garrison also skewers Hunter Biden, whom I would consider a fair target, considering that daddy's pardon let him off of accountability. However, considering 1,500 of Trump's surrogate children—the ones whom Garrison defends in his own work—got away with trying to violently overthrow the legitimately-elected federal government thanks to the same pardon power that gave Hunter a free pass, I'd say it's the equivalent of the Pacific Ocean being mad at a lake for being wet; I agree that it is, but you're so far away from the moral high ground here that you may as well be in Atlantis.

It all gives off the exact same vibes as (the repurposed) Pepe the Frog, the "Politically Incorrect" 4chan board, and the former "r/The_Donald" subreddit. Garrison's work evokes the meme culture around right-wing ideology, but also inspires it. According to a 2017 *Wired* article,[22] some "fans" of Garrison's work turned his images into anti-Semitic caricatures, which he at the time denounced, only furthering their drive to continue doing so. Meme culture, where remix is fair game, had taken Garrison's work to what was for him a new dimension. Eventually, as the very same *Wired* article indicates, he became part of the machine, openly spouting anti-trans, anti-gay, anti-feminist, and anti-Muslim sentiment in that same interview. (If you're a fan of his, those are probably all plus-marks.) And although I made the comparison of his work to Pepe the Frog *before* I read the profile, the article ends by making the exact same comparison.

So, you tell me: are memes really so different these days from political cartoons?

Why I Find It So Hard
to Live in the Present

June 12, 2025

I find that I have a hard time relaxing. The obvious explanation is the general sense of doom and gloom — fed by the news and the current events it reports on — that I feel about the world on a daily basis; that's something I know that is far from unique. That's part of it, no doubt; I mean, it's one of the reasons I've decided not to have biological children of my own.

I remember when 2021 came around, and it felt like things were normal once again in the United States. I believed we had expelled a tyrannical federal government and had staved off an attempt, led by the outgoing commander-in-chief, to overthrow a legitimately-elected successor government. Logically, I understood that my country and the world were still experiencing plenty of problems (the pandemic and the withdrawal from Afghanistan being the first two examples to come to mind), but for around nine months, things overall felt okay. In fact, it felt like the closest to normalcy we as a country had seen since 2016.

Then, my anxiety returned starting near the end of 2021 and increased significantly in 2022. Perhaps it started with the Texas Heartbeat Act and the judicial response to it, which indicated we were about to lose basic reproductive rights in this country. Then, my purple state of Virginia elected a Republican governor, lieutenant governor (they are elected separately, so can be from the opposite party of the governor), and attorney general, which hadn't happened since the 2009 election; this result also meant Virginia had fallen under the MAGA spell. (Virginia had previously voted for the Democratic presidential nominee every cycle since 2008.) Then, in February 2022, Russia invaded Ukraine, reintroducing the threat of nuclear war while the world was (and still is) imperiled by the climate crisis. Then, of course, more calamities, real and potential, came down the pipeline. The world we knew, that I thought we'd managed to save, felt like it had slipped away. Now, in 2025, I already have nostalgia for 2021.

However, recently I realized that the explanation above is incomplete. The second component of my restlessness is how I react to my anxiety about the world: it makes me want to experience as much as possible as quickly as possible, to make every moment count. I'm not doing this because I want to follow some hippie advice for an alleviation of my anxiety, such as "live in the moment, it's all that's guaranteed, and you'll stress a lot less." No; to be crass, it's a kind of fear-of-missing-out on experiences. It's because I feel like if I don't maximize my time, I'll lose out on what life has to offer before my time comes, and some days, it feels like that time could be any day now.

This emphasis not just on momentary living but on maximizing those moments does at times help me focus on tasks and accomplish them, but it has an immense downside: it takes away the breathing room, the quiet moments, the contemplative—and sometimes even meditative—parts of life. We're meant to take in information and experiences, but we need the time to process them; without that, we only experience life on a shallow level while simultaneously keeping ourselves in an excited, active state all the time. I switch very quickly between tasks on a daily basis, just to ensure that I don't miss out on opportunities, on ideas (like those for essays), or even on social connections. For example, I was in the middle of reading an essay from Evan Puschak's *Escape into*

Meaning, and receiving text messages at the same time, when I opened the Medium app to type the notes for this very essay so that I wouldn't forget the ideas that were flowing through my mind. (Come to think of it, I've done that a couple times recently; maybe *Escape into Meaning* is just a really good book for inspiration. It's definitely a good book, at least.)

Speaking of texting: most of us are always on call thanks to our smartphones, but because that's how to reach everyone else, and everyone else is in the same boat, we kind of collectively accept it; we even in a way force it upon ourselves while also having it forced upon us by social pressure. That's certainly not helping us to relax, either.

I still think, though, that anxieties about the state of the world, and the emotional responses we have to it, are the main reasons for our despair.

––––––––

Imagine that you are a person anxious about the future and convinced that the end is nigh, whether because nuclear war, environmental and social collapse, an AI takeover, or something else. Although you are convinced that there is no future, in this story you are given a glimpse of what life will be like 25-to-50 years from now. Let us imagine that what you see is not a wasteland, but a utopia; it turns out that all of your fears were for nothing.

Upon your return to the present, you tell of what you've seen to everyone you know, and it brings relief. The Doomsday Clock won't hit midnight, the climate won't get worse, nuclear war won't break out, etc. All is happy and good with the world.

But as time progresses, the future you saw, that you knew would come to pass, doesn't. Instead, the climate breakdown continues, more wars erupt, social and political instability increase. As you watch the world crumble in the way you once feared, you come to a realization: by learning about the positive future and thus having that guarantee that things would be okay, you and everyone else failed to take action on the problems, and this inaction caused the potential future to fall out of reach. Thus, it is a self-defeating prophecy, rather than a self-fulfilling one.

I think about this example when it comes to our present problems, and it reminds me that while the future is possible, it isn't guaranteed. We have to engage with these problems, force ourselves to fight for the better future that we want, and not simply hope that it will magically come to pass. Progress has never been achieved through passivity and acceptance; in fact, it's quite the opposite.

At the same time, we must each ensure we do not neglect ourselves physically and mentally in the course of this fight, because then we render ourselves ineffective activists. We also need to realize that we cannot each focus on every single issue and try to fix them all; instead, we should focus on one or two problems and do what is in our power to effect positive change around those issues. (We can also consider smaller actions to support a few other causes; maybe for one cause you will march in the streets, while for another you'll donate to an organization that can push for change in ways you can't.)

We also must focus on building genuine community with others, preferably away from screens. Without community, we are lost in sea of social emptiness, and we lose the human connection that makes us care about each other and the world at large.

It's not a cure-all, but it's a start.

"We the People" in 2025 America

June 14, 2025

In light of the recent protests in Los Angeles and other cities, as well as today's military parade and regal birthday, I wanted to briefly consider the idea of "We the People"—of the people's power—in (Project) 2025 America, where what's left of the federal government is currently in the process of ripping this country apart.

In "Politics as Theater and Ritual" (to which this essay is a semi-sequel), I said: "Without the support and consent of the people (or, at least, without the consent of a sufficient number of them), the law is meaningless, merely an ephemeral product of an ephemeral process."

Laws probably predate the written word, depending on how you define the term "law." Human societies, even small tribes (I'm using "tribe" in a very broad sense here), require some customs in order to maintain group cohesion, ensuring that threats to that cohesion—namely violations of group norms or threats toward other group members—can be resolved. Laws, then, are part of human nature.

On the other hand, as the Agricultural Revolution allowed tribes to settle in a single place and grow their numbers through more births and immigration, there was a need for a record-keeping system that didn't rely on human memory, which would include the ability to preserve group customs and pass

231

them down through generations and make them clear for anyone joining the group who did not have direct access to the makers of the law. Thus, writing was born.

However, the growth of large cities and empires, and the concomitant ability to dictate laws through writing (which meant leaders did not need to be present for their power to be exercised), meant that the power of the individual in those societies decreased substantially. Consider political power as being defined by the ratio of those in power to those outside of it—the bigger the ratio, the less power an outsider has within the system. So, the leadership class of a city has a much more disparate level of power compared to the average citizen than a tribal leader would have over other tribal members. A tribe has a mostly horizontal power structure, whereas complex, modern societies have a vertical power structure.

This is also one of the arguments for the "Great Man Theory of History," which essentially states that great leaders (who have, historically, overwhelmingly been men) are the defining force in a society. To use military power to exemplify this idea: the might of an army is what makes a siege possible, but it is the leader making the strategic calls who decides whether a siege succeeds. Take Napoleon, a strategic mastermind who, rare for modern political leaders, also led his troops in battle, just like Alexander the Great. On their own, without troops, these men would have accomplished nothing in the grand scheme of history, but it is their organization and use of their forces that merits them the credit and admiration of history. (So the theory goes, at least.)

The most obvious contrasting view of history is "history from below," which argues that larger forces, carried by the common people, are really what lead to historical events and changes; the leaders are more-so riding the wave of change than guiding it. This notion, in fact, is also supported by the political-power-ratio concept we introduced above: the bigger the disparity between the number of those in the leadership class and those outside of it, the more power the people have in aggregate compared to the leadership class, especially if they unite. Look to the French Revolution for a great example of this principle.

And this makes sense. What's the most effective surveillance society? It isn't our current, tech-obsessed nation-states. No, in fact, it's our old friend, the tribe. Everyone knows everyone else in a tribe, and thus people can slip through cracks much more easily in cities and empires than they can in tribes. However, the tribal surveillance was not a power imbalance, since all had the same power over each other, whereas now, the state has power over its citizens, and *that* is the actual main issue with modern-day surveillance societies. Again, the political-power-ratio question comes into play.

The huge benefit of tribes, which were the natural state of human affairs for at least 95% of our history, were that they were *communitarian*; laws and conflicts were dealt with hyper-locally, because that was the only way. What this meant, though, is that because everyone knew everyone, a sense of trust could form, one which could underpin that society and keep it cohesive. In the United States, at least, we used to have this sense with our local communities, as well. However, there are a few pressures which have torn at those communal fabrics:

1. The decline of local news has meant people are less informed about and connected to their local communities.
2. The advent of the Internet, especially social media, has allowed for people to build relationships with those far away. Normally, this wouldn't be in issue, but because this is now *in lieu of*, rather than alongside, the building of local connection, it adds to a sense of disconnection from one's physically-local community.
3. The nationalization of politics, where all focus is placed at the federal level, has exacerbated the sense that our communities — our tribes — are not those who live near us, but those who share our viewpoints; simultaneously, this turns those who don't share our viewpoints into our enemies, even if they are our neighbors.

I don't mean to make it sound like the United States (or any other country) was ever perfect, because you can pick any time in history and find people suffering, including in small, tribal communities. However, we are social creatures, and our societies function best when we are able to connect with one another.

It is our loss of this sense of community, our alienation from one another, that has allowed our politics to become divisive, with bad actors taking advantage of our disconnection to divide us even further and thus gain power for themselves by exploiting the political-power-ratio discrepancy. They win when we accept their power unquestioningly.

So, how do we revive and thrive? Well, we need to remember that ultimate political sovereignty in any location at any time comes from, and lies in, the people. It is not given, top-down, from the government. Therefore, if the people as an aggregate are against any government action, or stand to be harmed by government action, it is the government's duty to stand down. Any government which does not operate under this framework is by its very nature illegitimate, and it is the people's moral duty to alter or abolish it in favor of one which does follow it. We the people *still* have power, and always will. Tyrannical government will only exist if we do nothing. (Those involved in the Revolution — beyond just the Revolutionary War — were fighting for this exact reason.)

Government's sole justification for existence is to protect its people from harm. If in taking no action government allows harm to come to someone(s) who could have otherwise been protected, or (even worse) a government actively harms its citizens, that government has failed to justify its existence and has lost at least a part of its legitimacy. (Interpretation of this harm-prevention principle is up for debate, and is elastic in part on purpose; its main goal is to assert a claim against its opposite condition.)

Just remember this: it is up to the people to assert and defend their power.

On the Spectra: My Experience with Autism and Queer Identity

June 15, 2025

When I was seven years old, I was diagnosed with Asperger's syndrome, then a term for what is now classified as high-functioning autism. However, I would only find this out a full two years later, in third grade.

I was probably subconsciously aware that *something* was different about me compared to most of my peers, but I wasn't certain of it; after all, I could (mostly) function just fine in class, some distractibility and daydreaming aside. Some of that may have been due to my anti-epilepsy medication, Lamictal; when I temporarily went off of it during a 2007 hospital visit, my brain seemed to lift from a fog. My parents then kept me off that medication (we had a different anti-seizure medicine available at that point), and I went from being a somewhat-struggling student to a knowledge-loving, successful one in a few years.

After I was told of my diagnosis, though, I was intimately aware that I was different from my peers; in fact, I felt *damaged*, ashamed of my difference. It didn't help that during third and fourth grade, I would go to a separate classroom for part of the day, something my fellow students took notice of; they *knew* I was different. (Actually, it probably didn't help that in second grade, I had a seizure during class, which is definitely something they wouldn't forget, either.)

I would've continued to be pulled out of class in fifth grade, but by that point I had been out of my Lamictal-induced brain fog for a year, and I insisted, at only ten years old, that I remain in class the entire time. My parents were worried about the adjustment, but I was determined to take back a sense of control of my identity; I would be normal, damnit. My determination to succeed may have been built on insecurity and resentment, which is not something I'd ever recommend, but that chip on my shoulder was incentive to succeed; by the time I finished middle school, I'd developed a reputation as an exemplary student, something that continued into high school. In elementary school, I wasn't even sure if I would go to college; by the time I graduated high school, I was ranked 13th in my class of 327, and I had been accepted into the University of Virginia. I had made it.

It also helped that I had genuinely grown to enjoy learning and creating, starting with a love for storytelling that really took off in fourth grade, when I began writing stories for the first time. I would also read my dad's old college history textbook for fun sometimes; in an age before smartphones were universal and I had my own laptop, I barely knew what Wikipedia was, so this and other books were my best access to information. That love of learning certainly helped my success, as well.

I don't tell this story to brag; I tell it to set the stage for who I was when I had my first inklings, around 12 or 13, that I might not be straight. Because these experiences would weigh heavily on my journey toward self-acceptance in regard to my sexuality.

When I thought that I was possibly not straight, that I might in fact be gay, I was terrified. I wasn't afraid of going to Hell, since—despite my Catholic upbringing—my parents had always been accepting of gay people; in fact, one of my best friends in elementary school had two moms, and I never questioned whether that was normal, because my parents treated the situation the same way they would treat a straight couple. So, I was raised in anything but a homophobic home.

Still, I was raised in a society where, even if homosexuality was accepted, it was viewed as an aberration from the norm. Heterosexuality was the natural order of things, and gay people just couldn't help differing from that; it wasn't their fault that they were afflicted by differing desires. (I don't believe this now, but it was how I felt at the time.) As a teenager who was already acutely aware of his difference from neurotypicals, who—like all teenagers—was already struggling with his identity and sense of belonging, I couldn't be gay. It just wasn't possible. Well, even if it was *possible*, I wouldn't allow it.

Of course, there was also another complicating factor: I still had the occasional crush on a girl in middle and high school. As someone who was already a black-and-white thinker, combined with the fact that bisexuality was invisible in comparison to homosexuality, I thought: *No, I can't be gay; I like girls.*

It wasn't until college—when I had a completely fresh start in terms of a social atmosphere (since nobody around me had preconceived notions based on who I was in elementary, middle, or high school) and I met people of many different backgrounds—that I realized (1) that bisexuality was possible, and (2) I could be accepted (by certain people) for who I was without conforming to some stupid standard. Because of this, I was finally able to start coming out, beginning with my close friends in 2017.

———

I've come to learn that people on the autism spectrum are more likely to be non-heterosexual (including asexual and aromantic) and/or gender non-conforming compared to neurotypical people. To be honest, that surprised me at first because I know that people on the spectrum can be very black-and-white in their thinking; as I've indicated already, I definitely am. But it makes sense in a larger context: we are less likely to conform to social expectations that don't make logical sense. If we feel something, we might just be honest and say it, instead of conforming to rules of a social game that often don't make sense to us.

To use a personal example once more, I don't feel proud of being bisexual, nor do I feel proud of being autistic. Putting aside the issues I have with the emotion of "pride" (which can often have very negative consequences), neither my autism nor my sexuality are results of my actions; they're just part of who I am. That's how both of these should ideally be viewed, in my opinion. However, if "pride" is taken to mean "unashamed of being who I am," then I do take pride in both my neurodivergence and my sexuality.

Sometimes, my autism can even be an asset, something climate activist and fellow autistic individual Greta Thunberg has also observed. In my case, the hyperfixation mindset that comes with autism allows me to focus on certain tasks for extended periods of time, especially in the world of writing. None of these essays would exist without that ability to hyper-focus.

Other times, my autism can also give me a different lens through which to see the world. For example, while most people associate the Democratic Party with blue and the Republican Party with red, I associate the former with orange and the latter with green. Why? My best guess is that, when I learned the letters of the alphabet, I associated colors with each one, which is a form of synesthesia. "D" probably had an orange association, while "R" definitely had a green one, since my name begins with that letter and green has always been my favorite color; it isn't because I associate Republicans with money and greed.

Another example: how do you picture a calendar? If anything, it's probably either as a flip-book per month or as the kind of calendar on computers and smartphones. However, I picture a staple shape, with the staple facing right. The year starts at the top and moves left, then moves down the side, and finally goes toward the right; after December 31, it jumps back up to the top and the cycle begins all over again. Each month also has a color associated with it: January, June, and July are different shades of blue, February is red, March and May are green, April and August are purple, September is yellow, October is orange, November is yellowish-orange, and December is a dark green.

I can actually explain exactly where my calendrical associations come from: my first-grade classroom had a mat with this exact-same calendar layout, and I know that at least some of the monthly colors were the same on the mat as they are in my memory. Since that was an everyday object in my life, it became ingrained in my head as the canonical calendar, and I don't imagine that ever changing; it's been part of my life for 20 years at this point.

I've also recently learned that I have mild aphantasia, which is an inability to picture images in one's head. It's not total, because I can picture certain things (sometimes clearly), but my imaginings of humans, of specific details, are often *fuzzy*, like they're out of focus. This is why I often skip over character- and scene-descriptions in written stories that I read, and why my own prose storytelling is focused on describing character actions rather than appearances.

I do think my sexuality, a mix of bisexuality and asexuality (I've learned that I'm probably somewhat "demisexual") does give me a perspective on human sexuality that is far from common, although I would bet it's not unique. My autism may also have played a role in the development of my sexuality, as well.

––––––

On this Pride Month, I'm not "proud" of my autism or sexuality in the same way I'm proud of these essays, of the books I've written, or of the impact I've had on my students as an English teacher. However, I am proud to say that I am comfortable and confident in both of these elements of my identity, and despite all of the hatred and ignorance directed toward autistic individuals and queer people, I am not ashamed to be both.

How Rian Johnson Is Reviving
the Mystery Genre

June 16, 2025

While it's no secret that a rewatch of *The Last Jedi* soured my opinion on the movie, I am still a fan of Rian Johnson's work overall, and my admiration has actually grown, rather than decreased, since his *Star Wars* outing.

I first became aware of Johnson's work thanks to his announcement as director of what was then called *Star Wars Episode VIII*, but I'd previously encountered his directing thanks to *Breaking Bad*, most notably the episodes "Fly" and "Ozymandias." While Johnson wrote neither episode, his work in directing "Fly" demonstrates an ability to work outside the box, even with someone else's ideas; it was knowing this that first made me excited about him working on *Star Wars*.

As noted in "Who Is the True Creator of a Film?," it's difficult to assign "authorship" to a movie, especially big-budget ones with hundreds, or even thousands, of employees involved in some form of the creative process. However, whether we're using the lens of "Trident Theory" or its more general form, "Crater Theory," it's clear that Johnson is the main author of *The Last Jedi*, as he was both writer and director; at the very least, he had the largest voice in making the film, even if his voice wasn't the only one. So, if we're laying blame for that movie's faults, it should be at the feet of Rian Johnson.

However, that also means that when Johnson is able to write and direct a hit, we have to give him most of the credit. Starting with the success of his 2019 film *Knives Out* and continuing with its sequel, *Glass Onion*, plus the Peacock crime drama *Poker Face*, it's clear that Rian Johnson's love of mystery is helping to revive a once-dormant genre in the world of cinema and television.

(Don't worry; there are no spoilers for any stories discussed here. It takes a special kind of asshole to spoil the ending of a mystery story.)

The Benoit Blanc Series

When Johnson's *Knives Out* begins, it appears that Marta Cabrera (played by Ana de Armas) is the main character: we see events from her point of view, and we're meant to sympathize with her while looking down on the other murder suspects. When Daniel Craig's Cajun-like detective, Benoit Blanc, shows up, he is a blank to the audience (pun intended, maybe even on Johnson's part).

However, thanks to the success of the movie, it is Blanc who headlines subsequent entries in the franchise. Although *Glass Onion* is referred to as "A *Knives Out* Mystery," it really should be called "A Benoit Blanc Mystery"; the reason it wasn't is because of the branding that was established with the first movie, but in future it's possible that the series' star will be more heavily emphasized in the title material.

What was Johnson's inspiration?

Agatha Christie and the Classic Whodunit

It might surprise you to learn that Agatha Christie is the second best-selling lone writer in history, after William Shakespeare; they're both only outsold by the multi-author compendium that is the Christian Bible.

Edgar Allan Poe may have started the mystery genre with his three tales featuring C. Auguste Dupin; these also directly inspired the stories of the genre's most famous character, Arthur Conan Doyle's Sherlock Holmes.

(Other inspirations for the genre might be cited, but these two are the towering founders in cultural memory.) However, aside from four novels in the Holmes series, all canonical works featuring those two detectives are short stories.

While Wilkie Collins's *The Woman in White* and *The Moonstone* are novels which can be classified as mysteries, it was Agatha Christie who set the standard for the detective novel, starting with her 1920 debut *The Mysterious Affair at Styles*. In this book, she debuted her most famous character, Belgian sleuth Hercule Poirot, who moved to England as a refugee during the First World War. Her second-most-famous detective, Miss Marple, first appeared in a 1927 short story.

Christie's 66 detective novels—four more novels than there are Sherlock Holmes short stories and novels *combined*—defined the genre in the 20th century, and her sales domination speaks to her popularity. However, what really solidified her place in pop culture are the numerous adaptations of her works, especially on film. Most notably, there was *Murder on the Orient Express* (1974), *Death on the Nile* (1978), *The Mirror Crack'd* (1980), and *Evil Under the Sun* (1982). *The Mirror Crack'd* is a Marple adaptation, and the rest are based on Poirot novels.

It wasn't just these and other Agatha Christie films that influenced Johnson; there are other movie inspirations that he's cited. However, the classic whodunit owes its existence to Christie's standard, and thus she is the most prominent influence on Johnson, directly and indirectly.

Most obviously, Johnson's Benoit Blanc is a direct take on—but far from a ripoff of—Christie's Hercule Poirot, down to an eccentric, emphasized accent. At the climax of *Knives Out* (again, no spoilers… except saying that the mystery does get solved), Blanc assembles all of the characters into the same room, then reveals the solution. This is not a device invented by Poe or Conan Doyle; it is straight out of a Christie novel, all the way back to *The Mysterious Affair at Styles*.

On top of this, all of the films in the Blanc series—including the upcoming

Wake Up Dead Man — boast all-star casts, which is a trait of those classic Christie movies I listed above. The stars are as much of a draw as the story, and it's no different here; the emulation is intentional.

Poker Face

On its surface, *Poker Face* — the detective show Rian Johnson created for Peacock — is the complete opposite of the classic whodunit: whereas Johnson's movies walk us through a mystery and make the solution's revelation the climax of the story, *Poker Face* shows us the crime at the beginning of the episode; the drama then centers around how the show's lead character, human lie-detector Charlie Cale, will catch the criminal(s).

Credited as an executive producer and as the show's creator on all episodes, Johnson wrote episodes 1, 9, and 10, as well as directed episodes 1, 2, and 9, of the show's first season. Because of this, he can't be said to be the true author of the show as a whole in the same way he can be considered that for his Blanc movies, but his is still probably the most prominent voice in the show's development, and the show definitely wouldn't exist without him.

So, what are he and the rest of the creative team drawing from? Most prominently, the TV show *Columbo* (1968-1978; 1989-2003). Although it didn't invent the "inverted detective story" (also called a "howcatchem"), *Columbo* is probably the most well-known example of the genre, and it's the inspiration behind the structure of *Poker Face*.

The other noteworthy connection between *Columbo* and *Poker Face* is one that they both share with the Blanc series: an all-star cast. Whereas the Blanc mysteries feature an ensemble cast of notable stars in each installment, every episode of *Poker Face* features at least one notable guest star, often but not always the murderer, which is something else *Columbo* is known for.

Other Credit Where It's Due: Kenneth Branagh's Poirot

I'd be remiss if I acted like Rian Johnson is the sole example of someone drawing on classic mystery to revive the genre. The most notable other example is Kenneth Branagh's series of Hercule Poirot adaptations, the first film of which actually predates Johnson's work in the genre.

In 2017, Branagh released *Murder on the Orient Express*, wherein he also starred as Hercule Poirot, complete with a very campy but charming-in-its-own-way mustache. (Poirot, whose mustache is his most mentioned feature in the books, would either be delighted or horrified.) Branagh would reprise the role and the director's chair for both 2022's *Death on the Nile* and 2023's *A Haunting in Venice*. The movies also boasted star-studded casts which, like Johnson's movies, was a direct reference to the classic Christie films. In Branagh's case, the connection is more obvious because he is making modern Christie movies; his attempt to revive the mystery genre is to literally revive the classics, not just quote them.

Branagh's movies are adaptations of both the Christie books and the famous films; Johnson's work, on the other hand, is original. However, it is precisely in Branagh's deviations from the source material, in his original working of Poirot's stories, that his movies shine the brightest. We've seen better renditions of the actual stories of *Murder on the Orient Express* and *Death on the Nile*, but Poirot's unique test at the end of the former, and the new role of a returning cast member in the latter, are standout improvements. There is also a running storyline in the two movies regarding Poirot's backstory, which more explicitly explores his past in Belgium during the First World War—even if it clearly conflicts with what Christie set up in the books. Poirot is given more pathos than in the stories, where more often he is a vehicle for comedy and crime-solving than for complex characterization. That's okay, by the way; it isn't at all a knock on Christie's work, and her version of Poirot will always be the definitive one, and not just by its nature as the original.

Then there is *A Haunting in Venice*; to call it a loose adaptation of Christie's *Hallowe'en Party* is to be somewhat generous. Aside from shared character names, it is a completely original story that dips its toes into both psychological and supernatural horror. Even as someone who read the book specifically before the movie, I had no idea where the story would go. It's not often that I can say the third film in a trilogy is the best, but I can say that here with confidence. Branagh's first two outings have their moments, but more often they're just adaptations that allowed me to share my love of Christie with my mom, who has never read any of the Poirot books; *A Haunting in Venice* is genuinely unique, and it feels like a melding of Christie, Branagh (as both performer and director), and screenwriter Michael Green (who wrote the other two movies, as well). I can't think of a better way to bring new life to an old genre: a revival through a remix.

That's also, of course, what Johnson's work is—just in its own way.

In Defense of Public Bookcases

June 19, 2025

I'd been a fan of so-called "free little libraries" ever since I noticed them popping up in my area in the late 2010s. I always understood the concept not to be "take a book and bring it back," but instead "take a book if you'd like, or leave a book you wish to make available for others to take." I viewed it less as a community library and instead as a book exchange, where at its best my neighbors and I could cut out the middleman of a store and swap our books with one another. To me, this was the greatest appeal of the concept: bringing a neighborhood together, forming community connections.

My interest in the concept was supercharged, however, in summer 2022. At that time, a comics-focused YouTube channel, Cartoonist Kayfabe, introduced the "Comic Book Christmas in July" concept, where they encouraged their viewers to buy comic books and place them in public bookcases in their area, along with information about where to buy comics and learn more about them. The hope was simple: create more comics fans. (It also made sense that this would be a goal of the theirs, as both of the hosts—Jim Rugg and the now-deceased Ed Piskor—were comic-book creators themselves; new customers for the industry meant potential new customers for them.)

In doing this activity, I learned of several bookcases in my area, but I noticed as well that my neighborhood itself didn't have one. As someone who was (and remains) a huge fan of the idea, I decided that I would build one and place it outside of my house. My father and I built our custom book house over the course of a month or so (the work was intermittent, dependent on our work schedules), and finally installed it that October. We made it big enough to accommodate plenty of books, painted it the brightest red we could find (with some white accents) so that it would stand out even from a distance, and started the collection with some older books from our guest-room bookshelf. In the past 2 $1/2$ years, some of my biggest smiles have come from seeing people, especially families with younger children, stop by and either pick up or deposit books, because it means that something my dad and I made is having an impact, long-term at that.

That's also why, when I found out that there were critics of the concept, I was flabbergasted. Who could possibly have a problem with the idea of neighborhood book exchanges?

Well, according to the article "Against Little Free Libraries,"[23] the main critiques are that the concept represents a privatization of the public good that is a library, and oftentimes these book exchanges are placed not in areas which lack library access and are "book deserts" to begin with, but instead in wealthier neighborhoods with plenty of access to libraries and bookstores. It's worth reading the entire article if you can, because it goes into depth regarding the data the critics use and how they assessed the impact of these little libraries, along with some responses to their critiques.

The biggest point of agreement I have with the complaint is that these bookcases are often called "free little libraries" when, as one librarian says in the article, public libraries are also free. And I love my local libraries; I'm lucky enough to live in a county with ten of them, the most recent built in 2015. It would, no exaggeration, horrify me if my public bookcase were ever used as part of the excuse to defund my local libraries. Libraries are so important to disseminating knowledge, but they're also community spaces that bring people together; while I like that my neighbors use and visit my bookcase, I can't provide Wi-Fi, computer access, job-search help, restrooms, air-conditioning, or any of the other amazing resources that public libraries provide. Nor would I want to.

That's why don't I call what I built a "free little library." I call it a "book house," "book exchange," or "public bookcase" because its function, like I've said, is to facilitate the exchange of books between people, to de-commercialize and communalize that activity. The free exchange of privately-owned books is something that libraries do *not* do; they shouldn't be expected to, I should add, but that's precisely why these public bookcases — which are expressly *not* libraries, in my view — are so important.

I do also agree, however, with the critique that there is often a dearth of these exchanges in poorer areas. That is due precisely to the fact that these exchanges are a reflection of the communities in which they are built: they require resources to build and books to start their collections, both of which people who already have financial means can much more easily provide. There could be a push to have donors and volunteers respectively pay for and build exchanges in less-wealthy areas, but, as the article points out, that can also have its problems, especially in regards to the books which are then placed in the collection by the builders, as opposed to by the residents themselves. These exchanges' collections are meant to reflect their communities, and if even just the books which begin the set are reflective of a different community's values, then the bookcase is already failing its purpose. (This is partly what the article calls the colonialist elements of this process.)

Honestly, I don't have a simple solution for this problem. One possibility is to build them specifically around community spaces which every area would have; many of the schools in my area have a bookcase somewhere on their campus, and those get just as much traffic as the ones outside of homes, if not more. This way, students, parents, and teachers all have the ability to easily take or leave books when they visit for school-related purposes, and because teachers and students can come from such diverse backgrounds, the collection can come to reflect those disparate experiences. Yes, schools should also each have a library whose books also reflect their students' needs, but again, these book exchanges should be seen as a supplement to, rather than a replacement for, the resources that a library can provide to a community.

That's really the most important word here: *community*. That's why I loved the public bookcases I came across, and why I and so many others have built one. But that's also why libraries themselves are so important: because of how well they serve their areas, including by creating a space where communities can coalesce and form. Those of us who love the concept of the bookcase probably already love libraries, as well, but we should always emphasize the ways in which our work is augmenting the mission of the public library, rather than attempt—even unintentionally—to replace it.

How False Binaries Divide Us

June 20, 2025

With Juneteenth just passed and Pride Month still going strong, I've thought a lot about people who have been traditionally seen as outside of the mainstream, outside of acceptability, whether because of their race, their sexuality, their gender identity, or something else. Though thankfully there are exceptions, humans have historically not treated positively those who look and act differently from them. This in-group, out-group mentality underpins every type of intolerance.

But sometimes even people in minority groups fail to grasp nuances in identity, instead embracing the opposite side of the false binary that the intolerant majority have forced upon the world. One must be either gay or straight, White or Black (or White and non-White), male or female, etc.

I've spoken before about being both autistic and bisexual; the former has at times led me to thinking in a binary manner, a yes-no, but the latter has helped me realize that when it comes to elements of identity, things are a lot more complicated than I or many others would expect. I have actually spoken to gay men who think that I'm just a fellow gay man unwilling to call himself gay. I've encountered straight women who have lost interest in me once they've learned that I'm not straight, probably for the same reason. I think this prejudice goes back to the dichotomy of gay versus straight, and the accompanying argument in favor of gay rights: that people are born gay and thus are just being who they are. Bisexual men seem to demonstrate that there are some "gay" men who can "choose" to be straight, to act according to the "natural" way of things, and thus can be seen as a threat to gay rights. But we're not; we're neither straight nor gay, instead falling somewhere in between the two. (I can't forget to mention that there are also, of course, asexual individuals.)

I see this same argument playing out right now when it comes to the demonization of transgender individuals, and the insistence that there are only two sexes, male and female. To most people, this might seem like a logical conclusion to come to, since gender is baked into our society at such a core level, from gender roles to restrooms to clothing, etc. Even if we accept the response that gender is how one expresses themselves (for example, in how they dress and act) while sex is biological, we still haven't captured the fault in our definition of sex.

Okay, how might we define "male" and "female" biologically? The snarky answer is to say that males have penises and testicles, while women have vaginas and uteruses (among other differences). But what about intersex people? There are instances where people are born with both male and female genitalia, and even if only one of the two is functional, that still doesn't fall neatly into the male-female binary, since males traditionally only possess a penis and genitalia and women a vagina and uterus.

Could we instead go off of chromosomes, where a male is XY and a woman is XX? Well, then what about people born XXY, XXYY, XYY, XXXY, or even XXXYY? How would we classify those people neatly into being either male or female?

I recognize that the genital and genetic examples above are uncommon (though estimates place intersex individuals at about 1–2% of the population), but they demonstrate that the classifications we make—even the ones that seem dictated by nature—are not always as neat as we'd like them to be. No, a transgender woman isn't capable of giving birth or having a period, but neither are all cisgender women. We don't say "oh, you're infertile, therefore you're not a real woman" or "oh, you had to get your uterus removed due to cancer, you're not a real woman." Because those are intuitive to us, and the people in those situations still *look like* (and that's key here) women to outside observers.

And then there's race.

Now, I'm a pale White male individual, and aside from being mistaken as Jewish on occasion, I have never had someone assume I'm anything other than White. (I'm not saying Jewish people are *not* White, but depending on who you ask, the definition varies.) However, my paternal grandfather is Puerto Rican, with some Taíno, African, and European heritage all mixed together. Because my dad's mom is Italian, and my mom's family is Irish, I can pass for being completely White; to be fair, if I'm not allowed to put both "White" and "Hispanic" on forms, I will just put "White," since that's over 75% of my makeup, and because that's what I look like.

I was aware from a young age, though, that my father looked "different" from a lot of other dads. I grew up in a very-predominantly White area, and that meant that all of my friends' fathers looked… well, clearly White. My dad has an olive skin tone that, growing up at first, just seemed normal to me. But then one day, when my mom, dad, and I were at a store, I noticed a White family together, and then a Black family together, and then I looked at my parents. My mom was clearly White like that other family, but I couldn't categorize my father. So, I asked him: "Dad, are you Black?" Dad explained to me that no, he wasn't, and that he considered himself White.

Years later, I was reminded of that when I came across a 1940 census entry which classified my Puerto Rican grandfather and his parents and siblings as "Negro." Within that same month, I happened to watch the movie *Loving*, about the interracial couple whose court case, *Loving v. Virginia*, struck down interracial marriage bans in the United States. One of their children is the same age as my father, and so hearing the children called "abominations" hit home differently than it would have a year earlier. To consider the possibility that my father and his siblings would have been considered abominations had they been born in Virginia, the state where I was born 30 years after the *Loving* decision, was haunting. (I don't know if Virginia would have considered my Italian grandmother to be White, but they definitely wouldn't have considered my Puerto Rican grandfather to be, especially considering his classification on that census.)

The very existence of mixed-race individuals is a threat to the false narrative that White supremacists peddle, that nature made the races separate and intended to keep them that way. Mixed-race people are both the colonizer and the colonized in certain societies. They also go against the idea of cultural purity and of human separation based on race, culture, religion, etc. Not only are they living testaments to the potential of human unity, but they themselves are a new, hybrid cultural foundation.

In my grandfather's case, he has a mix of Taíno (native Puerto Rican), African, and European ancestry because some of his ancestors were Puerto Rico's original inhabitants, others were forcibly brought there from Africa as slaves, and his Spanish ancestors were part of the group that wiped out and enslaved the other two, respectively.

In the realm of religion, while Catholicism is the most common one in Latin America, it was also mixed with certain native traditions once it was foisted upon and then adopted by the oppressed in those nations. For example, Santa Muerte is not a saint recognized by the Catholic Church, and she originates from Aztec traditions of a death goddess, but she is as real to the Mexican Catholics who worship her as any other saint is, despite the Catholic and Evangelical churches condemning her worship.

Spanish is the language of most Latin American nations because Spanish was imposed by the colonizers, but it's now become an integral part of the culture in Latin America, and thus is the opposite of invalidated-due-to-colonialism. I lament the culture lost due to colonialism, but we have something new now, and we must work with the complicated beauty that it creates.

For an even better linguistic example, see Haitian Creole, a mixture of French and African languages that went from a pidgin (a simplified form of language) spoken in Haiti to a fully-fledged language of its own, now spoken by around 10–12 million people. While it is by far the most spoken creole language, the fact that there is an entire category of this type of hybrid language speaks to their widespread existence, and while creole tongues may carry the scars of colonialism, they also represent both a synthesis of cultures and the current lived reality for millions of people.

I bring the linguistic examples up because, initially, this essay was sparked by one word: "Latinx." There is a question of whether this word is or is not an instance of linguistic imperialism from the English-speaking world. One of the responses in defense of the word was that Spanish itself was a colonial artifact. While I agreed that this was true, I also felt that it failed to grasp the nuance, failed to see that the lines between dominant and dominated were not as clear now as they were when Spanish was first forced upon the natives and the slaves. I realized then that we become so focused on defining who is and is not a victim, on establishing this sharp divide, when there are people who, in terms of gender, sexuality, or race, do not neatly fit into the boxes prescribed by society. Because of that, to those in power especially, these people and their culture are seen as a threat.

Race, gender, and sexuality have their basis in reality (in terms of appearance and behavior), but they are just as much cultural constructs as they are real; it isn't their existence that matters as much as how we as humans act upon those concepts. However, I don't believe that just saying "racism is over," "gender is complicated," and "it's okay to be gay or bisexual" is the way forward, precisely because these concepts have had and continue to have real impacts on how humans are treated. My suggestion, instead, is that we learn to embrace these complications and work toward making these surface-level differences irrelevant to how people are treated by their societies.

A Complicated Picture of Stan Lee

July 31, 2025

My family owns a copy of a drawing, one that features a bunch of newspaper cartoon characters in a cartoon Independence Hall, as if they're there to sign the Constitution. The reason my family has a copy of this is because one of the signers, John Prentice, was my father's step-father, as I've mentioned in other essays. Most cartoonists signed roughly under their work, or at least one of their works if multiple appeared in the image. (Charles Schulz signed under Snoopy while Jim Davis signed under Garfield, for example. Prentice's signature appears under an image of Rip Kirby, a realistic character who looks a little out of place in this very cartoonish atmosphere.) However, there is one signature of a non-cartoonist that appears on the page: Stan Lee, who signed under Spider-Man.

Before I knew John Prentice had at one point worked with Jack Kirby, this was the closest connection I could make between him and the architects of the Marvel machine that would come to dominate the movies in the 2010s. Because of this, I used this image as part of an introduction to a class I was teaching on superhero films after 9/11; wasn't it cool that I had this indirect family connection to Marvel? Well, as it turns out, the professor who sponsored my class (since I was still a student) was a comic-book aficionado, and he told me after class that (1) Stan Lee didn't draw Spider-Man like that, and when he did draw the character, it was usually for conventions, and (2) it looked like the style of John Romita, Sr. Sure enough, there was a Spider-Man newspaper comic that ran from 1977 to 2019 called *The Amazing Spider-Man*, and between 1977 and 1981, it was drawn by John Romita, Sr. However, unless Romita, Sr. returned for this special occasion, it wouldn't have been his work, since this was made around 1987. It's possibly the work of Fred Kida, who drew the strip from 1981 to 1986, or by Stan Lee's younger brother, Larry Lieber (Lieber was Stan's birth name), who drew the strip from 1986 to 2018.

But it's only Stan Lee's signature on the page.

———

Stan Lee is a complicated figure in Marvel Comics history. As the face of the company from the 1960s to the 1980s, Lee was given most of the public credit for the many comics Marvel published that were hits with readers, from the Fantastic Four to Spider-Man to Hulk to the Avengers to the X-Men, etc. However, in more recent years it's emerged that Lee probably took more credit than he was due, and that the artists at Marvel sometimes did much of, or most of, the writing, with Stan only providing an idea or a plot synopsis to get them going, then coming in and polishing or adding dialogue, narration, and sound effects.

Personally, I don't believe Marvel would have succeeded without Lee's leadership, and I do think he was integral to the process of creating the comics, but it seems clear that the artists who did most of the day-to-day work never got the full credit they deserved. Jack Kirby is the quintessential example, but there are others, like Steve Ditko, co-creator of Spider-Man and fundamentally the sole creator of Doctor Strange.

Having admired Lee ever since I learned about him due to the cameos he made in so many Marvel movies, I at first believed he'd been an equal partner with his artists in helping build the Marvel comics universe into the grand tapestry that Marvel Studios would use to construct the Marvel Cinematic Universe starting with *Iron Man* in 2008. (Fittingly enough, though, just like Tony

Stark's first Iron Man suit, it was initially built with scraps. Marvel had sold off the movie rights to its most popular characters, but because no one had been interested in Iron Man enough to make a movie, Marvel had his movie rights when they began planning their unprecedented movie-series experiment.) However, as I learned more, I realized that Lee took more credit than he probably deserved, and from that point on I began admiring the artists he worked with more than I admired Lee himself.

It's why I'm conflicted when I look at the poster. I see a roster of incredible cartoonists, and am honored that a relative of mine is on there, even if we're just related by marriage. Then I see Stan Lee's signature; he's probably the most well-known signer by name, yet unless he drew the Spider-Man himself, I view his signature as a kind of stolen cartoon valor: if he didn't draw it, he doesn't deserve his name on the page with the rest of the artists. It feels like one more theft of the credit due to someone else.

Of course, there may also be an innocent explanation. Perhaps the drawings were made first, then the artists were asked to sign later, and the Spider-Man artist wasn't available to sign, so Stan signed instead.

However, Stan's past history of credit-taking is what gives this idea doubt. Maybe it's slightly better if it were his brother's artistic work, but still, the problem mostly remains.

This isn't the largest controversy in comics history or anything like that, but… it represents something. Some of the other signers made fortunes off of their work, while others (like John Prentice) were simply hired hands who never could receive the same payday as a strip creator like Charles Schulz or Jim Davis (the latter of whom allegedly owned a Garfield-themed private jet). However, none are as remembered now as Stan Lee is. Did he really have to step into the artists' territory and pretend he'd drawn something he hadn't?

Or am I just misinterpreting the intent and overthinking this whole thing?

Ancient and Modern Numerology

July 31, 2025 [*]

Throughout recorded human history, we have been obsessed with finding a connection between numbers and people. As soon as we were able to start writing down numbers instead of just doing math verbally, math became more complex, but we also began finding meaning in the numbers.

From the standpoint of "writing as magic," this actually makes perfect sense. Early writing systems would easily have been viewed as magical, since writing allowed the transmission of thoughts from one person to another without anything needing to be spoken, a complete departure from the tens of thousands of years of previous human experience. It's worth noting that Sequoyah, inventor of the Cherokee writing system, viewed European writing as "talking leaves," and that his fellow Cherokee were initially skeptical of his invention, perhaps viewing it as a kind of dark magic. Once they learned more, however, they would quickly embrace the writing system.

The practice of assigning mystical properties to numbers is called "numerology" (also known as "arithmancy"), while the specific form of fortune-telling based on a person's name is "onomancy," though this doesn't always involve numbers.

---

[*] Published after "A Complicated Picture of Stan Lee" on the same day.

I guarantee, however, that you've encountered at least one example of numerology: the number 666.

666 and Emperor Nero

The use of "666" as the "number of the beast" comes from the Book of Revelation, wherein writer John of Patmos says (from the World English Bible):

> *He who has understanding, let him calculate the number of the beast,*
> *for it is the number of a man. His number is six hundred sixty-six.*

What John is doing here is encoding a message to his followers using numbers. He cannot say directly that Nero is the beast; John was already exiled to Patmos due to Roman persecution of Christians, so inviting the direct wrath of Nero (or his imperial successors) was not in his best interest. So, he uses *gematria*, which is the practice of converting text into numbers.

In Hebrew, "Nero Caesar" is "NRON QSR" (in the Latin-alphabet equivalent) and each Hebrew letter converts to the following: 50 200 6 50 100 60 200, which sums to 666. Notably, "NRO QSR," which appears in other manuscripts, leads to the sum of **616**, which may have been the original number of the beast. The fact that both versions seem to point to Nero indicate that either he or a future Roman emperor, such as Domitian, is probably the beast referred to. ("Nero" could have been synecdoche for Roman emperors generally, which I note because it's possible that Nero was already dead when Revelation was written.)

A Modern System

One day in the recent past, I was working in Microsoft Excel and noticed that once you added more than 26 columns, they would be labeled "AA, AB, etc." and I wondered: how long would it take to get to three "digits" under that system? (In contrast, Microsoft Word's list feature goes from Z to AA to BB, which shortens the list of possibilities considerably.) In order to find out, you have to think about how our base-10 system works.

In base 10, 1,111 is simply $1 \times 10^3 + 1 \times 10^2 + 1 \times 10^1 + 1 \times 10^0$. In any number system written with modern Western numerals, "10" really just means the first number where you have to use a zero and reuse the 1 for the first time. In base 2, it's "2," base 3 it's "3" and so on. The difference with our base-26 system is that we don't have a zero, so when we hit 26 (Z) we don't go "A0" on 27 but "AA," the equivalent of skipping 10 and going straight to 11.

But the principle still applies. "ABC" is the same as $1 \times 26^2 + 2 \times 26^1 + 3 \times 26^0$, the last of which we can really just write as "3" since anything to the power of zero is just 1, and anything multiplied by 1 is itself. (Keeping the 26^0 simply aligns it with the system.) Our result: **731**.

You can also work backwards, going from numbers to the alphabet equivalent. Let's use the infamous 666 as an example.

First, we have to divide 666 by 26, which gives us about 25.6, but we really only care about two things: the number before the decimal, and whether or not there is a decimal. Since "25" is Y, we know that our number is Y-something. We also know that we're only dealing with two digits, since our result is lower than 26. (If it were more, we'd be dealing with three digits.) So, we take 25×26, which is 650, and subtract that from 666, which gives us a remainder of 16. As "P" is the 16th letter of the English alphabet, our number is "YP" in this new system.

Funny: *Yersinia pestis* (aka *Yp*) is the scientific name of the bacteria that causes plague. Was John of Patmos secretly predicting future plagues, like the Black Death?

Of course not. But it speaks to interesting coincidences you can find with numbers when you play with this system. The problem is, if you're already seeking patterns and are conspiratorially minded, this will probably only make that paranoia worse. (If it makes you rest more easily, 616 = WR, which I can't connect with anything related to the plague. Maybe someone else could, though.)

You can also take your initials and find a unique number. The nice thing about this system compared to, say, where you would add $1 + 2 + 3$ if a person's initials were ABC, is that order matters. Someone with the initials CBA would have a completely different number in this system, whereas in the other one they and ABC would both be equal to 6. Only those who shared all of your initials would share the same number if we did it the new way. (You could do this for your full name, as well, but you're going to get a **MASSIVE** number. That's how exponential growth works.)

On the other hand, if you start with a number and want to know the letters that correspond to it, but it goes beyond two digits, the system I showed you before still works. Let's try it with a larger number: 2,025 (our current year).

$2,025 / 26 = 77.885$, which is higher than 26, so we need to divide it again. Since we only care about what's before the decimal, we can simply go $77 / 26 = 2.962$. This indicates that our first letter is *B*, since that's the 2nd letter of the alphabet. Since $2 \times 26^3 = 35,152$, we know we're not in the 4-letter terrain, so we need to do $2 \times 26^2 = 1,352$. $2,025 - 1,352 = 673$, which we then have to divide by 26 again: $673 / 26 = 25.885$. Our second letter is *Y*. $25 \times 26 = 650$, so $673 - 650 = 23$, which gives us our final letter, *W*. Therefore, the initials which correspond to the year 2025 are BYW. I wonder if Brigham Young University did anything special last year; it would be a funny coincidence if so.

A potential error may arise and see you get too low too quickly. For example, $10,282,000 = $ VLZAN. Had I tried to find the letters the normal way, I'd have gotten 22×26^4, then 13×26^3, but then I would have already reached 37, which is much lower than even 1×26^2, which indicates a problem. Instead, we have to do 12×26^3, which solves the problem and allows us to obtain the full answer. The issue arises when a Z is involved, because $Z \times 26^n$ gives you 26^{n+1}, which is what confuses the math. So, if this arises, just go one lower letter on the step when you encounter this problem, and know that the last letter of the alphabet is to blame.

———

I'll leave you, then, with a puzzle to solve, in the tradition of John of Patmos, but using this system instead of the Hebrew one:

We fear the coming of 1984, as foretold by Orwell in 1948. But 1984 has already come, and it has come a second time. Take the millennium from 1984, but then take it past our new millennium, and you shall see what Orwell feared.

An Example of the
Beauty in Mathematics

Unless we're incredibly familiar with math's use in art, we tend not to think of math as being capable of producing beauty. However, in deeply exploring a seemingly simple mathematical observation over the course of six years, I came to see first-hand just how beautiful and elegant math could be.

———

In my senior year of high school (the same year of my discovery that I really enjoyed calculus), I had a seemingly-innocuous realization: the area and perimeter of a square are always treated separately, but since they're both in terms of the measurement of the side, s, you could eliminate that variable and just relate them to each other. The relation is as follows:

$$A_{square} = \frac{p^2}{16}$$

where p is the perimeter.

Little did I know where this would take me. But, for the time being, it remained in the back of my head, something that fascinated me because it *felt* like I had made a unique discovery, even though logically someone must have figured this out long before me.

You couldn't make this relation with a rectangle, because you would be dealing with two independent variables: the length and the width. However, rectangles are also integral to the next step of the discoveries I made going off of this perimeter-area relationship.

In my first year of college, when playing around with numbers in regards to areas of rectangles and squares, I made two realizations: (1) the maximum area one could cover with a given perimeter, p, if only allowed to make a rectangular shape, would be by using a square. (2) As one changed length and width in separate directions, the difference between each new area and the area of the perfect square would drop off each whole-number iteration (2.1) by every odd number between each iteration, and (2.2) by the square of the difference between ideal side length, s, and one of the sides of the new rectangle, l and w. Thus:

$$A_R = A_{square} - (\frac{l-w}{2})^2$$

where A_R is the area of the rectangle. Because the difference between length and width would be *twice* the difference between one of those variables and the side measurement of a perfect square, you have to divide that difference by 2, hence the denominator.

Restating variables, one would get:

$$\frac{l-w}{2} = \sqrt{A_{square} - A_R}$$

Because we have an easy way to shift between perimeter (which remains unchanged) and a square's area, we can easily determine what A_{square} is. As we already have A_R, we can easily determine what this will be.

For the sake of ease of display, let this be the case:

$$\frac{l-w}{2} = Q = \sqrt{A_{square} - A_R}$$

Because length and width must be additive or subtractive of Q (depending on which is the bigger number), we can thus make our final calculations. Let us set l to be the bigger number. Hence:

$$l = \sqrt{A_{square}} + Q \text{ and } w = \sqrt{A_{square}} - Q$$

because the square root of A_{square} gives us the side measurement of the perfect square. (The above equation is also a "difference of squares," because the product of l and w will be $A_{square} - Q^2$.) But we know that the square root of A_{square} is equivalent to $\frac{p}{4}$, so we can thus say:

$$l = \frac{p}{4} + \sqrt{A_{square} - A_R} \text{ and } w = \frac{p}{4} - \sqrt{A_{square} - A_R}$$

And that is where it remained for many years. It became a party trick, where people could pick two numbers, give me them multiplied together (the area) and twice their sum (the perimeter), and I could work backward using this relationship to figure out which numbers they had originally chosen, even if they were decimal.

But then, on July 17, 2022, I grew curious: at what point does area equal the perimeter? I knew there would have to be a point where that was the case because if one takes a side length and maximizes it by placing all of the perimeter in that direction, then the other side goes to 0, and therefore the area is 0. Since maximum area is always greater than perimeter when side measurements are greater than 1 (and maximum area is always *less* than perimeter when side lengths are less than 1), then there must be a point between the maximum area and 0 where the area and perimeter intersect.

How could we figure that point out? Well, let us consider the rectangular formulas:

$$A = l \times w \text{ and } p = 2l + 2w$$

We want to generalize a formula that can answer our question by just in-putting the numbers. So, we must rearrange one of the formulas. We will rearrange the perimeter identity, and solve for w:

$$w = \frac{p}{2} - l$$

Proceeding further, we then plug in the right-hand side into the area equation for w:

$$A = l \times \left(\frac{p}{2} - l\right)$$

Thanks to distribution, we obtain:

$$A = -(l^2) + \frac{p}{2}l$$

Because we want to solve for "zeroes" (i.e. when *area* and *perimeter* are equivalent), we can move A over, set the whole thing equal to 0, and multiply both sides by -1:

$$l^2 - \frac{p}{2}l + A = 0$$

We have to treat $\frac{p}{2}$ and A not as variables but as constants, since if we were manipulating them with specific numbers in mind that's what it would be. But we can use the quadratic equation:

$$x = \frac{-b \pm \sqrt{b^2 - 4ac}}{2a}$$

to solve for our zeroes. In this case, $a = 1$, $b = -\frac{p}{2}$, and, for the case we want to solve, $c = A = p$, so:

$$l \,\&\, w = \frac{\frac{1}{2}p \pm \sqrt{(-\frac{1}{2}p)^2 - 4p}}{2}$$

Plug in your perimeter, and your two answers will give you the length and width at which point the area and the perimeter are exactly the same.

But then, on the morning of July 18, 2022, I realized that this could be generalized, and in doing so could provide a more elegant-looking solution for what I had been trying to do years before. After all, this is only a special case where *area* equals *perimeter*. A more general case would just be:

$$l \,\&\, w = \frac{\frac{1}{2}p \pm \sqrt{(-\frac{1}{2}p)^2 - 4A}}{2}$$

because $c = A$, but A does not equal p.

This would give us the lengths and widths of all possible versions. But we can rearrange what's under the square-root sign:

$$\left(-\frac{1}{2}p\right)^2 - 4A = \frac{p^2}{4} - 4A$$

267

and then rearrange a little bit more:

$$\frac{p^2}{4} - 4A = \frac{p^2 - 16A}{4}$$

This then gives us:

$$l \,\&\, w = \frac{\frac{1}{2}p \pm \sqrt{\frac{p^2 - 16A}{4}}}{2}$$

Remove the $1/4$ out of the square root by realizing its square root is $1/2$, and now you have:

$$l \,\&\, w = \frac{\frac{1}{2}p \pm \frac{1}{2}\sqrt{p^2 - 16A}}{2}$$

Factor out the $1/2$ from both:

$$l \,\&\, w = \frac{1}{2}\left(\frac{p \pm \sqrt{p^2 - 16A}}{2}\right)$$

Then we multiply the $1/2$ across the bottom of what's inside the parentheses, turning our denominator into 4. This gives us the final equation:

$$l \,\&\, w = \frac{p \pm \sqrt{p^2 - 16A}}{4}$$

It's astounding, because it relates geometry and algebra in such a concise way that is in and of itself quite beautiful. Geometry, in the case of length-and-width relationships, is a concrete case of something that algebra abstracts with variables, that being the relationship between two numbers in two specific ways. Those ways, in geometric terms, are area and perimeter.

Realize also that, when you're dealing with a square, $p^2 = 16A$, making that portion go to zero and having length & width (in that case the same value) be equal to $\frac{p}{4}$, which is the same as saying the measurement of one side, s. Otherwise, the difference between the perimeter's square and 16 times the area of the rectangle will give you how much you need to add or subtract from the ideal side measurement to find length and width.

It's the exact same work performed by the original equations, with the simple difference between how the variables under the radical are phrased. *That's it!* Somehow I independently (though again, almost certainly not uniquely) stumbled upon an astounding geometry-and-algebra relationship without realizing it for more than half-a-decade.

————

The following is a very famous math expression:

$$e^{i\pi} + 1 = 0$$

This is considered the most beautiful formula in mathematics, and an example of mathematical elegance, because it combines five of the most fundamental numbers into one relation: Euler's constant, e (≈ 2.72), the imaginary unit (the square root of -1), pi (≈ 3.14), 1, and 0. You don't have to be familiar with math beyond that to appreciate the beauty of the equation (I know almost nothing about how or why it works).

While I don't think my discovery is as elegant as the relation of five fundamental mathematical constants in one equation, I do find it beautiful in its own way, and I submit it as another example of math's ability to aesthetically and intellectually astound.

The Family Man (2000) and Forgotten Memories

Being born in the late 1990s, I grew up in a time when social media was only on the horizon, yet my childhood was remarkably well-documented by my parents, between home videos and photographs. I know that I am far from the only person of my generation who can say this (although I may have an advantage over many, since being an only child meant I had all the focus), but it is something that has only really been possible for a couple of generations.

Before photography, the capturing of visual memories could only happen in drawings, paintings, and other such media; this meant that only the most important events in the lives of wealthy or powerful people—such as weddings and family portraits—would be commemorated. Memories outside of this could be documented in writing, sure, but when, say, a child were reading about their early years, the ones for which they have no memories, they would essentially be creating memories using their imagination. Their imaginings would be based in reality, but would look completely different from how it happened.

To use another example from my own life: when my father told me about how his second-grade teacher asked him to be in a performance of *Oliver!*, I pictured my elementary-school hallway and classroom as the location where he was asked to do this. I didn't picture his school; how could I, considering

I'd never seen it? And while I didn't picture my own teachers in place of his, I know I wasn't picturing what she actually looked like, because I'd never seen a picture of her before.

It's only with especially realistic pictures, like photographs, that we can look upon our old, forgotten selves as if that younger version were in front of us. Somehow, these lines on a photograph or pixels on a screen are able to act as portals to an otherwise-lost world. They can't capture exactly what it was like to live then, but they can capture those moments, those faces, those expressions.

This is even more true, of course, with home videos. They may have been fodder for TV shows (see *America's Funniest Home Videos*), but they also let us see and hear ourselves as children. It's so common today, with digital video cameras and then smartphones, for us to record our lives, that we forget how revolutionary it is.

Nothing has ever quite captured this feeling, however, better than the 2000 Christmas-adjacent movie *The Family Man,* starring Nicolas Cage and Téa Leoni. The film sees Cage's character, a billionaire Wall Street businessman, wake up on Christmas morning in the suburbs of New Jersey, and comes to learn that this is a vision of a life he would have led had he stayed with his then-girlfriend instead of going to London to pursue business, a decision which caused the end of their relationship.

What could easily be a bland knockoff/reimagining of *A Christmas Carol* is instead one of the most moving holiday films I've ever watched. (I called it "Christmas-adjacent" because Cage stays in this alternate reality well past Christmas, and thus the holiday is not the focus, except in a vague thematic sense.) There is one scene in particular, however, which stands out as both a great display of Cage's acting ability and a central moment in terms of the film's theme. Cage's character, Jack, watches a home video recorded in this alternate reality, one which depicts a past birthday celebration for his wife; at the party, a past, alternate version of him sings a schmaltzy, off-key song to his

271

wife, in front of a crowd, about how much he loves her. At first, the modern-day Jack has an embarrassed snideness about him as he realizes his alternate, younger self is about to start singing. "Oh no," he mumbles, as he holds a drink in his hand. "*Oh*," he bemoans as his video-self begins to sing. But as the video plays on, he goes silent; the movie switches back and forth between the video and Jack's reaction to it, as he begins to tear up. In that moment, he views a memory that he never lived, and he realizes the kind of life that he could've lived had he chosen that same love over his business career 13 years before.

I get that same way when looking over old pictures in family photo albums and old home videos on tape. Some of the memories I lived and forgot (no way would I remember going to the beach at only a few months old, for example), while others are from times before I was born. But I'm just like Jack, either way: I see a happy past that no longer exists, and of which I have no memory. The baby in those pictures truly is a different person, and the man and woman in their late twenties to late thirties are strangers to me, even though they're my parents.

I don't think these older times were perfect, by any stretch of the imagination, but I mourn them nonetheless because the people in those memories no longer exist. I will never have the chance to meet my parents when they first met, when they shared vinyl records with one another, when they made home-made gifts for each other (like my mom printing out old newspaper records of my dad's sports victories from microfilm and putting them together in a scrapbook). I love my parents, but I can't help but be sad to know that I will never meet those versions of them. I also wish I could go back to my childhood and see with my own eyes what I was like as a child, because I imagine I would have a better understanding of why I am the person I've become, for good and for bad.

I think that's why *The Family Man* hits me so hard emotionally. It's a movie about the life its main character, Jack, can never live, shown to him through a glimpse. Near the end of the movie, he is thrust back into reality, but it's not a surprise to him. His guardian angel appears to him, just as Jack is beginning to really enjoy this life with his wife and two kids, and tells him that this is all about to end. That night, he says goodnight to his two children, but almost as if they're about to die, or if he is; in a way, that's exactly what will happen, since these children don't exist in his reality. After that, he tries desperately to stay awake, knowing that sleep will bring him back to the real world, but ultimately, he does fall asleep, and when he wakes up, he's lost that life forever. The movie ends with he and his ex-girlfriend (his wife in the alternate reality) catching up, and it's implied that they might end up having a life together, after all. However, it won't be that life that he caught a glimpse of, with their two children, with his specific relationship with his in-laws, with his job as a tire salesman. That's what's tragic about it all: he has a second chance, but that second chance can never be the same as the first, and he can never get that first chance back.

Just like Jack, I can't go back in time and change the past. I can't force my younger self to impart the wisdom I have now, to tell him to appreciate what he has and to see things more positively. I can't go back in time and save my parents' marriage. I can't go back in time and keep some of that happiness alive — even though I've come to realize that things were never perfect.

But I can work with what I have in the present, and if there's any positive message that *The Family Man* has to impart, it's really that one. I can work with what I have and do the best that I can. I can appreciate the memories I have, and the ones I've forgotten or never formed but which were preserved anyway, while not letting them define me or my present state. I can try, to the best of my ability, to make my own happiness.

———

For a long time, I did have a very clear, early memory, and although it's mostly faded now, I can still vaguely see it. I'm probably about six months old, and my mom is putting me in my crib — I know this isn't a false memory because of how clear it was, and because I correctly remembered the side of my room where the crib was. I don't know why this memory was preserved, among so many possibilities, or why it lasted so long. I'd like to believe it was because I was comforted by my mom's presence, that I felt so content that even a decade later I could recall that moment like it happened yesterday. Even though Mom was the working parent and Dad the stay-at-home one (which itself, having a stay-at-home parent, is a luxury far from universal), she made sure that we had the nights and weekends together. We'd get up early on Saturday to watch *PBS Kids*, she'd read to me at night, she'd be the silly mom at times, and she'd help arrange playdates, among other things.

Even though their relationship with each other was complicated when I was growing up, I was blessed to have both a mom and a dad who raised me well, looked out for me, and who would do anything to both protect me and help me thrive. Looking back at those memories brings a mixture of sadness and happiness, but I'm glad that I have the ability to look back on those times thanks to the photos and videos that my loving parents started taking before — but which picked up a lot after — they had me.

Incentive Structures Rule the World

In teaching, one lesson you have to learn on the job is how to get students to work with you, especially once they reach their teenage years. When there are 20–30 of them and only one of you, there's no way to keep total control over every student every second of a class period, so it's critical to incentivize cooperation with you and with their peers. In thinking about this on a daily basis, I came to a realization that incentive structures don't just apply to the classroom: they're everywhere! Seriously, you can analyze all situations involving human behavior — and even some *not* involving human behavior — through the lens of incentive and disincentive structures.

Most of the obvious incentive structures today center around money. Take, as one example, clickbait, which is a headline and/or a picture designed to tempt a viewer to click on it, whence the "bait." Now, I avoid clickbait and rage bait (similar, but designed simply to upset, because that also prompts engagement) as much as I can. Being upset, negative, cynical, etc. isn't keeping me more informed or leading me to make positive changes; it's just making me upset, negative, lethargic, depressed, etc. But the proliferation of that negative content, especially rage bait, reflects an incentive structure that rewards that kind of content because it gets more views and thus more ad dollars for the hosting site. The people creating this sensationalistic content could be genuine nutcases who happen to attract attention and the site's promotion of them increases their influence and access to resources, or they've gamed the algorithm and have tailored their behavior to maximize engagement. Either way, an incentive structure has dictated and/or reinforced their actions. As many have observed, it's a modern version of tabloid journalism, which itself was a descendant of yellow journalism—the difference now is that websites, unlike newspapers, have access to so much more specific information about their viewers that they can tailor their content even more toward whatever gets the most engagement, and they can do so a lot quicker than a medium reliant on print.

I'll admit it: even I have engaged in clickbait-y titles and taken some unorthodox stances in order to attract attention. When I worked for the entertainment website Screen Rant as a "list writer" (my content focused around articles like "10 Things You Didn't Know About [the newest superhero movie]"), I would pitch ideas based on what had been successful in the past. While I can't reveal the exact incentive structure, I can say that articles which got above a certain amount of engagement earned a small bonus, which didn't hurt. However, I still would have pursued those higher numbers even without the bonus, because I was proud to have more people viewing something I wrote. There was a non-monetary reward to it, as well, which is something we cannot discount when thinking about how incentive structures affect our lives.

But that's just one example. How about another, this one in politics?

The 2010 Supreme Court decision of *Citizens United v. Federal Election Commission* is bad, but people tend to think it's bad because it lets rich people buy elections or gives them an outside voice. This may be true, but it isn't the only way that this decision allows for money to corrupt the process. Once again, we must turn to the lens of incentive structures, and consider a scenario which can demonstrate the point.

Say we have ten candidates in a field. No candidate knows what the donors want. Each candidate takes their stand, and presents their case to the public, where the donors (big and small) are watching. The one who best addresses the desires of the donors will take in the most money, right? In evolutionary terms, they're given the resources to "reproduce" (i.e. stay politically viable). The increased attention placed on said candidate would also likely increase their political lifespan.

If the candidate is elected, their actions may very well seem to reflect their donors' wishes, but that could just as easily be because their genuine views were the ones most in alignment with the wealthiest and/or most giving donors, and that alignment provided them with the resources to stay viable. There is no corruption in the traditional sense in this scenario (assuming the candidate was genuine in their beliefs from the beginning, and did not change their stances in order to get more support), but money has still influenced the outcome of election and of policy, because the resource-givers had an outsized influence on a process that is meant to reflect the people's voices equally.

Of course, if a candidate switches positions because they recognize a stance's popularity with the donors, that is a dishonest move; without a tit-for-tat that both the candidate and the donor have agreed to, it isn't corruption, but again is still reflective of money's influence. People have correctly identified the problem, but I don't think they often consider the different ways that this problem could present itself; if we view this through the lens of incentive structures, we realize that our problem is more than just one involving legalized bribery. (It could also help the push for some public funding of elections, but that's a scenario worth exploring in a different essay.)

Under this view of incentive structures, we can even go a bit more radical and argue that democracy and capitalism are incompatible because their requirements and incentive structures act at cross-purposes. Functional democracy, in the sense of people having a say in their government, requires a degree of selflessness, because the public is being asked to consider the well-being of the community; they might not always do this, but they should, ideally. On the

277

other hand, capitalism encourages selfishness, the accumulation of resources for oneself; any philanthropy is the choice of the individual wealth-hoarder. Yes, it's great that some billionaires are able to help fund needed causes, and no, I don't always have faith that the government would do a better job with that money than the billionaire would (just look at our current government, a den of thieves and despots), but that charity is at the billionaire's whims. Perhaps other wealth magnates will instead put their money toward causes that are anti-democratic, like conservative mega-donors Philip Anschutz, Sheldon Adelson, and the Koch brothers. These people may or may not have malicious intent, but they do (or did) have massive resources that have helped them dictate American policy through the causes to which their money goes (or went). Their incentive? Well, maximize profit; some Christian donors may also seek to force their faith onto the American public, but at the end of the day, it's about increasing their accumulation of wealth and power, as those two things reinforce each other. That is a feature, not a bug, of the capitalist system. Now, in an interconnected, globalized world where their money can do the most harm far away from where they live, or (like with climate change) will have the most devastating impact after they've died, they have no personal incentive to refrain from this destructive behavior. In fact, it's the opposite: they get to reap the rewards without dealing with any of the consequences. That is a poor incentive structure for maintaining a just, democratic society.

But this can also backfire. If enough people are disincentivized to support a system, then they may end up overthrowing the system and its managers, like when the French and Russian revolutions broke out. Regardless of how you feel about post-Revolution France or the Soviet Union, you can't deny that the rise of those societies was a direct result of the old orders failing to incentivize people to keep supporting them.

Finally, let's consider a personal example of how incentive structures can affect human behavior: diaries versus blogs. A diary is traditionally defined by its privacy, in that only the writer (and maybe a select few trusted individuals) will see its contents, whereas a blog is written for the express purpose of speaking to as wide of an audience as possible. One who keeps a blog would not, for instance, share confidential information on themselves or others in the same way they might do so with a diary. On top of this, if the blog were popular, then it might create income for its writer, and thus, the writer would be incentivized to maximize engagement, because whether they're supported by ads or by donors, blogs are only financially viable if they attract attention. Consider as well the example of family-vlogging channels (the video equivalent of a blog both figuratively and literally — the word "vlog" is a portmanteau of "video" and "blog"), where viewers are promised a sort of public home video series. However, vlogs can never be true home movies, because families could not share with the public all that they could share on private home movies; on top of this, the behavior of the family is driven by the engagement-maximization incentive, so the behavior is not "natural" in the way it would be if the content were filmed simply for at-home viewing and memory purposes.

While I didn't keep a blog in college, I did keep a diary, one that I updated almost daily. After my first semester of college, I happened to mention it to my parents, and then I realized that it might be fun to let them read the first-hand account of my college experience. Of course, there were plenty of elements I'd have to remove for the sake of keeping them to myself, but since it was just my parents, I wasn't worried about sharing private information the same way that I would if I were to post my diary publicly. So, I made a copy, scrubbed parts of it that I didn't want them to read, and then sent it to them. It turned into a semesterly thing during my second year of college, and then a monthly thing during my third year; it was almost like sending a newsletter to my parents.

The nice thing about my diary-sharing was that it allowed my parents to get a glimpse into my day-to-day life and thoughts in a way they'd never really been able to before, and I think it actually brought us closer. I even looked forward to the monthly ritual of making a copy of that month's diary, highlighting in pink the passages only Mom would read, highlighting in orange only the passages my Dad would read (those were their favorite colors), and high-lighting in green what I would remove from both versions. (Unhighlighted text was what they could both read.) Thanks to this system, however, I was able to still write for myself, since I knew I could remove anything I wanted to keep private from their version, but I'd also be incentivized to add more detail and explanation because I knew, right from the start, that I wasn't just writing for myself. This way, my record of my college years *after* I started sharing it with my parents was more complete than it was before, when I was just writing for myself as a fun distraction.

Taking our cue from the above examples regarding private versus public memory archives, we could reference Marshall McLuhan's famous phrase "the medium is the message" and say that "the incentive drives the message."

You can apply the incentive-structure lens to almost any element of human behavior and get something informative from that exercise. We've seen just a few examples of how it reveals some of the core behavioral motivations behind the actions we take, both as individuals and as larger groups. Perhaps this will help you have a new view on life and all of its complexities.

Post-Script

While not an "update," since this essay was never published, I did still want to make note of something I thought about after finishing this essay but which would not fit within anything that had already been written: games are more than just the perfect example of incentive structures. Games are incentive structures incarnate. As I said in *Narrative in Action*, "Games have rules and are situated within a frame of requirements … With games, it's as important what constraints are placed on the players as what they are allowed to do." Due to this, we can view games as our best example of incentive structures, or we can see incentive structures as creating game-like conditions on everyday life.

How We Could Reform the Electoral College Without Eliminating It

The United States Electoral College is charged with electing the President and Vice President of the United States for a four-year term beginning on January 20 of the year following the election. Although this has not always been the case, the winner of each state is given the total number of electoral votes based on the popular vote; all states are first-past-the-post, and all but Maine and Nebraska are winner-take-all in terms of the electoral votes. While this system made sense in the early history of the republic, it now acts as an undemocratic force which can override the votes of the majority or plurality of the American people. While this has led to calls for abolition from Democrats and activists, Republicans support the current system because it gives them an advantage in presidential elections, and would not be amenable to voting for a constitutional amendment abolishing the system. This paper proposes a reform which would make the Electoral College align more closely with the popular vote, would make nearly all states competitive for both parties (and even third party candidates), and yet would not change the outcome of any election from 2000 to 2020. These three elements provide benefits to both parties and, more importantly, to the American people as a whole, whose votes would immediately become more valuable in almost every state, and thus, power would flow back to the public for whom the elected work.

History of the Electoral College

When proposing a new Constitution to replace the Articles of Confederation, one of the many questions facing the delegates was how to elect the chief executive of the new government. Proposals from popular-vote to having Congress elect the candidate were considered, but ultimately, the system put in place assigned a number of votes to each state based on the number of senators and representatives a given state had in Congress. However, states were free to decide for themselves how to choose the electors in the first place. For several of the first presidential elections, a few states did not even hold a popular vote in their state; instead, the state legislature chose for whom the electors would vote.

When considering the structure of government at the time, however, this idea isn't surprising. While the House of Representatives has always been elected by the people, the Senate was initially elected by each state legislature choosing the senator. It wasn't until the 17th Amendment that senators would be directly elected by the public. Thus, the Electoral College was not a system designed to prevent tyranny, as was suggested by some in the wake of the 2016 election. Instead, it was designed as a bulwark against populism and a way of keeping some power in the hands of the states, many of which were wary of a new, more powerful national government.

In the 1800 election, Thomas Jefferson and Aaron Burr tied in the Electoral College, because at that point, electors cast two votes for president, rather than one for president and one for vice president. This meant that the House of Representatives would choose the next president, per the Constitution, and after 36 ballots, Jefferson became president and Burr vice president. This experience, however, led to the 12th Amendment, which, among other things, differentiated electoral votes into one for president and one for vice president; this also helped adjust the electoral process to account for political parties, which the Founders hadn't anticipated — and which George Washington excoriated in his Farewell Address.

In the 1824 election, no candidate carried a majority in the Electoral College, although Andrew Jackson won the most popular votes. However, once the election went to the House, John Quincy Adams was elected president. Allegations that Adams made a "corrupt bargain" with the Speaker of the House, Henry Clay, energized and angered Jackson's supporters. In 1828, Jackson would unseat Adams and go on to serve two terms as president. This is the last time a "contingent election," as it is called, was held in the House.

In the 1860 election, while Abraham Lincoln won a majority of the Electoral College, he only won around 40% of the popular vote, due to a four-way race in which each of his opponents saw noteworthy support. While Lincoln was elected under the system as it worked, it shows, in hindsight, another example of the Electoral College being out of sync with popular sentiments.

In the 1876 election, Samuel J. Tilden won the majority of the popular vote, but lost the Electoral College to Rutherford B. Hayes, the first time in American history that this would happen. Hayes became president, but only after agreeing to end Reconstruction in American history's second "corrupt bargain," which would have disastrous consequences for African-Americans for generations.

Just 12 years later, the 1888 presidential election saw the defeat of Grover Cleveland's re-election to Benjamin Harrison, even though Cleveland won more of the popular vote than Harrison. Cleveland and Harrison would rematch in 1892, with Cleveland winning back his seat and becoming the first president to serve non-consecutive terms.

A split between the Electoral College and the popular vote would not happen again until 2000, wherein George W. Bush lost the popular vote by around 500,000 votes, but managed to win the Electoral College by carrying the state of Florida with the smallest margin of victory by far (somewhere between 500 and 1,000 votes). This victory was only solidified by a Supreme Court decision, in *Bush v. Gore*, which stopped a recount which might have put Gore ahead in Florida, and which marks the first time a presidential election was possibly decided by the Supreme Court; despite how extreme the court has titled away from the Constitution since 2016, that decision is still one of the court's most divisive in history.

Finally, in the 2016 election, despite winning the popular vote by around 3 million votes, Hillary Clinton lost the Electoral College to Donald Trump.

The Problems with the Electoral College

It is Unrepresentative

The Electoral College, as evidenced in the previous section, does not necessarily align with the will of the people as a whole. Majoritarianism is a genuine concern that any healthy democracy needs to guard against, but the solution is not minority rule, either.

It Encourages a Focus on Only Certain States

However, another problem with the Electoral College is that it encourages candidates to focus most of their energy on swing states which sway elections, and thus, indirectly, to ignore most states, either because the state is a probable or guaranteed win or a probable or guaranteed loss. What about the Democrats of Mississippi, or the Republicans of California? As far as each candidate is concerned, their specific interests don't matter because their votes will not benefit their preferred candidate. Yes, Republicans in a blue state still have their chosen candidate win if he wins the Electoral College, but there's no incentive to appeal to those voters *in particular*. Despite what it seems, not all voters in a single party agree on everything, and the interests of rural voters and urban voters can vary quite a bit even if they favor the same party.

A Critique of the National Popular Vote Interstate Compact

The most popular solution proposed for fixing the Electoral College is the National Popular Vote Interstate Compact (NPVIC), wherein states pledge their electoral votes to the candidate who wins the majority or plurality of the popular vote in the country.

While it seems to solve the issue of the Electoral College being unrepresentative, it does so in a way which imposes improper representation in another way. If, for example, voters in a given state voted for Candidate B, but Candidate A won the popular vote, then that state would have to override its own citizens' wishes and have its electors vote for Candidate A, if it's part of the NPVIC. We ought not to replace one wrong with another.

On top of this, it does not do anything to solve the issue of swing-state focus, because it does not encourage candidates to change behavior and appeal to different factions of the country. In fact, it *rewards* candidates who focus on strategic areas, because all it does is reaffirm the popular vote. The president ought to be accountable to a broad swath of the country, not just his base in safe and swing states.

Because of this, I do not support the NPVIC, and instead propose my own solution.

My Solution: Divided Electoral Votes

Introduction

Maine and Nebraska, as of this writing, allow for their electoral votes to be split, as opposed to the winner taking all of the votes. In their cases, two votes go to the winner of the statewide popular vote (correlating to the two electoral votes for the two senators), while each House district has its own vote that can be won separately. This is how Donald Trump won an electoral vote from Maine in 2016 and 2020 (his only one in New England), and how Barack

285

Obama and Joe Biden both won an electoral vote from Nebraska in their respective presidential campaigns.

Some reform proposals have suggested implementing this system nationwide, and that may seem like a great solution, except for one glaring problem: gerrymandering. This undemocratic practice already allows for skewed House races, and if implemented across the country to determine the winners of electoral votes, state legislatures will only be even more emboldened to draw lines to their ruling party's benefit. Any state which does not engage in the practice, then, has put its ruling party at a competitive disadvantage if states controlled by the opposition have done so.

The question becomes, then, can we implement this in a way that maximizes the divided-electoral-vote scheme's benefits while minimizing its drawbacks? The answer is *yes*.

My System Explained

Imagine, if you will, a hypothetical state (we'll call it ST, for short) which has 10 electoral votes. In a presidential election, Alan wins 49% of the popular vote, Betty wins 35% of the vote, and Carl wins 15% of the vote. (1% went to other candidates, write-ins, etc.) Under a normal system, ST would give all 10 votes to Alan and call it a day.

However, under my system, you would take the percentage each losing candidate obtained, multiply it by the number of electoral votes available, and round down to the nearest whole number. (The rounding down is to ensure no undue lower rounding is placed upon the winner, thereby potentially rounding up to an extra vote for the losers.) The result is how many electoral votes the losing candidate obtains. Once all of these numbers have been subtracted from the total, the remainder is given to the winner. So, in this case, Carl would win one vote from ST, Betty would win three, and Alan would get the remaining six.

Therefore, the more electoral votes a state has, the lower the percentage needed to obtain an electoral vote. For instance, in California in 2020, because it had 55 electoral votes, a candidate only needed to obtain roughly 2% of the state's votes in order to obtain an electoral vote. This also means that nearly every state is in play for both a Democrat and a Republican, because the votes are divided proportionately. The fewer votes a state has, the higher the threshold, though, so states with only three electoral votes would require a candidate to win over 33% of the vote to get an electoral vote.

What happens if two candidates are tied in terms of electoral votes, even if one candidate won more votes in total? Well, there are a couple ways we could handle this. If only two candidates obtained any votes, the winner of the two is rounded up to the nearest non-tying number, while the loser is rounded down to the nearest non-tying number. If three or more candidates each won a vote, the lowest-scoring candidate would give up a vote to the candidate in the tie who won more popular votes, and so on until there is no tie.

In order to demonstrate how this model would work, I've looked at every presidential election from 2000 to 2020 (the 2024 election had not occurred when I ran this data), as well as the 1984 and 1992 elections, calculated the new vote totals based on this system, and compared the results to both the national popular vote of that year and of the actual Electoral College results.

Presidential Election Simulations

1984 (Walter Mondale vs. Ronald Reagan)

The 1984 election is the biggest landslide, in terms of the number of electoral votes received by a single candidate, in American history. In the contest, Ronald Reagan won 525 electoral votes by winning the popular vote in every state except for Minnesota and the District of Columbia, which meant that his opponent, Walter Mondale, received 13 electoral votes. This is why I wanted to apply my system to the election; I knew that it wouldn't change the outcome, but I had a hunch that it would make those outsized electoral results closer to the actual national popular vote difference.

Using the data in Figure 1 (see the end of this essay), only Alaska, D.C., and Wyoming would still award all of their electoral votes to a single winner, while the rest would split their votes between the two candidates. The new results would grant 343 electoral votes to Reagan and 195 to Walter Mondale, 63.75% vs. 36.25%. This still indicates a landslide for Reagan, and even gives him a boost compared with the popular vote, but it is much closer to the 58.77% vs. 40.56% popular vote.

1992 (Bill Clinton vs. George H.W. Bush vs. Ross Perot)

The other 20th-century presidential election to which I wanted to apply my system was the three-way race in 1992, because it is the first time since the modern two-party system evolved that a third-party candidate received a substantial portion of the popular vote. Like in 2016, this indicates a dissatisfaction with the two major parties.

In the real 1992 presidential election, Bill Clinton received 370 electoral votes, George H.W. Bush received 168, and Ross Perot zero votes (despite the fact that Perot received about 19% of the popular vote).

Figure 2 demonstrates that, had the system applied, Clinton would have received 253 votes, Bush 210, and Perot 74; compared to the popular vote, Clinton and Bush get boosts and Perot sags, but his votes still count for something—specifically, they ensure that neither of the two major candidates receives the required 270 votes. Because of this, the election for president would be thrown to the House, and the election for vice president would be thrown into the Senate.

Because Democrats controlled the Senate at the time, we can assume that Al Gore would win a majority of the votes and become vice president.

However, even though Democrats had a majority in the House, this doesn't guarantee that Clinton would win the House. Why? Well, because in presidential contingent elections, states each get one vote, regardless of the number of representatives, and so a candidate has to receive 26 votes to win the presidency. A state's vote is determined by the vote of the majority of a state's House delegation.

After a survey of all 50 House delegations in 1992, it was revealed that 26 state delegations were majority-Democrat (Vermont's sole representative, Bernie Sanders, was an independent but I imagine he would have voted for Clinton), so in fact, Clinton would also have won the election. (The states of Arizona, Arkansas, Nevada, Connecticut, Idaho, New Hampshire, Kansas, Maine, Maryland, Rhode Island, and South Carolina had tied delegations; the rest were Republican-majority.)

So, no, the outcome of the election would not be different from the actual 1992 election; however, had the Senate makeup been different, you would have had a Republican or Reform-Party vice president to a Democrat president. On the other hand, a different House composition would have changed the presidential outcome, something that will come into play with our 2016 simulation.

2000 (Al Gore vs. George W. Bush)

The 2000 election was a saga that divided the nation at the outset of the new millennium, and until 2016 it was the go-to, quintessential example for why the Electoral College is abominable. First, there was the neck-and-neck race in Florida, then there was *Bush v. Gore* which essentially saw the Supreme Court take partisan sides and choose their preferred candidate over letting the actual Florida recount play out (notably, each side seemed to swap judicial philosophies for this one decision), and then, in hindsight, there was the blame on Ralph Nader for helping put Florida in jeopardy.

In the real election, Bush won thanks to his declared victory in Florida; had Gore won that state, Gore would have won the election. However, there is no contention that Gore won approximately 500,000 more votes than Bush in the popular vote; again, hence why it became so divisive.

The incredibly surprising outcome of applying my system to this race, as shown in Figure 3, is that it would have made Bush *clearly* the winner, even if Gore won more votes in Florida, because of how Bush performed in other states. Noticeably, while Gore's percentage is only a few tenths of a point off, Bush gets an almost 3-point boost from his popular-vote totals, percentage-wise. The final results are 273–262–3, with Nader getting two votes from California and one from New York.

Obviously, this election would still not represent the will of the majority, but had Gore been operating under this system, he might have campaigned differently, and perhaps that small difference would have changed the outcome.

2004 (John Kerry vs. George W. Bush)

The 2004 election was close in terms of the electoral votes, with Bush winning 286 electoral votes to John Kerry's 251. Under the system, as Figure 4 demonstrates, only five votes would transfer to Kerry, for a final count of 281–256, or 52.23%–47.77%, closer to the actual popular-vote percentage of 50.73%–48.27%.

2008 (Barack Obama vs. John McCain)

Like in 1984, there was no question that Barack Obama would still walk away the winner under the new system, because his original victory was so large. Sure enough, according to Figure 5, Obama still wins, but by an incredibly closer margin than he won in 2008 with his 365–173 win against McCain. In this model, Obama gets a boost compared to the popular vote, but so does McCain. Both numbers are also very close, though.

2012 (Barack Obama vs. Mitt Romney)

Like in 2008, the 2012 election becomes a lot closer than the large margin of victory for Barack Obama, which in reality was 330–203. In Figure 6, the victory is instead 279–259, putting Obama only ten votes away from losing the electoral vote. Romney gets a boost compared to his popular vote totals, but the most noteworthy thing is that Obama's popular-vote percentage is 51.06%, while his new electoral-vote percentage is 51.86%, which is very close!

2016 (Hillary Clinton vs. Donald Trump)

Now comes the final big one. The actual results (not counting faithless electors from either party) are 306–232. When I starting running the data for this one, I knew the numbers would be closer, but I wasn't sure if it would flip to a Clinton win, remain with a Trump win, or have neither candidate win a majority, the last of which felt unlikely.

In my system, Libertarian candidate Gary Johnson won a vote from Texas and two from California, while Green candidate Jill Stein won one vote from California. It's nowhere near Ross Perot's 74 votes, but it is more than Ralph Nader's 3 votes in 2000, and thus still represents a higher dissatisfaction with the two major candidates than in other races.

After accounting for third parties, the final totals were 266 for Clinton and 268 for Trump, meaning that neither one wins the majority of the vote. Also worth noting, however, that a lack of these third parties in the race wouldn't lead to a Clinton win, at least based on available electoral votes; it would put both candidates at 269, since Trump would get the Texas vote and Clinton the three California votes.

Either way, a contingent election would be held in the House and Senate. I'm comfortable betting that a Republican-controlled Senate would elect Mike Pence as vice president, and the delegation breakdown in the House, based on party control at the time, would probably lead to a 32–18 Trump victory, which is even more lopsided, percentage-wise, than it was in real life.

So, no, this system would have changed the outcome in 2016, just like it would not have changed the 2000 and 1992 ones, even though it changes the dynamics of them. However, the change in dynamics is precisely why this analysis is valuable. Had the Clinton campaign known that red states were in play for some of their votes, and had they known that Trump could've captured states that were part of the "Blue Wall" even if he didn't win them, they might not have tossed aside certain states or taken others for granted. I can only make this projection based on the data available from the actual elections, but it's inconceivable to think that the split-vote system wouldn't incentivize different campaign tactics.

2020 (Joe Biden vs. Donald Trump)

The 2020 election was an exact flip of 2016 in terms of electoral votes obtained by either party, with a Biden victory coming in at 306–232. As Figure 8 makes clear, Biden and Trump both get boosts compared to the popular vote (Biden gets a boost of 1.49%, Trump a much smaller 0.49%), but unlike 2016, when neither candidate gained the majority, it's a clear Biden victory this time, even under this new system, with the new tally being 284–254.

Conclusion

Under this new system, candidates would be encouraged to seek out voters in states they traditionally wouldn't campaign in, because those votes would have a bigger impact on elections in this system. This in turn would lead to a more representative and less divisive view of the country; there are almost no more blue or red states, but purple states. It would also be to the benefit of both parties, as Republicans still retain a slight advantage while also turning blue states competitive, while Democrats have less of a hurdle to overcome with the Electoral College and, on top of that, now have red states which are competitive. Now, almost every vote counts because almost every state is up for grabs. Even third parties have a chance to capture some votes; even if their share likely would never translate into a presidential win, they can be represented.

NOTES: All of the following information for the popular-vote percentages in each of the tables was gathered from Wikipedia; while the website is not always completely accurate, these numbers have been checked by multiple editors and were taken from trustworthy sources.

EC is the electoral vote obtained by a Democrat (**D**) or Republican (**R**) in a given election. **%V** is the percentage of the popular vote obtained in each state by a given candidate. **Adj.** is the adjusted number of electoral votes received in each state under the new system I proposed in the essay.

FIGURE 1 – **1984**

state	EC, D	EC, R	%V, D	%V, R	Adj. D	Adj. R
AL		9	38.28	60.54	3	6
AK		3	29.87	66.65		3
AZ		7	32.54	66.42	2	5
AR		6	38.29	60.47	2	4
CA		47	41.27	57.51	19	28
CO		8	35.12	63.44	2	6
CT		8	38.83	60.73	3	5
DE		3	39.93	59.78	1	2
DC	3		85.38	13.73	3	
FL		21	34.66	65.32	7	14
GA		12	39.79	60.17	4	8
HI		4	43.82	55.10	1	3
ID		4	26.39	72.36	1	3
IL		24	43.30	56.17	10	14
IN		12	37.68	61.67	4	8
IA		8	45.89	53.27	3	5
KS		7	32.60	66.27	2	5
KY		9	39.37	60.04	3	6
LA		10	38.18	60.77	3	7
ME		4	38.78	60.83	1	3

293

MD		10	47.02	52.51	4	6
MA		13	48.43	51.22	6	7
MI		20	40.24	59.23	8	12
MN	10		49.72	49.54	6	4
MS		7	37.46	61.85	2	5
MO		11	39.98	60.02	4	7
MT		4	38.18	60.47	1	3
NE		5	28.81	70.55	1	4
NV		4	31.97	65.85	1	3
NH		4	30.95	68.66	1	3
NJ		16	39.20	60.09	6	10
NM		5	39.23	59.70	1	4
NY		36	45.83	53.84	16	20
NC		13	37.89	61.90	4	9
ND		3	33.80	64.84	1	2
OH		23	40.14	58.90	9	14
OK		8	30.67	68.61	2	6
OR		7	43.74	55.91	3	4
PA		25	45.99	53.34	11	14
RI		4	48.02	51.66	1	3
SC		8	35.57	63.55	2	6
SD		3	36.53	63.00	1	2
TN		11	41.57	57.84	4	7
TX		29	36.11	63.61	10	19
UT		5	24.68	74.50	1	4
VT		3	40.81	57.92	1	2
VA		12	37.09	62.29	4	8
WA		10	42.86	55.82	4	6
WV		6	44.60	55.11	2	4
WI		11	45.02	54.19	4	7
WY		3	28.24	70.51		3
RESULTS	13	525			195	343
%	2.42	97.58	40.56	58.77	36.25	63.75

FIGURE 2 – **1992**

state	EC,D	EC,R	%V, D	%V, R	%V, I	Adj. D	Adj. R	Adj. I
AL		9	40.88	47.65	10.85	3	6	
AK		3	30.29	39.46	28.43		3	
AZ		8	36.52	38.47	23.79	2	5	1
AR	6		53.21	35.48	10.43	3	2	
CA	54		46.01	32.61	20.63	26	17	11
CO	8		40.13	35.87	23.32	5	2	1
CT	8		42.21	35.78	21.58	5	2	1
DE	3		43.51	35.31	20.44	2	1	
DC	3		84.64	9.10	4.25	3		
FL		25	39.00	40.89	19.82	9	12	4
GA	13		43.47	42.88	13.34	7	5	1
HI	4		48.09	36.70	14.22	3	1	
ID		4	28.42	42.03	27.04	1	2	1
IL	22		48.58	34.34	16.64	12	7	3
IN		12	36.79	42.91	19.77	4	6	2
IA	7		43.29	37.27	18.71	4	2	1
KS		6	33.74	38.88	26.99	2	3	1
KY	8		44.55	41.34	13.66	4	3	1
LA	9		45.58	40.97	11.81	5	3	1
ME	4		38.77	30.39	30.44	2	1	1
MD	10		49.80	35.62	14.18	6	3	1
MA	12		47.54	29.02	22.74	7	3	2
MI	18		43.77	36.38	19.30	9	6	3
MN	10		43.48	31.85	23.96	5	3	2
MS		7	40.77	49.68	8.72	2	5	
MO	11		44.07	33.92	21.69	6	3	2
MT	3		37.63	35.12	26.11	2	1	
NE		5	29.40	46.58	23.63	1	3	1
NV	4		37.36	34.73	26.19	2	1	1
NH	4		38.86	37.64	22.56	3	1	
NJ	15		42.95	40.58	15.61	7	6	2

NM	5		45.90	37.34	16.12	4	1	
NY	33		49.72	33.88	15.75	17	11	5
NC		14	42.65	43.44	13.70	5	8	1
ND		3	32.18	44.22	23.07		3	
OH	21		40.18	38.35	20.98	9	8	4
OK		8	34.02	42.65	23.01	2	5	1
OR	7		42.48	32.53	24.21	4	2	1
PA	23		45.15	36.13	18.20	11	8	4
RI	4		47.04	29.02	23.16	3	1	
SC		8	39.88	48.02	11.55	3	5	
SD		3	37.14	40.66	21.80	1	2	
TN	11		47.08	42.43	10.09	6	4	1
TX		32	37.08	40.56	22.01	11	14	7
UT		5	24.65	43.36	27.34	1	3	1
VT	3		46.11	30.42	22.78	3		
VA		13	40.59	44.97	13.63	5	7	1
WA	11		43.40	31.96	23.68	6	3	2
WV	5		48.41	35.39	15.91	4	1	
WI	11		41.13	36.78	21.51	5	4	2
WY		3	33.98	39.56	25.56	1	2	
RE-SULTS	370	168				253	210	74
%	68.77	31.23	43.01	37.45	18.91	47	39	14

FIGURE 3 – **2000**

state	EC, D	EC, R	%V, D	%V, R	Adj. D	Adj. R
AL		9	41.57	56.48	3	6
AK		3	27.67	58.62		3
AZ		8	44.73	51.02	3	5
AR		6	45.86	51.31	2	4
CA	54		53.45	41.65	30	22
CO		8	42.39	50.75	3	5
CT	8		55.91	38.44	5	3

DE	3		54.96	41.90	2	1
DC	2		85.16	8.95	3	
FL		25	48.84	48.85	12	13
GA		13	42.98	54.67	5	8
HI	4		55.79	37.46	3	1
ID		4	27.64	67.17	1	3
IL	22		54.60	42.58	13	9
IN		12	41.01	56.65	4	8
IA	7		48.54	48.22	4	3
KS		6	37.24	58.04	2	4
KY		8	41.37	56.50	3	5
LA		9	44.88	52.55	4	5
ME	4		49.09	43.97	3	1
MD	10		56.57	40.18	6	4
MA	12		59.80	32.50	9	3
MI	18		51.28	46.15	10	8
MN	10		47.91	45.50	6	4
MS		7	40.70	57.62	2	5
MO		11	47.08	50.42	5	6
MT		3	33.36	58.44	1	2
NE		5	33.25	62.25	1	4
NV		4	45.98	49.52	1	3
NH		4	46.80	48.07	1	3
NJ	15		56.13	40.29	9	6
NM	5		47.91	47.85	3	2
NY	33		60.21	35.23	21	11
NC		14	43.20	56.03	6	8
ND		3	33.06	60.66		3
OH		21	46.46	49.97	9	12
OK		8	38.43	60.31	3	5
OR	7		46.96	46.52	4	3
PA	23		50.60	46.43	13	10
RI	4		60.99	31.91	3	1

state	EC, D	EC, R	%V, D	%V, R	Adj. D	Adj. R
SC		8	40.90	56.84	3	5
SD		3	37.56	60.30	1	2
TN		11	47.28	51.15	5	6
TX		32	37.98	59.30	12	20
UT		5	26.34	66.83	1	4
VT	3		50.63	40.70	2	1
VA		13	44.44	52.47	5	8
WA	11		50.16	44.58	7	4
WV		5	45.59	51.92	2	3
WI	11		47.83	47.61	6	5
WY		3	27.70	67.76		3
RESULTS	266	271			262	273
%	49.44	50.37	48.36	47.86	48.7	50.74

FIGURE 4 – **2004**

state	EC, D	EC, R	%V, D	%V, R	Adj. D	Adj. R
AL		9	36.84	62.46	3	6
AK		3	35.52	61.07	1	2
AZ		10	44.40	54.87	4	6
AR		6	44.55	54.31	2	4
CA	55		54.31	44.36	31	24
CO		9	47.02	51.69	4	5
CT	7		54.31	43.95	4	3
DE	3		53.35	45.75	2	1
DC	3		89.18	9.34	3	
FL		27	47.09	52.10	12	15
GA		15	41.37	57.97	6	9
HI	4		54.01	45.26	3	1
ID		4	30.26	68.38	1	3
IL	21		54.82	44.48	12	9
IN		11	39.26	59.94	4	7
IA		7	49.23	49.90	3	4

KS		6	36.62	62.00	2	4
KY		8	39.69	59.55	3	5
LA		9	42.22	56.72	3	6
ME	2		53.57	44.58	3	1
MD	10		55.91	42.93	6	4
MA	12		61.94	36.78	8	4
MI	17		51.23	47.81	9	8
MN	9		51.09	47.61	6	4
MS		6	39.76	59.45	2	4
MO		11	46.10	53.30	5	6
MT		3	38.56	59.07	1	2
NE		2	32.68	65.90	1	4
NV		5	47.88	50.47	2	3
NH	4		50.24	48.87	3	1
NJ	15		52.92	46.24	9	6
NM		5	49.05	49.84	2	3
NY	31		58.37	40.08	19	12
NC		15	43.58	56.02	6	9
ND		3	35.50	62.86	1	2
OH		20	48.71	50.81	9	11
OK		7	34.43	65.57	2	5
OR	7		51.35	47.19	4	3
PA	21		50.92	48.42	11	10
RI	4		59.42	38.67	3	1
SC		8	40.90	57.98	3	5
SD		3	38.44	59.91	1	2
TN		11	42.53	56.80	4	7
TX		34	38.22	61.09	12	22
UT		5	26.00	71.54	1	4
VT	3		58.94	38.80	2	1
VA		13	45.48	53.68	5	8
WA	11		52.82	45.64	6	5
WV		5	43.20	56.06	2	3
WI	10		49.70	49.32	6	4

		3	29.07	68.86		3
WY		3	29.07	68.86		3
RESULTS	251	286			257	281
%	46.65	53.16	48.27	50.73	47.77	52.23

FIGURE 5 – **2008**

state	EC, D	EC, R	%V, D	%V, R	Adj. D	Adj. R
AL		9	38.74	60.32	3	6
AK		3	37.89	59.42	1	2
AZ		10	45.12	53.64	4	6
AR		6	38.86	58.72	2	4
CA	55		61.01	36.95	35	20
CO	9		53.66	44.71	5	4
CT	7		60.59	38.22	5	2
DE	3		61.94	36.95	2	1
DC	3		92.46	6.53	3	
FL	27		51.03	48.22	14	13
GA		15	46.99	52.20	7	8
HI	4		71.85	26.58	3	1
ID		4	36.09	61.52	1	3
IL	21		61.92	36.78	14	7
IN	11		49.95	48.91	6	5
IA	7		53.93	44.39	4	3
KS		6	41.65	56.61	2	4
KY		8	41.17	57.40	3	5
LA		9	39.93	58.56	3	6
ME	4		57.71	40.38	3	1
MD	10		61.92	36.47	7	3
MA	12		61.80	35.99	8	4
MI	17		57.43	40.96	11	6
MN	10		54.06	43.82	6	4
MS		6	43.00	56.18	2	4

MO		11	49.29	49.43	5	6
MT		3	47.25	49.51	1	2
NE	1	4	41.60	56.53	2	3
NV	5		55.15	42.65	3	2
NH	4		54.13	44.52	3	1
NJ	15		57.27	41.70	9	6
NM	5		56.91	41.78	3	2
NY	31		62.88	36.03	20	11
NC	15		49.70	49.38	7	8
ND		3	44.62	53.25	2	1
OH	20		51.50	46.91	10	10
OK		7	34.35	65.65	3	4
OR	7		56.75	40.40	5	2
PA	21		54.49	44.17	12	9
RI	4		62.86	35.06	2	2
SC		8	44.90	53.87	3	5
SD		3	44.75	53.16	1	2
TN		11	41.83	56.90	4	7
TX		34	43.68	55.45	14	20
UT		5	34.41	62.58	1	4
VT	3		67.46	30.45	3	
VA	13		52.63	46.33	7	6
WA	11		57.65	40.48	7	4
WV		5	42.59	55.71	2	3
WI	10		56.22	42.31	6	4
WY		3	32.54	64.78		3
RESULTS	365	173			289	249
%	67.84	32.16	52.93	45.65	53.72	46.28

FIGURE 6 – **2012**

state	EC, D	EC, R	%V, D	%V, R	Adj. D	Adj. R
AL		9	38.36	60.55	3	6

AK		3	40.81	54.80	1	2
AZ		11	44.59	53.65	4	7
AR		6	36.88	60.57	2	4
CA	55		60.24	37.12	35	20
CO	9		51.49	46.13	5	4
CT	7		58.06	40.73	5	2
DE	3		58.61	39.98	2	1
DC	3		90.91	7.28	3	
FL	29		50.01	49.13	15	14
GA		16	45.48	53.30	7	9
HI	4		70.55	27.84	3	1
ID		4	32.40	64.09	1	3
IL	20		57.60	40.73	12	8
IN		11	43.93	54.13	4	7
IA	6		51.99	46.18	3	3
KS		6	38.05	59.66	2	4
KY		8	37.80	60.49	3	5
LA		8	40.58	57.78	3	5
ME	4		56.27	40.98	3	1
MD	10		61.97	35.90	7	3
MA	11		60.65	37.51	7	4
MI	16		54.21	44.71	9	7
MN	10		52.65	44.96	6	4
MS		6	43.79	55.29	2	4
MO		10	44.38	53.76	4	6
MT		3	41.70	55.35	1	2
NE		5	38.03	59.80	1	4
NV	6		52.36	45.68	4	2
NH	4		51.98	46.40	3	1
NJ	14		58.38	40.59	9	5
NM	5		52.99	42.84	3	2
NY	29		63.35	35.17	19	10
NC		15	48.35	50.39	7	8

ND		3	38.70	58.32	1	2
OH	18		50.67	47.69	10	8
OK		7	33.23	66.77	2	5
OR	7		54.24	42.15	5	2
PA	20		51.97	46.59	11	9
RI	4		62.70	35.24	3	1
SC		9	44.09	54.56	3	6
SD		3	39.87	57.89	1	2
TN		11	39.08	59.48	4	7
TX		38	41.38	57.17	15	23
UT		6	24.69	72.62	1	5
VT	3		66.57	30.97	3	
VA	13		51.16	47.28	7	6
WA	12		56.16	41.29	8	4
WV		5	35.54	62.30	1	4
WI	10		52.83	45.89	6	4
WY		3	27.82	68.64		3
RESULTS	203				279	259
%	61.34	37.73	51.06	47.20	51.86	48.14

FIGURE 7 – **2016**

state	EC, D	EC, R	%V, D	%V, R	Adj. D	Adj. R
AL		9	34.36	62.08	3	6
AK		3	36.55	51.28	1	2
AZ		11	44.58	48.08	4	7
AR		6	33.65	60.57	2	4
CA	55		61.73	31.62	35	17
CO	9		48.16	43.25	6	3
CT	7		54.57	40.93	5	2
DE	3		53.09	41.72	2	1
DC	3		90.86	4.09	3	
FL		29	47.82	49.02	13	16
GA		16	45.64	50.77	7	9
HI	4		62.22	30.03	3	1

303

ID		4	27.49	59.26	1	3
IL	20		55.83	38.76	13	7
IN		11	37.91	56.82	4	7
IA		6	41.74	51.15	2	4
KS		6	36.05	56.65	2	4
KY		8	32.68	62.52	2	6
LA		8	38.45	58.09	3	5
ME	3	1	47.83	44.87	3	1
MD	10		60.33	33.91	7	3
MA	11		60.01	32.81	8	3
MI		16	47.27	47.50	7	9
MN	10		46.44	44.92	6	4
MS		6	40.06	57.86	2	4
MO		10	38.14	56.77	3	7
MT		3	35.75	56.17	1	2
NE		5	33.70	58.75	1	4
NV	6		47.92	45.50	4	2
NH	4		46.98	46.61	3	1
NJ	14		55.45	41.35	8	6
NM	5		48.26	40.04	3	2
NY	29		59.01	36.52	19	10
NC		15	46.17	49.83	6	9
ND		3	27.23	62.94		3
OH		18	43.56	51.69	7	11
OK		7	28.93	65.32	2	5
OR	7		50.07	39.09	5	2
PA		20	47.46	48.18	9	11
RI	4		54.41	38.90	3	1
SC		9	40.67	54.94	3	6
SD		3	31.74	61.53		3
TN		11	34.72	60.72	3	8
TX		38	43.24	52.23	16	21
UT		6	27.46	45.54	2	4
VT	3		56.68	30.27	3	
VA	13		49.73	44.41	8	5
WA	12		52.54	36.83	8	4
WV		5	26.43	68.50	1	4

		10	46.45	47.22	4	6
WI		10	46.45	47.22	4	6
WY		3	21.88	68.17		3
RESULTS	232	306			266	268
%	43.12	56.88	48.20	46.10	49.63	49.81

FIGURE 8 – **2020**

state	EC, D	EC, R	%V, D	%V, R	Adj. D	Adj. R
AL		9	37.09	62.91	3	6
AK		3	42.77	52.83	1	2
AZ	11		49.36	49.06	6	5
AR		6	34.78	62.40	2	4
CA	55		63.48	34.32	37	18
CO	9		55.40	41.90	6	3
CT	7		59.24	39.21	5	2
DE	3		58.74	39.77	2	1
DC	3		92.15	5.40	3	
FL		29	47.86	51.22	13	16
GA	16		49.47	49.24	9	7
HI	4		63.73	34.27	3	1
ID		4	33.07	63.84	1	3
IL	20		57.54	40.55	12	8
IN		11	40.96	57.03	4	7
IA		6	44.89	53.09	2	4
KS		6	41.51	56.14	2	4
KY		8	36.15	62.09	2	6
LA		8	39.85	58.46	3	5
ME	3	1	53.09	44.02	3	1
MD	10		65.36	32.15	7	3
MA	11		65.60	32.14	8	3
MI	16		50.62	47.84	9	7
MN	10		52.40	45.28	6	4

MS		6	41.06	57.60	2	4
MO		10	41.41	56.80	4	6
MT		3	40.55	56.92	1	2
NE	1	4	39.17	58.22	1	4
NV	6		50.06	47.67	4	2
NH	4		52.17	45.36	3	1
NJ	14		57.33	41.40	9	5
NM	5		54.29	43.50	3	2
NY	29		60.87	37.74	19	10
NC		15	48.59	49.93	7	8
ND		3	31.78	65.12		3
OH		18	45.24	53.27	8	10
OK		7	32.29	65.37	2	5
OR	7		56.45	40.37	5	2
PA	20		49.85	48.69	11	9
RI	4		59.39	38.61	3	1
SC		9	43.43	55.11	3	6
SD		3	35.61	61.77	1	2
TN		11	37.45	60.66	4	7
TX		38	46.48	52.06	17	21
UT		6	37.65	58.13	2	4
VT	3		66.09	30.67	3	
VA	13		54.11	44.00	8	5
WA	12		57.97	38.77	8	4
WV		5	29.69	68.62	1	4
WI	10		49.45	48.82	6	4
WY		3	26.55	69.94		3
RESULTS	306	232			284	254
%	56.69	43.31	51.30	46.80	52.79	47.21

REFERENCES

1. CDZA. "Fresh Prince: Google Translated." *YouTube*, 15 January 2013, https://www.youtube.com/watch?v=LMkJuDVJdTw&pp=ygURY2 R6YSBmcmVzaCBwcmluY2U%3D;

2. Philips, Matthew. "Religion: God's Word, According to Wikipedia." *Newsweek*, 14 March 2010, www.newsweek.com/religion-gods-word-according-wikipedia-91377

3. "Plutos 1 - Alarm in the Night (Translation)." Translated by crashryan, *Comic Book Plus*, 5 January 2014, www.comicbookplus.com/?dlid=39406

4. "La Araña Verde (Spanish Language Books)." Category created by mr_goldenage, *Comic Book Plus*, www.comicbookplus.com/?cid=2737 (NOTE: Later, the translation was moved to a different section of the website for "scanilations," so this link only leads to the originals now.)

5. Guardian staff reporter. "Karl Ove Knausgaard Webchat – Your Questions Answered on Self-Loathing, Love and Jürgen Klopp." *The Guardian*, 17 October 2016, www.theguardian.com/books/live/2016/oct/13/karl-ove-knausgaard-webchat-some-rain-must-fall-my-struggle

6. Goldsmith, Annie. "Joe Biden's Photographer on Campaigning during COVID, and Earning a Candidate's Trust." *Town & Country*, 26 October 2020, www.townandcountrymag.com/society/politics/a34454754/joe-biden-photographer-adam-schultz-campaign-covid-interview/

7. Sullivan, Kate. "How One Photographer Shapes the Way the World Sees Joe Biden." *CNN*, Cable News Network, 13 March 2021, www.cnn.com/interactive/2021/03/politics/joe-biden-photographer-cnnphotos/

8. Green, John. "How many drafts do you do?" *John Green*, www.johngreenbooks.com/where-i-get-my-ideas-inspiration-and-general-writing-stuff

9. u/Bersnardo. "Saint Dismas and the ending [Spoilers]" https://www.reddit.com/r/uncharted/comments/4kk3i3/saint_dismas_and_the_ending_spoilers/

10. Wikipedia. "Video Games as an Art Form." Wikimedia Foundation, en.wikipedia.org/wiki/Video_games_as_an_art_form

11. In Praise of Shadows. "The Most Controversial Novelization of All Time." *YouTube*, 2 June 2023, www.youtube.com/watch?v=eBBXHFNKT_c

12. Hernández, Alec, and Summer Concepcion. "JD Vance Says 2021 Comments about Giving More Votes to People with Kids Were a "Thought Experiment."" NBC News, 11 August 2024, www.nbcnews.com/politics/2024-election/jd-vance-allotting-votes-people-children-thought-experiment-rcna166140

13. McCloud, Scott. "Designing for the Device." *Scott McCloud Journal RSS*, Scott McCloud, 16 December 2014, www.scottmccloud.com/2014/12/16/designing-for-the-device/

14. Norris, Richard, and El Csawza. "Alan Moore Interview, 1988." *{ Feuilleton }*, 21 February 2009, www.johncoulthart.com/

feuilleton/2006/02/20/alan-moore-interview-1988/ (Interview was originally published in *Strange Things Are Happening*, vol. 1, no. 2, May/June 1988.)

15. Vylenz, Dez and Moritz Winkler, directors. *The Mindscape of Alan Moore*. Shadowsnake Films, 2004.

16. Eisner, Will. *Will Eisner's Shop Talk*. Dark Horse Comics, 2001 (page 211).

17. Harvey, R.C. "What Jack Kirby Did." *The Comics Journal*, April 1994, pp. 61–73.

18. Flannery, Mary Ellen. "Pay, Planning Time & More: What Collective Bargaining Means in Virginia." *Nea.org*, 2025, www.nea.org/nea-today/all-news-articles/pay-planning-time-more-what-collective-bargaining-means-virginia

19. Lieberman, Mark. "MAP: Where School Employees Can and Can't Strike." *Education Week*, 16 March 2023, www.edweek.org/leadership/map-where-school-employees-can-and-cant-strike/2023/03

20. Tornoe, Rob. "Pulitzer change leaves illustrators feeling slighted." *Editor & Publisher*, 1 May 2022, www.editorandpublisher.com/stories/pulitzer-change-leaves-illustrators-feeling-slighted,229083

21. Garrison, Ben. "CAN YOU HEAR US NOW? JAN6 PROTEST." *Rogue Cartoonist Ben Garrison*, 7 January 2021. https://grrrgraphics.com/can-you-hear-us-now/

22. Grey Ellis, Emma. "The Alt-Right Found Its Favorite Cartoonist—And Almost Ruined His Life." *Wired*, 19 June 2017, https://www.wired.com/story/ben-garrison-alt-right-cartoonist/

23. Capps, Kriston, "Against Free Little Libraries." *Bloomberg*, 3 May 2017, https://www.bloomberg.com/news/articles/2017-05-03/down-with-little-free-library-book-exchanges

ACKNOWLEDGEMENTS

This book represents over two years of work, from writing my first essay on Medium to putting the finishing touches on this manuscript. As always, there are plenty of people who have made this project possible.

First, I would like to thank Robert Tomlin, the math teacher who suggested I first try writing for Medium. While I never monetized my essays, like he suggested at the time, this book would never have existed without his suggestion to write for the site in the first place.

The students I had at my first high school, from the regular classroom visitors to the honorary students to the ones who always had a positive attitude in class. This book was dedicated to them because of how much they influenced its creation and how much they impacted my life. Thank you to all of them.

Thank you to all of my former fellow teachers at Henrico High School. You made my first teaching placement so wonderful, and I'm grateful to have known all of you.

I would like to thank my parents, Al and Sharon Ten, who have always encouraged my writing, my curiosity, and my love for learning.

Thank you to Chris Irving, whose guidance and friendship has been beyond generous, and I'm so grateful for all of your help.

I send my thanks to the examples set by Scott McCloud and Evan Puschak;

although I have met neither of them and neither knows I exist, they both have had an immense influence on my thoughts regarding media analysis.

Finally, thank you to all of those who have read any of my Medium essays. Your support, even if just in a view, kept me on the site and encouraged me in making this collection.

ABOUT THE AUTHOR

Ryan Ten has been writing creatively since he was ten years old. When he's not writing, or working on media projects, he's either reading, watching YouTube, listening to podcasts, volunteering, or working at his full-time job.

www.ingramcontent.com/pod-product-compliance
Lightning Source LLC
Chambersburg PA
CBHW070805180626
46818CB00001B/116